DELUSIONAL STATES

༄༅

Delusional States is the first in-depth study of state-making and social change in Gilgit-Baltistan, a Shia-majority region of Sunni-dominated Pakistan and a contested border area that forms part of disputed Kashmir. For over seven decades, the territorial conflict over Kashmir has locked India and Pakistan in brutal wars and hate-centred nationalisms. The book illuminates how within this story of hate lie other stories—of love and betrayal, loyalty and suspicion, beauty and terror—that help us grasp how the Kashmir conflict is affectively structured and experienced on the ground. Placing these emotions at the centre of its analysis, the book rethinks the state–citizen relation in deeply felt and intimate terms, offering a multi-layered ethnographic understanding of power and subjection in contemporary Pakistan.

It argues that Gilgit-Baltistan's image within Pakistan as an idyllic paradise elides how the region is governed as a suspect security zone, and dispossessed through multiple processes of state-making including representation, militarization, sectarianized education, and biodiversity conservation. The book charts this rule of state and empire as delusion, demonstrating how the region's inhabitants nevertheless struggle to promote a progressive vision of ethics and politics. From political activists and preachers to poets and pastoralists, citizen-subjects in the region are demanding inclusion not only in terms of political rights—an aspect that over-determines the discourse on Kashmir—but also through struggles for religious recognition and ecological sovereignty which they feel is integral to a meaningful life of dignity.

A powerful contribution to studies of citizenship, development, and Muslim sociality in South Asia, the book additionally offers distinct theoretical insights in the fields of social movements, education, cultural studies, and political ecology.

Nosheen Ali teaches at the Institute for Educational Development, The Aga Khan University, Pakistan. She is the founder of *UmangPoetry*, a digital humanities archive for documenting contemporary poetic knowledges in South Asia, and *Karti Dharti*, an alternative learning space for ecological inquiry.

DELUSIONAL STATES

❦

FEELING RULE AND DEVELOPMENT IN PAKISTAN'S NORTHERN FRONTIER

NOSHEEN ALI

CAMBRIDGE
UNIVERSITY PRESS

University Printing House, Cambridge CB2 8BS, United Kingdom

One Liberty Plaza, 20th Floor, New York, NY 10006, USA

477 Williamstown Road, Port Melbourne, vic 3207, Australia

314 to 321, 3rd Floor, Plot No.3, Splendor Forum, Jasola District Centre, New Delhi 110025, India

79 Anson Road, #06–04/06, Singapore 079906

Cambridge University Press is part of the University of Cambridge.

It furthers the University's mission by disseminating knowledge in the pursuit of education, learning and research at the highest international levels of excellence.

www.cambridge.org
Information on this title: www.cambridge.org /9781108497442

© Nosheen Ali 2019

This publication is in copyright. Subject to statutory exception and to the provisions of relevant collective licensing agreements, no reproduction of any part may take place without the written permission of Cambridge University Press.

First published 2019

Printed in India by Nutech Print Services, New Delhi 110020

A catalogue record for this publication is available from the British Library

ISBN 978-1-108-49744-2 Hardback

Cambridge University Press has no responsibility for the persistence or accuracy of URLs for external or third-party internet websites referred to in this publication, and does not guarantee that any content on such websites is, or will remain, accurate or appropriate.

CONTENTS

List of Maps and Figures	VII
Acknowledgements	IX
List of Abbreviations	XI
Introduction	1

PART I: Representation and Repression

1. Unimagined Communities in the Eco-body of the Nation — 31
2. Loyalty, Suspicion, Sacrifice: Feeling and Force under Militarism — 77

PART II: Education and the Politics of Faith

3. Challenging School Textbooks: The Sectarian Making of National Islam — 113
4. Sectarian Imaginaries and Poetic Publics — 153

PART III: Saving Nature, Saving People

5. The Nature of Development: Neoliberal Environments and Pastoral Visions — 195
6. Books vs. Bombs? Humanitarian Education, Empire, and the Narrative of Terror — 231

Conclusion: The Great Media Game	257
Bibliography	265
Index	297

MAPS AND FIGURES

Maps

I.1 The city of Gilgit and the village of Shimshal, in relation to Gilgit-Baltistan — 22

1.1 Section from 'Pakistan: Showing Administrative Districts' — 51

1.2 'Pakistan: Showing Administrative Division' — 52

1.3 Section of 'Pakistan: Political Divisions' — 55

1.4 Map of Pakistan used in the book *Pakistan* — 56

Figures

3.1 Page from *Meri Kitab* (My Book), Class 1 — 128

3.2 Page from *Art and Drawing*, Class 7 — 129

4.1 Dancers and musicians perform before the polo match at the Silk Route Festival, Gilgit, 2006 — 165

4.2 Poetry festival held at the Karakoram International University, Gilgit, 2006 — 188

5.1 A village settlement in central Shimshal — 205

ACKNOWLEDGEMENTS

To acknowledge is a political act, and a particularly consequential one when one is researching a heavily surveilled, border territory.

How do I acknowledge anyone when I cannot freely name the allies from Gilgit-Baltistan who made this research possible? Anonymously, hence, to my wonderful friends, hosts, and colleagues in Gilgit-Baltistan, I offer my eternal gratitude. Thank you for your immense generosity, your warm support and knowledge-sharing, for looking out for me and after me, for showing me how to be. I kept the promise.

This book is dedicated to my parents, who despite gendered social worries, always supported me in my rebellious, out-of-the-way journeys. The research and writing for the book has been supported by the Charlotte W. Newcombe Doctoral Dissertation Fellowship, the Mellon/ACLS Early Career Fellowship, and the Cornell University Graduate Fellowship in Peace Studies.

ABBREVIATIONS

ADP	Annual Development Programme
AJK	Azad Jammu and Kashmir
AK	Azad Kashmir
AKDN	Aga Khan Development Network
BNF	Balawaristan National Front
CAFOs	Concentrated Animal Feedlot Operations
CBNRM	Community-Based Natural Resource Management
CCHA	Community Controlled Hunting Area
CIA	Central Intelligence Agency
CPEC	China–Pakistan Economic Corridor
DC	District Commissioner
DFO	District Forest Officer
DMT	District Monitoring Team
FANA	Federally Administered Northern Areas
FATA	Federally Administered Tribal Areas
FC	Frontier Constabulary
FCNA	Force Command Northern Areas
FCR	Frontier Crimes Regulation
FMCC	Field Monitoring Coordination Cell
FWO	Frontier Works Organisation
GBDA	Gilgit Baltistan Democratic Alliance
GBLA	Gilgit-Baltistan Legislative Assembly
GBNA	Gilgit-Baltistan National Alliance
GECA	Gojal Educational and Cultural Association
GEF	Global Environment Facility
GIS	Geographic Information System

ID	Identification
IMF	International Monetary Fund
ISI	Inter-Services Intelligence
IUCN	International Union for Conservation of Nature
JI	Jamaat-e-Islami
JUI	Jamiat Ulema-e-Islam
KANA	Kashmir Affairs and Northern Areas
KKH	Karakoram Highway
KIU	Karakoram International University
KNM	Karakoram National Movement
KNP	Khunjerab National Park
LoC	Line of Control
MNAs	Members of the National Assembly
MoU	Memorandum of Understanding
NA	Northern Areas
NALA	Northern Areas Legislative Assembly
NALC	Northern Areas Legislative Council
NCCW	National Council for Conservation of Wildlife
NGO	Non-Governmental Organization
NLI	Northern Light Infantry
NWFP	North-West Frontier Province
NAPWD	Northern Areas Public Works Department
PIA	Pakistan International Airlines
PMA	Pakistan Military Academy
PML (N)	Pakistan Muslim League (Nawaz)
PPP	Pakistan People's Party
PRT	Provincial Reconstruction Team
PTV	Pakistan Television
SCI	Safari Club International
SCO	Special Communication Organization
SNT	Shimshal Nature Trust
SSP	Sipah-e-Sahaba Pakistan
TCT	Three Cups of Tea
TJP	Tehrik-e-Jafaria Pakistan
UN	United Nations
UNCIP	United Nations Commission for India and Pakistan
UNDP	United Nations Development Programme

UNEP	United Nations Environment Programme
UNESCO	United Nations Educational, Scientific and Cultural Organization
US	United States
USAID	United States Agency for International Development
VC	Vice Chancellor
WCNPPA	World Congress on National Parks and Protected Areas
WWF	World Wide Fund for Nature

INTRODUCTION

☙❧

In 1993, when I was a student of grade eight in a private school in Lahore, our class was divided up in four groups for a geography project on Pakistan. The group of which I was a part had to make a sculptural map of Pakistan, demonstrating the diverse physical and social qualities of its landscape. And so we had set about carving our country with stuff like styrofoam, cotton, and cardboard. In the final map that we made, the region of Gilgit-Baltistan—then the 'Northern Areas'—had remained unlabelled and unpeopled, marked only with mountains made of clay.

Even today, nature remains the primary modality through which Gilgit-Baltistan is understood within the Pakistani national imagination. Its magnificent peaks and breathtaking valleys invoke within Pakistanis a simultaneous sense of emotional attachment and proud ownership, permitting them to claim Pakistan as 'beautiful'. But while Gilgit-Baltistan is externally produced as an idyllic tourist destination, it is internally managed as a suspect security zone. This is because the region is internationally considered as part of the disputed area of Kashmir—a territory that both Pakistan and India claim, and have turned into the most militarized zone in the world over the last seven decades. This is also because Gilgit-Baltistan is the only Shia-dominated political unit in a Sunni-dominated Pakistan.

Ironically, at the heart of the territory of Kashmir—which Pakistan claims on the basis of its 'Muslim' identity—lies the region of Gilgit-Baltistan which contradicts this identity by being home to a different kind of Muslim than that endorsed by Pakistani nationalism. Such territorial and religious anxieties transform Gilgit-Baltistan from a place of mythical beauty into a zone of treachery, proudly claimed yet disavowed at the same time. Meanwhile, the inhabitants of the region express a strong yearning for recognition and inclusion within the Pakistani nation-state, and feel a deep love and loyalty towards it—only to find themselves constantly alienated and betrayed. This book charts such dynamics of attachment and alienation, placing at its centre the emotionalities—of love and betrayal, loyalty and suspicion, beauty and terror—that help us grasp how the Kashmir conflict is affectively structured and experienced on the ground. After all, Kashmir is not just a matter of national security in India and Pakistan, but a place that has become the emotional heart of these nationalisms. How this 'heart of hostility' translates into political subjection and intimately felt struggle in the terrain of Gilgit-Baltistan is the story that I wish to narrate in this book.[1]

THE ANGUISH OF LOVE

Pakistan ne hamaray ehsasaat ke saath khela hai!
'Pakistan has played with/manipulated our emotions!'

This is a refrain that is often heard in Gilgit-Baltistani protests against the Pakistan state, and came up repeatedly during my interviews in the region. People in Gilgit-Baltistan attribute their political predicament not just to the lack of rights as a result of being entangled in the Kashmir dispute, but fundamentally to the lack of 'trust' *(bharosa/aitmad)* in the region by the Pakistani state authorities, which signifies a 'betrayal' *(bewafai/dhoka)* of the region's own 'love' *(muhabbat)* and 'loyalty' *(wafadari)* to Pakistan. As one interviewee commented to me, the real problem is that 'Pakistan is not *sincere* with us'.[2] Across the border, in Srinagar, Kashmiris voice-related grievances against the Indian state: 'They [Indians] *can't feel or represent* our sentiments'.[3] Such feeling-thoughts compel us to rethink the state–citizen relation in deeply emotional and intimate terms, in place of purely legalistic logics. This is especially true in conflict zones like Kashmir, where the attitudes of aggressive hyper-nationalism and struggles of self-determination have become immersed in multiple emotional histories. These emotional structures, histories, and experiences are central for gaining a grounded understanding of the Kashmir conflict, as well as of the state–citizen dynamic in general.

Let me recognize at the outset that this dynamic, as well as the emotionality of rule and resistance, operates differently in the different regions that form part of the conflict of Kashmir. In Gilgit-Baltistan, intriguingly, love is a compelling constellation through which we may chart how the dynamic of citizenship operates on the ground. In order to grasp the politics of love and emotional attachment in the case of state-making in Gilgit-Baltistan, it is crucial to first note the profound significance of love in the very structuring of individual subjectivity and social being in South Asia. If South Asian legends, poetic thought, and popular culture particularly from Pakistan and north India are an indicator, then we might say that the history of all hitherto existing society is not the history of class struggles, but of love struggles.[4] The struggles of legendary lovers—from Heer Ranjha to Mirza Sahiban, Laila Majnun to Sassi Punnu, and Shirin Farhad to Sohni Mahiwal—form the foundational motif in the dominant literary traditions of the Perso-Indian cosmopolis from the medieval period onwards. Narratives of love-martyrs embodied the paradigmatic theme of separation and union, but also that of defiance and rebellion against patriarchal, priestly, and class oppression.[5] Performed through poetic storytelling and illustrated through painting, the power of love in these narratives embraced a transcendental spirit of piety and collective oneness, and served to define the moral universe and cognitive hearts of local populations. If language reflects the life-worlds of its speakers and their frames of meaning and value, then we might grasp how cherished love is by witnessing the many modes of referring to a beloved soul: *yaar, jaan, jaaneman, jigar, dost, rafeeq, habeeb, sanam, sajan, dildar, dilbar, piya, mehboob, saaqi, saheb, saiyaan, mahi, mitwa, mitr*—at least nineteen terms just in the Gujrati-Urdu-Hindi tongue that I am familiar with.

Alongside a devotional affection and life-consuming desire for the beloved, expressive traditions of love in South Asia are necessarily inscribed with themes of anguish and alienation—particularly since the beloveds are always obstructed by hostile environments. Moreover, love is deemed to characterize all human and human–divine relations, not just the affair of romance. As Gold (2006) notes in the illuminating edited volume *Love in South Asia: A Cultural History*, idioms of love tend to be more expansive in South Asia and are used to describe not only spiritual love, as has been widely recognized, but also intimately felt community ties and ecologies. These factors take us closer to the argument that I wish to make here: that it this expansive, cultural–poetic constellation of love which is being drawn upon by Gilgiti subjects, as they articulate their feelings of love, loyalty, and longing for the Pakistani nation/state. It is because of the pathos of this same paradigmatic constellation that they speak of insincerity, betrayal, and *be-wafai*— no-loyalty—in return. This doubleness in relation to love is even indicated by the term *khelna*, which is referred to in the quotation at the beginning of this section. The Urdu word *khelna* means the light-hearted, joyous play that is involved in love, but depending on the way it is used, it can simultaneously mean a kind of insincere play, a pretense, and ultimately, the state of manipulated love.

It is precisely this state of manipulated love that Pakistan has come to represent in Gilgit-Baltistan, in betrayal of the true love that Gilgitis feel they have expressed towards the country. This longing for love, attachment, and national belonging is a formative factor that is often eclipsed in analyses of power and state-making, which are often focused on disciplinary practices of rule and regulation. Of particular relevance here is James Scott's now canonical work, *The Art of Not Being Governed* (2009), in which he argues that hill communities in upland Southeast Asia and Northeast India have historically been focused on evading centralized state authority, and it is only the result of top-down practices of internal colonialism that successive states have brought them under their rule—a process that has accelerated since the 1950s. Gilgit-Baltistan is not unlike Scott's description of hill peoples at state frontiers, but here the chronicle of internal colonialism—while extremely present and pertinent—is simply insufficient. Already out-of-the-way subjects are not trying to run away further, but longing to belong. Their strong desire for inclusion and recognition is a yearning for identity in a world where modernity and the nation-state—no matter how evident their violences are—remain both seductive and enchanting, and a necessary existent without which no vision of life is deemed possible. In Gilgit-Baltistan, this yearning is also historically linked to the affective power of a moral Muslim community promised in the form of Pakistan in 1947, which was deemed more appealing than either Hindu-ruled Kashmir or Hindu-dominated India at the moment of partition.

Such a yearning is not only unexplainable within Scott's framework, but also within that of Judith Butler (1997), who productively raised the question of love, the psyche, and the formation of the subject in *The Psychic Life of Power*. Recognizing that love is what is missing from Althusser's theorization of rule and regulation, Butler rightly guides us that passionate attachments form the psychic ground of power. And yet this attachment seems to be always a disciplinary cultivation. While not denying the possibility of a narcissistic attachment to subjection, I wish to highlight that we also need to recognize the possibility of an affirmative attachment constituted by desire and surrender. This is offered in the language of the heart, and deemed to be abused through the language of force and the law. It is precisely because social emotionality in South Asia inhabits this sensibility of love-offerings, moral community, and affective expectations, that leaders like Gandhi and Baccha Khan—who embraced a politics of love—had such a deep resonance across South Asia. And it is also for this reason that the local struggles for substantive citizenship that I discuss later in the book—poetic, faith-based, and ecological—are fundamentally tied to the ethical–emotional aspirations of promoting *insaaniyat* (humanism) instead of prejudice and ecological stewardship instead of greed.[6]

In *Muslim Becoming*, Naveeda Khan (2012) productively brings our attention to the question of aspiration in Pakistan. Yet her analysis seems to be limited to the striving for a better Muslim-ness that Pakistanis seem to be constantly engaged in. This emphasis occludes attention to other kinds of ethical–political struggles that may be linked to Islam—such as the faith-based movement for textbook reform that I discuss in Chapter 3—but cannot be exhausted only by reference to Islamic discourses and theological argumentation between differently pious subjects. The understanding of Pakistani subjects as 'Muslims' tends to somehow pigeonhole them as pious-or-not, and fails to attend to how they negotiate the state as political, cultural, and development subjects. Moreover, while Khan's emphasis on skepticism also rings true for everyday, middle-class life in Pakistan, it nevertheless fails to capture the sense of anguish that is actually felt due to devastated, betrayed aspirations in the state.

This is perhaps most visible, not from the Lahori streets at the heart of Punjab which form the ethnographic site for Khan, but from marginal, Gilgiti ones in Pakistan's borderlands. Such border territories also make more visible the contradictions that lie at the core of nationalism and state-making in Pakistan.

DELUSIONAL STATES

Several scholars have explored the socio-political and class-centred basis for the emergence of Pakistan, unravelling the constructed idea of Islamic nationalism which eventually came to be identified as the basis for the country's creation.[7] Post-1947, this ideological fixation with Islam as the *raison d'être* of the Pakistani nation was transformed and coupled with an ideological obsession with India, the presumed opposite of an Islamic Pakistan. Notwithstanding the contradictions of such a vision—such as the presence of many more Muslims in India and the familial ties that continued across a yet-to-be-consolidated border—the portrayal of India as an aggressive, overbearing enemy came to constitute a central pillar of state-formative ideology as propagated in particular by military leaders in Pakistan. In this portrayal, the Pakistani state is deemed to face a permanent existential threat from India, and must constantly battle to uphold the glory of Islam as well as its own glory as a Muslim state.

It is often recognized that such hawkish national imaginaries in Pakistan have served to entrench military interests by helping to justify high defense expenditures, a prioritization of the needs of military personnel, as well as direct military intervention in politics. What is less emphasized and theorized is the sheer extent of *delusion* that such an imaginary inculcates in the political and social order. This sense of delusion might be especially visible in the case of Pakistan, but is certainly not limited to it. Rose (1996) has long alerted us to the fundamental role of fantasy in the construction of modern nations and states. Fantasy, though, almost feels too light a term for the kind of paranoid state sensibilities we have actually witnessed in the twentieth- and twenty-first century. Particularly under conditions of the 'war on terror', it would not be far-fetched to argue that delusion has become a global condition of stateness, sustained by simultaneous beliefs of persecution and grandeur and also instrumentalized to justify extreme surveillance regimes as well as highly militarized societies.

The delusional state is most evident, in fact, in a context that is considered decisively incomparable to Pakistan in terms of classic comparative analysis: the United States. Given the historical, political, and economic connections between the US and Pakistan since 1947, the comparison is perfectly apt and necessary. In making this comparison, I am following Philip McMichael (1990) where he critiques the ahistoricity of the conventional comparative method and argues for a historically grounded 'incorporated comparison' approach that reveals the relationality of social processes.

One of the most illuminating theses on the US as state of delusion is offered by Ann McClintock in *Paranoid Empire* (2009). Reflecting on the obscene specters of violence embodied by Guantanamo and Abu Ghraib—'shadowlands of empire', as she compellingly calls them—McClintock argues that the US as empire and nation-state 'has entered the domain of paranoia' where 'fantasies of global omnipotence' combine with 'nightmares of impending attack'. Her elaboration of this double-edged nature of paranoid power is worth quoting at length here:

> ... for it is only in paranoia that one finds simultaneously and in such condensed form both deliriums of absolute power and forebodings of perpetual threat. Hence the spectral and nightmarish quality of the 'war on terror', a limitless war against a limitless threat, a war vaunted by the US administration to encompass all of space and persisting without end. But the war on terror is not a real war, for 'terror' is not an identifiable enemy nor a strategic, real-world target. The war on terror is what William Gibson calls elsewhere 'a consensual hallucination', and the US government can fling its military might against ghostly apparitions and hallucinate a victory over all evil only at the cost of *catastrophic self-delusion* and the infliction of great calamities elsewhere.[8]

I would like to expand McClintock's insightful argument by contending that the shadowlands of empire generated by such 'catastrophic self-delusion' are not limited to post-9/11 extraordinary prisons. Nation-states likes Pakistan have long served as shadowlands of empire. As Saadia Toor demonstrates in *The State of Islam: Culture and Cold War Politics in Pakistan* (2012), the state in Pakistan has been intimately structured by US foreign policy since its inception, and it continues to be implicated in the nightmarish violence under US-led terror wars that have been so foundational to global political rule in the new millennium. Coached and contained as a Cold War ally, Pakistan has come to mirror its imperial master in its delusional, omnipotent sense of power combined with a perpetual threat of engulfment. In both contexts, the delusions and their spectral violence are not spontaneous responses to incidences of attack, but rather outcomes of a long-standing paranoid state militarism that justifies itself through the social production of fear.

In the specific context of Pakistan, the machinery of paranoia and surveillance has expanded to such an extent that a Pakistani journalist has fittingly termed the country as the 'Intelligence Republic of Pakistan' in place of its official label—the Islamic Republic of Pakistan. Nowhere is this paranoid state of permanent existential threat deemed more at stake than in disputed Kashmir, where the twin imperatives of defending Islam and defending the border against India converge. And within Kashmir, Gilgit-Baltistan poses a particularly vexed territorial and religious anxiety because its majority-Shia populace contests the dominant Muslim sensibility that a Sunni-ized Pakistani state has sought to normalize for its citizens. How does the delusional state play out in this fraught region? In addressing this question in the book, my purpose is to shift attention away from the trite narrative of how regionalisms constantly threaten the imagined order of the nation-state. Instead, I provide an ethnographic glimpse of the lived practices through which the state-citizen relation is made, felt, and reworked in the most contested border zone of Pakistan.

Feelings are central to the story of state-citizen relations that I wish to tell, not only because the state and its regions are imagined through particular emotional logics, but also because rule is desired and inhabited emotionally by state subjects.[9] Love, trust, and betrayal is one aspect of how this dynamic is felt in Gilgit-Baltistan, as discussed in the previous section. The other linked dynamic is that of loyalty and suspicion, and in the book, I demonstrate how this dynamic unravels in the context of state-formative processes of militarization and sectarianization. Gilgiti male subjects are not just loving but also especially loyal, and this has to do with the history of male employment as military wage-labour in this frontier region. The 'political economy of defence' in Pakistan—a foundational framing for understanding the Pakistani 'state of martial rule'[10]—is thus underpinned and buttressed in Gilgit-Baltistan by a political economy of feeling. This is a state where militarization is critically linked to livelihoods and cultural orientations, shaping popular understandings of life and politics and hence reordering people's identities and aspirations. These aspects of the cultural–economic politics of militarization have been most compellingly explored in the context of the United States by the pioneering feminist scholar Catherine Lutz (1999, 2004), and it is thus the US again, which provides a frame of connection and comparison for me as I attempt to understand the militarized reality in Pakistan.

My key argument is that the employment of Gilgit-Baltistani men in the military creates loyal subjects who have come to revere the military and the military-state, hence producing the conditions of possibility for continued military authoritarianism in the region. At the same time, the activities of the intelligence agencies—key creators and enactors in the delusional state—constantly render people into permanent suspects and sources of threat. Suspicion is thus integral to the emotional structure of state power as people are *assumed* to be suspect *by definition* because they live in a Shia-majority, disputed border zone. This presumed suspicion is translated into a regime of monitoring and intimidation by the military–intelligence establishment, for which the suspicion serves as a convenient rationale for maintaining its own political and economic authority. More worryingly, the military–intelligence state also accomplishes its rule by promoting suspicion *amongst* citizens, most notably between the Shia and Sunni communities in Gilgit through state-backed sectarianizing discourses and practices. These practices have led to heightened feelings of emotional ill-will amongst these communities, and have damaged the cultures of pluralism that have historically dominated the region. Apart from suspected subjects, thus, the delusional state also produces suspicious subjects.

This strategy has further served to create the effect and affect of Gilgit-Baltistan as a quintessentially sectarian space where Shia–Sunni conflict can 'erupt' anytime unless prevented by an ever-vigilant, supposedly neutral state. Brimming with sectarian sentimentality, the people of Gilgit-Baltistan are thus imagined as irrational and non-political—as in, they are considered incapable of being proper political subjects and agents. By sectarianizing citizenship and politics, the question of substantive citizenship rights in Gilgit-Baltistan is thus trumped, reinforcing the securocratic interests of the state in relation to Kashmir. Ultimately, the political economy of feelings based on loyalty and suspicion results in a militarization of citizenship in Gilgit-Baltistan. It embodies forms of emotional regulation that are paradoxical yet not contradictory: loyalty to an employment-giving military integrates people into the nation and accomplishes rule by creating consent, while suspicion services state power by emotionally disintegrating the region and hindering the possibilities of regional political solidarity and resistance.

BETWEEN BEAUTY AND TERROR

Far from being a harbinger of order, thus, the delusional state in Pakistan ironically thrives by producing a state of disorder—one that is very much perceived as such by Gilgit-Baltistani subjects and constantly critiqued for its duplicity and dangerousness. The spectacular deception of the state, however, is erased in the national imaginary because the region itself is projected as the source of danger instead of state policy. Delusion after all is always underpinned by denial. Simultaneously, the political repression and religious manipulation in Gilgit-Baltistan is invisibilized by the continued representation of the region as a mythical space of immense beauty. Indeed, in national texts and self-imaginings, the region's mountains, glaciers and forests are made central to the very definition of the physical structure, geographical landscape, and ecological constitution of the Pakistani nation and state. This aesthetic politics of nature constitutes another aspect of the affective production of state power in Gilgit-Baltistan, as the imagination and incorporation of the region within the Pakistani nation/state is centrally grounded in the emotional attachments invoked by nature. If maps produce the geo-body of the nation—as Winichakul (1997) has argued—then representational practices surrounding the ecology of particular regions serve to constitute what I call the eco-body of the nation, converting natural splendor into territorial essence and epitome.[11] Moreover, I demonstrate how this eco-body is configured on the ground through transnational conservation and development projects such as national parks, and examine the ways in which they are resisted and re-imagined by Shimshali villagers in Gilgit-Baltistan.

The ecological terrain of struggle is especially significant as it is one that is often overlooked both in studies of Pakistan as well as of Kashmir, ridden as they are with the standard plot of geopolitical security and religious militancy.[12] The last two decades, however, have seen the emergence of a significant body of scholarship on Kashmir that has challenged the domination of a security-centered narrative. Most relevant for my work is scholarship that offers an ethnographic and critical–literary perspective on the Kashmir conflict, emphasizing aspects such as the representation of Kashmir in cultural discourse in India,[13] the social production of the jihadist in Azad Kashmir,[14] the interplay of militarization and humanitarian development in Kargil,[15] law as a site for control and protest,[16] artistic resistances to the violence in Kashmir,[17] and gendered performances in Kashmiri human rights struggles.[18]

Within ethnographic works on Kashmir and Pakistan, my approach is especially aligned with Ravina Aggarwal's work on Ladakh—*Beyond Lines of Control* (2004)—and Magnus Marsden's *Living Islam* (2005) which focuses on Chitral. Both texts examine the lived experience of regional and religious identity in postcolonial contexts that are closely related to Gilgit-Baltistan. Importantly, they also push the boundaries of representation for these contexts beyond folkloric description, romanticized landscapes, and portrayals of tribal life. While Aggarwal illuminates the ways in which marginalized Ladakhi subjects negotiate life in the shadow of the Kashmir conflict, Marsden attends more to the meaning of being Muslim in the Islamicizing context of Northern Pakistan. These texts, however, pay less attention to the ways in which life and identity in these border regions is profoundly structured by the processes of state-making, and the emotionalities that form the ground of such processes—aspects that I emphasize in this book. Moreover, research on Kashmir and Northern Pakistan often tends to ignore how deeply national state-making practices are reinforced and underpinned by neoliberal and imperial politics. In Pakistan's case in particular, I have already highlighted the relevance of the US in grasping delusional state rule and military cultural politics. The terrain of international development in Gilgit-Baltistan similarly cannot be understood without attending to the transnational politics of capital, ecology, and empire.

In the final section of the book titled 'Saving Nature, Saving People', I thus probe both the politics of international biodiversity conservation as well as the politics of imperial humanitarian development. Taking the popular book *Three Cups of Tea* as a point of entry, I demonstrate how feelings of humanitarian care and compassion are used for justifying imperial, military projects of education and counter-insurgency in Gilgit-Baltistan, thus extending my analysis of how militarism is sustained through a political economy of feeling. I further demonstrate how a depoliticized and dehistoricized narrative of the war on terror—a quintessentially delusional one—is produced through a therapeutic tale of humanitarian development in Gilgit-Baltistan that juxtaposes American goodness and character against the constructed ignorance and extremism of the Muslim other.

Hence, while I begin the book by showing how Gilgit-Baltistan is produced as a space of beauty, I end it by elaborating how it simultaneously becomes reduced to a fearful and dangerous space of terror. Oscillating between beauty and terror, loyalty and suspicion, and love and betrayal—opposing yet complementing, overlapping and overflowing—I chart the multiple emotional registers through which state and imperial projects are instantiated and locally negotiated in Gilgit-Baltistan.

THE REGION

Gilgit-Baltistan is often described as a region at the crossroads of South Asia and Central Asia, since it is located between the borders of India, Pakistan, China, and Afghanistan. Criss-crossing the Hindu Kush, Himalayas, and Karakoram mountains, the region of Gilgit-Baltistan covers an area of approximately 72,500 square kilometres and is divided into ten administrative districts—Gilgit, Ghizer, Astore, Ghanche, Shigar, Hunza, Nagar, Diamer, Skardu, and Kharmang. The mountainous and glacial terrain of the region constitutes a key catchment area for the Indus river, which is often described as the lifeline of agriculture in Pakistan. Indeed, the Indus derives around 72 per cent of its mean annual flow from rivers in Gilgit-Baltistan.[19] The region sustains a predominantly agro-pastoral population of around one million, which is spread across some 700 villages and belongs to at least five indigenous ethno-linguistic groups–Shina, Balti, Burushaski, Wakhi, and Khowar. Each of these groups has a multifaceted socio-political and cultural history, including princely dynasties, linguistic patterns, customs, epics, and festivals. Each group also practices distinct kinship relations, and complex intergroup dynamics that vary from valley to valley in this extensive terrain. Apart from stunning peaks, the landscape of the region is defined by fields of wheat, maize, buckwheat, barley, potato, and walnuts amongst other crops, grazing spaces, as well as a variety of fruit orchards. Compared to other areas in Pakistan, land distribution in Gilgit-Baltistan tends to be fairly equal with the average land holding per household being around one hectare.[20] Non-farm employment in businesses, banks, development organizations, and an expanding local government has steadily risen since the completion of the Karakoram Highway (KKH) in 1979 which provides the central link between the region and the rest of Pakistan.

Once home to animistic traditions and Buddhism, the religious landscape of Gilgit-Baltistan is today shaped by the Shia, Sunni, Ismaili, and Nurbakhshi interpretations of Islam. There is a flourishing culture of intellectual discourse in the region, signified by activities such as progressive seminars, critical publications, and literary festivals. People in Gilgit-Baltistan deeply enjoy traditional music and dance, alongside polo which is the region's most popular sport. Gilgit-Baltistan is also renowned as a tourist destination and global biodiversity hotspot. It is incredibly rich in plant and wildlife diversity, supporting several rare and endangered species such as the markhor (*Capra falconeri*) and snow leopard (*Uncia uncia*). Over the last three decades, several conservation organizations as well as other non-profits have initiated development projects in the region.

Historically, the territories that today form Gilgit-Baltistan were under the dual sovereignty of the British as well as the Maharaja of Kashmir, while in practice many of the areas were dominated by feudal kingdoms that had significant independent control over their terrains. In 1935, the areas that came under the rule of the Kashmiri Maharaja—the Gilgit *wazarat* as it was called—was leased by the British from the Maharaja of Kashmir for a period of sixty years. On 1 August 1947, the last Viceroy, Lord Mountbatten, prematurely terminated the lease, effectively returning the region to Maharaja

Hari Singh who was the ruler of Jammu and Kashmir at the time of partition. When the rulers of the princely states of India were given a choice to accede to either Pakistan or India, Maharaja Hari Singh of Kashmir allegedly decided in favor of India on 26 October 1947. The predominantly Muslim population of the Gilgit region resented the collapsing of their territory under 'Kashmir' and opposed the accession of their land to India by a Hindu Maharaja whose sovereignty over their region was already contested by local rulers. Dogra rule from Kashmir was disliked by locals for several reasons: people perceived themselves to be ethnically distinct from Kashmiris, Muslims were underrepresented in Kashmiri armed forces, and there was a prohibition on slaughtering cows.[21] On 31 October 1947, the local paramilitary force called the Gilgit Scouts—led by its British commandant Major Brown—initiated a revolt against the governor of the Jammu and Kashmir state stationed in Gilgit, Brigadier Ghansara Singh, and arrested him with the help of the Muslim soldiers of the Jammu and Kashmir armed force.[22] The territory around Gilgit was thus liberated through a mutiny, and on 1 November 1947, local military and political leaders declared a new independent state centered in Gilgit. This independence was short-lived, however: the leaders of the rebellion and the members of local ruling families realized that the region's security as well as their personal interest would be better served with the Muslim-majority Pakistan. They acceded to Pakistan within two weeks, although 1 November is still celebrated in the region as *yaum-e-azadi*—the 'day of freedom' from the Dogra state of Kashmir.

While the political leadership of Pakistan accepted the accession of the Gilgit region, it did not formally incorporate the region into its territory due to ongoing tensions with India over the control of Jammu and Kashmir. Challenging Hari Singh's accession, the Pakistani government argued that Kashmir's rightful place was in Pakistan due to its Muslim-majority population. It therefore provided support to Pakhtun tribesmen who had invaded Kashmir—ostensibly to liberate and annex Kashmir—but more likely motivated by 'opportunity, bravado, and possibly hunger' instead of Pakistani nationalism.[23] India and Pakistan subsequently became embroiled in a full-fledged war over Kashmir. Aided by local resistance, the Pakistani armed forces obtained control of over 13,297 square kilometres of Kashmir that came to be known as 'Azad Jammu and Kashmir' (AJK)—Azad Kashmir in short—within Pakistan. On 13 August 1948, the United Nations Commission for India and Pakistan (UNCIP) passed a resolution that called for a ceasefire between the two countries, the withdrawal of troops from Kashmir, and the holding of a UN-sponsored plebiscite in both Indian and Pakistan controlled Kashmir to determine the political will of its people. In accordance with this resolution, a ceasefire line was established in July 1949 that separated Indian-controlled Kashmir from its Pakistani counterpart but the agreement to demilitarize and to conduct a plebiscite is yet to be realized.

In April 1949, representatives of the Government of Pakistan, Azad Kashmir, and All Jammu and Kashmir Muslim Conference signed the 'Karachi Agreement' which allowed for Gilgit-Baltistan—then called the 'Northern Areas'—to come under the purview of a Pakistani Political Agent who also controlled the North-West Frontier Province (NWFP), while Azad Kashmir was granted significant autonomy. This Agreement is much maligned in Gilgit today, for it had no representation from Gilgit-Baltistan and sealed the fate of the region by enabling direct Pakistani rule without permitting any democratic rights.

It is important to note that the 1949 UNCIP resolution as well as subsequent UN negotiations regard the region of Gilgit-Baltistan as part of disputed Kashmir, in contrast to the opposition to a political future with Kashmir which was expressed at the moment of partition. The status of Gilgit-Baltistan has thus become intricately intertwined with that of Kashmir. As a disputed border zone, the region is claimed by both Pakistan and India and is internationally considered as forming 86 per cent of Pakistan-controlled Kashmir.

While India denies that there is any dispute and lays total claim to all regions that once came under the purview of the state of Jammu and Kashmir, Pakistan officially regards Kashmir as a 'disputed territory' and a 'frontier undefined'. State-led media campaigns in Pakistan continually raise awareness about the plight of Indian-controlled Kashmir, offer solidarity, and reassert Pakistan's support for Kashmiri *haq-e-khud-iradiyat*—the Kashmiri right to self-determination. Hence, the place of Kashmir in Pakistani state-building is defined by a curious saviour nationalism—a nationalism that is geared towards saving a community, place or people, which is not yet wholly part of the nation. This saviour rhetoric of nationalism on Kashmir has its problems, of course, because it is ultimately motivated by self-interest and seeks to win over more territory and people into the boundary of the Pakistani nation and state. It is also problematic because the emphasis on Indian atrocities in Pakistani media has historically been central to the production of a militarized ethos in Pakistan, in which Indian violence against Kashmir is used to create support for Pakistani military domination by whipping up anti-India sentiment. Yet in the peculiar case of Kashmir, the saviour nationalism of Pakistan has a liberatory dimension and potential as well because unlike the Indian stance on Kashmir, it is predicated on advocating self-determination for the subject population. In discourse at least—and discourses are real and impactful—the official policy of Pakistan on Kashmir remains cognizant of Kashmiri aspirations and rights through its emphasis on the region as a disputed territory with the promised right to a plebiscite. This is not just reiterated to the Pakistani public internally, but was most recently reinforced by Pakistani ambassadors internationally as India escalated its brutal violence in Kashmir in the latter half of 2016. It is not insignificant to Kashmiris that Pakistan is often the only country raising the issue of Kashmiri self-determination in international forums.

Of course, Pakistan gets a kick out of reporting Indian brutalities abroad, and itself has a record of suppressing dissent in Azad Kashmir and Gilgit-Baltistan, both of which continue to be principally ruled through the Pakistani central government as well as the military-state that I discussed in the previous section. Importantly, whether the question is that of Azad Kashmir or Gilgit-Baltistan, there tends to be an 'intellectual silence' on both these regions within academic and policy debates in Pakistan.[24] This is reflective of the larger social and emotional imaginary in the country, within which Kashmir figures primarily as a place where Indian soldiers commit atrocities, and where Pakistanis seek to support and save their Muslim brothers and sisters. Pakistan even observes a 'Kashmir Day' on 5 February every year—a holiday that is meant to express solidarity with Kashmiris fighting against Indian oppression. Kashmir is thus not just a territory that the Pakistani state desires, and one that is used to fuel a massive military apparatus. Like a flag or an anthem, a particular interpretation of the *masla-e-Kashmir* (Kashmir Problem) has been turned into a potent, emotional symbol of the Pakistani nation itself and the struggle for the liberation of Kashmir has become a legitimating ground for performing Pakistani nationalism. That this saviour nationalism is built on the backs of a terrible state policy of repression and sponsored militancy in Pakistan-administered Kashmir as well as in Pakistan at large is rarely brought to public vision. In the following section, I highlight my own surprises, tensions, and realizations as I struggled to understand and research the political and social life of conflict in Gilgit-Baltistan.

NAVIGATING THE FIELD

Before commencing my dissertation research in Gilgit-Baltistan in 2003, I had visited the region several times as a tourist and as a development worker. In particular, I had stayed with a local family in Gilgit for three months in the summer of 2001, as an intern at an environmental non-profit. This was an incredible learning experience, as I had the opportunity to conduct fieldwork in fifteen villages of the region on issues of gender relations, the built environment, and community development. Hence, when I decided to return to Gilgit-Baltistan as an academic researcher, I had some degree of confidence in my ability to navigate the field context—even if my topical focus was now far more political. I was worried too, of course: an American colleague had tried to dissuade me from my research, informing me about how previous academics interested in political processes in the region had been harassed by the Pakistani intelligence agencies and were eventually unable to complete their work. But these researchers were of foreign origin. I felt that as a Pakistani with previous development experience in the region, I was more of an 'insider' as compared to a foreigner who would clearly be perceived as an 'outsider'. Things would surely be easier for me. As it turned out, this was sheer naiveté on my part.

At the most basic level, I had anticipated but not quite grasped the difference between going to a remote, largely rural context as a non-governmental organization (NGO) worker and as an independent researcher. City folk who are engaged in internships and consultancies in Gilgit find themselves in a framework of facilitation that is comfortable and privileged. The local NGO provides housing, transport, and, most importantly, a meaningful status. Now that I was in Gilgit as an academic, these basic necessities of inhabiting a place had to be accomplished, instead of being assumed. My housing arrangements were always in flux, and involved stays with two wonderful host families, crashing at friends when one host family had moved to Islamabad and the other had guests, a girls' hostel, and a teaching resource centre that provided lodging. Transport was now about catching the public Suzuki, Wagon, or taxi, instead of a four-wheel drive that picks and drops. The fact that I was a young, unmarried, female researcher made matters more complicated. For example, my stay in the girls' hostel was short-lived as I often had to be out in the evenings, interviewing men, and this was deemed to affect the reputation of the hostel. On a few occasions, the driver in a Suzuki could be uncomfortably frank and inquisitive, as an unaccompanied, privileged-looking Pakistani woman catching public transport is not a common sight in Gilgit.

But these were minor adjustments, compared to the major dilemma I faced: the constant suspicion of what an independent, unmarried Pakistan woman was *really* doing in Gilgit-Baltistan. That I, out of my own accord, wanted to research the political predicament of Gilgit-Baltistan for my PhD thesis was often considered entirely implausible. The most popular local theory for my existence was that I was looking for a suitable boy to marry. People I met joked with me about whether I was 'researching' prospective grooms, and I was always amusedly assuring them that I had no such intentions. It was hard to be amused, though, when people starting suspecting me of being a spy.

The first time a Gilgiti suggestively brought up my potential 'Indian' backing, I was so shocked that I started laughing—till I realized that the accusation was serious and I was expected to defend myself. In 2005, I was interviewing Sajid, an activist and development practitioner based in Gilgit. I was introduced to him through a friend of mine who was Sajid's relative and a prominent journalist of the region. Sajid also knew me through the host family with whom I had stayed in Gilgit in 2001 during my internship. Hence, I was not a random person who had just arrived at his door. And yet, Sajid kept asking me circuitous questions about whether my 'assignment' was in any way sponsored by a 'neighbouring country'. When I tried to convince him that this was my sixth trip to the region and I got interested in its politics out of my own curiosities, he said: 'I would like to believe you. But I have never met a Pakistani who has genuinely showed concern for Gilgit-Baltistan. You come here to rule us, or for tourism and NGO work. No one talks about rights.'

My conversation with Sajid was also an early indicator of the difficulties that lay ahead for me in the research process. I had to get accustomed to the discomfiting reference of 'you Pakistanis' which often emerged in my interviews, and which constructed me as representative of a callous and unjust Pakistan. The spying allegations only multiplied to include the possibility that I could be a Pakistani spy, or worse, an American spy as I studied at an American university. The history of my predecessors worked to validate local mistrust. People in Gilgit were all too familiar with academic researchers who had ultimately turned out to be foreign spies. I was frustrated, and even hurt, when I discovered that a couple of people whom I had interviewed, befriended, and trusted, still suspected me of being untrustworthy. Eventually I realized that this suspicion was more structural than personal. It was an index of what social relationships had become in Gilgit, and characteristic of conflict zones more generally that have become engulfed with spies and surveillance.

It was this context of surveillance that eventually compelled me to cut my stay short. While I managed to conduct research in the region, my plans for an extensive stay in the region were disrupted by the 'messages' that I started receiving through two friends who were assisting me in my research. They had been 'approached' regarding my activities, and were told that I must cease my interviews and leave the region. When one of them really pleaded with me, I left—but I kept returning for shorter periods. I did not want to get in trouble, but I especially did not want to bring any harm to my facilitators.

Sociological and ethnographic research in Gilgit is also deeply affected by the region's sectarianized context—a topic that I discuss at length in Chapters 3 and 4. I was often asked about my sectarian identity at the beginning or during an interview, if the interviewee had not already discovered it through his or her own sources. My identity as an Ismaili Muslim often allowed my Shia and Sunni respondents to open up to me, especially when discussing matters of sectarianism. Ismailis in Gilgit are both admired and resented for their highly educated, liberal ethos, as well as the economic advancements that the community has made as a result of the work of the Aga Khan Development Network (AKDN). But Ismailis are also often perceived as peace-keepers in a volatile place. It is not unusual, for example, for an Ismaili judge to be appointed to mediate a dispute between Shia and Sunni parties in Gilgit.

Interestingly, my sectarian reception in the region transformed mid-way through my research, after I got married. That I now had a Pakistani husband was most comforting for my Gilgiti friends—it meant that I was a normal, family-oriented person, not an itinerant, Americanized woman. But the fact that I had married someone who grew up in a Sunni household was met with visible displeasure from several of my Ismaili acquaintances, even as many more remained perfectly accepting. Shia friends remained the same towards me, while Sunni friends and respondents were decidedly pleased. In fact, on two separate occasions, Sunni friends who were helping me with my research introduced me with pride to Sunni interviewees: '*Ab yeh humari ho gai hain*' (now she belongs to us).

This begins to point to the gendered nature of my research in Gilgit-Baltistan as well. In terms of access, being a woman did not pose any significant difficulty as I could interview both men and women freely, and travel to any region that I wished to visit. In terms of attitude, however, I sometimes had to contend with patriarchal notions of women's worth and work. A female, Pakistani researcher asking questions about 'sensitive' issues was considered absurd by some male acquaintances, who referred to me as a 'little girl' and were non-serious, dismissive, or patronizing towards my efforts. I was told by men and women that instead of talking about politics, I should work on topics such as folklore or work for an NGO. While such attitudes were upsetting at the time, it is important to emphasize that they were also quite rare. My research more generally received affirming and enthusiastic support from colleagues, mentors, friends, and respondents in Gilgit-Baltistan. They appreciated the fact that I was working on an under-studied topic, and that I had chosen to work as a visiting lecturer at the local, government-run Karakoram International University. My identity as a Karachite also proved to be a surprising source of connection with several male and female respondents. Whenever I said 'Karachi' in response to the ubiquitous question about my place of origin, I was almost always met with a nostalgic smile followed by details about the months or years someone had 'sat' in Karachi.

My place in the Gilgiti social landscape was also aided by my clothing decisions. For the duration of field research, I had decided to cover my head with a dupatta and wear full sleeves kurtas. This made me more comfortable in my surroundings, and it also met the approval of people around me. But fitting into local culture as a researcher is more complicated than adopting 'local dress', as I learnt gradually. One afternoon, for example, I was walking a short distance from one NGO office to another on a public road, with a local female friend Asmara. NGO offices are spaces where the usual Gilgiti norms of women's dress are somewhat relaxed, so women who might cover their heads in the bazaar may not be compelled to do so in the office premises. When Asmara and I walked out of the first NGO, I promptly covered my head— as had become second nature to me anytime I was in public space. Asmara followed suit, but a little while later, lightly said, '*Yaar* why did you cover your head? I have to do it because of you.' Completely stunned, I replied, 'What? I do it because of *you*! And to fit in! You know well I don't cover my head in Karachi.' She said, 'Yes, I know why you do it, but this is a short road and I don't think we need to cover our heads here. Who made these rules anyway? Are we not decent like this? Why is clothing a sign of respect, and not behavior?' Gendered norms are thus not static, and are constantly shifting as men and women struggle to negotiate with and manoeuvre societal expectations. On several occasions after this conversation, I accompanied Asmara to new public spaces—such as a restaurant in the bazaar—where it was not common at the time for local women to dine without men, or to dine at all. Asmara also suggested that I should stop covering my head so that people around me who appreciated my research would see that a woman could be honourable without covering her head. While I did not heed this advice for the sake of consistency, my conversations with Asmara nevertheless helped me gain a deeper appreciation of how ethnographers find themselves inserted into everyday negotiations of culture and power.

Let me now share details of my specific research location and approach (Map I.1). While I have travelled, stayed and researched in several parts of Gilgit-Baltistan over the last 15 years, the ethnographic ground of this book is primarily formed by two sites: the city of Gilgit which is located in Gilgit district and forms the key political and administrative center of Gilgit-Baltistan, and the village of Shimshal which is located at the extreme end of Hunza district alongside the Pakistan–China border.

Gilgit city has a population of approximately 200,000, while the Shimshal village is inhabited by around 1,700 residents. When I refer to 'Gilgitis' in the book, the reference is to those who reside in Gilgit, but it must be clarified

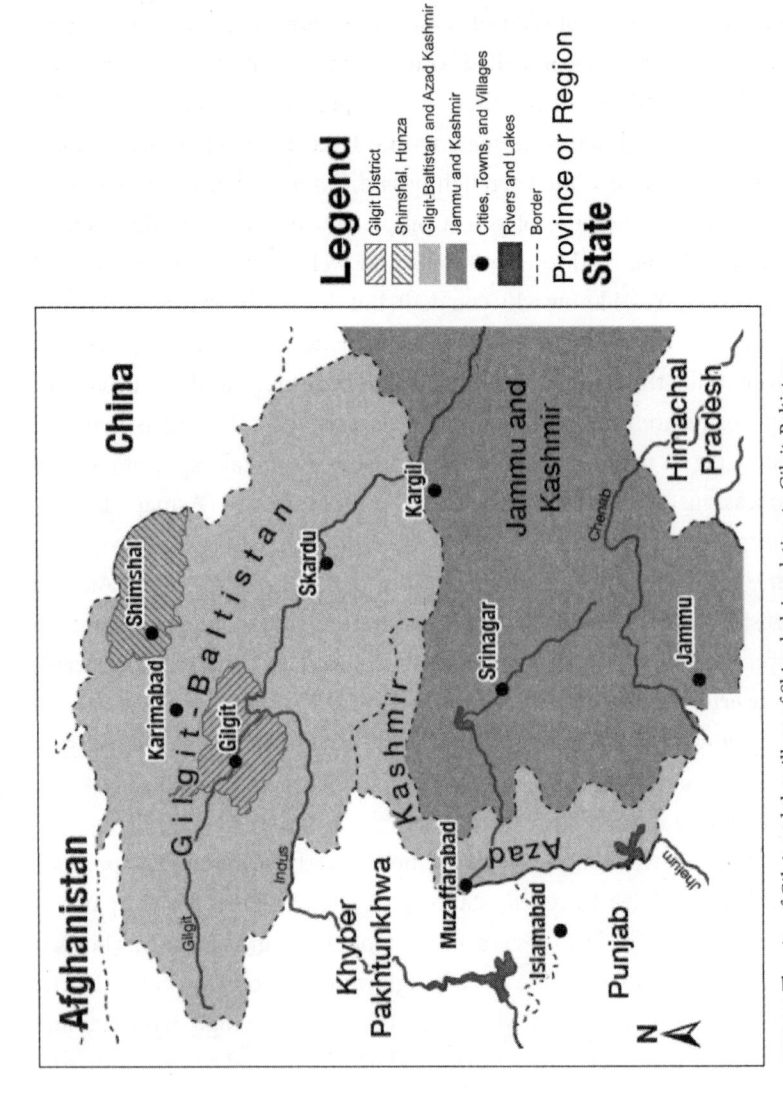

MAP I.1 The city of Gilgit and the village of Shimshal, in relation to Gilgit-Baltistan.
Source: Map by Moacir P. de Sa Pereira. Made with Natural Earth. Free vector and raster map data@naturalearthdata.com.
Note: Map not drawn to scale and may not represent authentic international boundaries.

that the inhabitants of Gilgit belong to all parts of Gilgit-Baltistan. Even families living in Gilgit for two generations might still trace their origin to Astore, Ghizer, Hunza, Skardu, or other regions of Gilgit-Baltistan where they may continue to have land, relatives, and an alternate residence. As indicated earlier, extended stays in the border region of Gilgit-Baltistan for investigating 'sensitive' topics was risky both for myself and for my research subjects. Hence, I conducted my research over a period of nine months during several trips to the region between 2003 and 2007, with the longest one lasting from August to November 2006. Serving as a visiting lecturer at the Karakoram University in Gilgit offered me a meaningful local status, and greatly facilitated my research due to the generous support of faculty and students. To understand state power and social struggle in Gilgit-Baltistan, I used a combination of ethnographic methods including participant observation, documentary analysis—of government data, historical texts, religious pamphlets, NGO reports, political magazines, and poetry collections—as well as open-ended interviews with over fifty respondents. The interviewees included political and social activists, development workers, members of the local state administration and legislature, journalists, pastoralists, shopkeepers, poets, preachers, students, teachers, mothers, and women from ordinary families. Many of my respondents were men, partly because public politics and activism continues to be dominated by men in the region. Most of my friendships, however, were with women who enormously aided in deepening my perspective on the local experience of state power, sectarianism, and development in the region.

THE JOURNEY OF WRITING

Feelings are not only central to the state–citizen relation but also active in the process of research and publication. To claim my own citizenship within academic worlds, I have often been asked to 'change the tone' of my work—a tempering that is of thoughts, feelings, and ultimately, of politics. An analysis that cares is often deemed feeble and unacceptable. Specifically, the transnational lens of my work which incorporates the US and Pakistan in a single analytic frame causes deep discomfort to white reviewers, who prefer that my analysis remain confined to the 'local'. In the historical moment that we find ourselves in, it is easy and popular to believe that Pakistan is exceptionally messed up, and hence evidence to the contrary is dismissed, while bringing in the extraordinary violence of the US into the picture is actively thwarted. My critique of US imperialism and humanitarianism in Chapter 6, for example, was deemed by some reviewers to be 'irrelevant' to understanding Pakistan and Gilgit-Baltistan, by others to be too 'indignant'. One reviewer felt that my discussion was 'crude' and polemical. My language could be more 'nuanced'—which meant, not as direct. Hence, political anger and inconveniently historicized critique that feels and exposes imperialism has little place in 'objective' social scientific knowledge till it is pacified and sanitized. This impulse to sanitize was reflected perfectly in the response of yet another reviewer of this work, who felt that the words 'imperial' and 'empire' in my text should be deleted altogether—something that goes against the very premise of this book in which Gilgit-Baltistan and Pakistan are situated squarely within the imperial context of the Cold War and the war on terror. In these judgments that pass for reviews, the positionality and politics of the reviewers remains unquestioned, while the authors are asked to *tone down* their writing in order to prove the seriousness and objectivity of their research.

What I am describing here is reflective of the larger policing mechanisms within academic systems of power. A critical–progressive text, grounded in inconvenient facts, argument, and empathy might trigger deep unease and fear from imperial others—emotional responses that themselves protect the status quo, and yet remain unacknowledged and masked in review processes that privilege the imperial perspective as neutral, and sabotage perspectives that inquire. When such perspectives, theory, and critique come from a Pakistani, brown, Muslim woman in this historical conjuncture, it strikes as a talking back that is resisted in subtle and overt ways while never being exposed as such—because the problem of *reactionary emotion* is quietly transferred to the author instead of the imperial reviewer. It is also felt as an assertion of equality and confidence that must be tamed and contained. Such punitive gate-keeping of feminist knowledge from colonized people of colour, reinforces the racial, gendered, and religious biases that are already rampant within deeply embedded structures of the world and academia.[25] And it is akin to patriarchal forms of disciplining that require women to be nice, polite, emotionally cautious and subdued, and politically conformist and non-confrontational. The irony, of course, is that privileged reviewers cannot identify the emotional terrain of their own privilege, and reflect on their deep-seated power that has historically deprived diverse voices of legitimacy, and suppressed them through tone and content policing. This deprivation and suppression is the bedrock of academic imperialism.

Resisting this imperialism to the extent permissible within the very structures of academia, I begin the narrative struggle in this book with Chapter 1 which examines the power of representation and the representation of power in Gilgit-Baltistan. I demonstrate how the region is centrally imagined in Pakistan through the lens of natural beauty, and how its physical landscape serves to produce the eco-body of the Pakistani nation-state. I further interrogate how knowledge about the territory of Gilgit-Baltistan has been historically regulated through discursive modes of illegibility, framing the way the region was named the 'Northern Areas', the way it was mapped, and the way in which it continues to be represented in the Pakistani constitution, census, and textbook. Chapter 2 explores the contested meanings of militarization in Gilgit-Baltistan. I analyse the multiple ways in which the military–intelligence regime—the most potent face of the Pakistani state in Gilgit-Baltistan— occupies bodies, discourses, and subjectivities in the region, and emphasize the emotional regulation through which this power is entrenched. In Chapter 3, I investigate the gradual sectarianization of the state and citizenry in Gilgit-Baltistan, detailing how inter-sect relations in the region have been radically transformed through international and national mobilizations of political Islam. Focusing on the realm of education, I discuss how in the early years of Pakistan the place of Islam in Pakistan's education system embraced a social justice orientation, thus offering liberatory possibilities. However, gradually, different visions of Islam came to be constructed as normal in the Pakistani curriculum. I then discuss how Sunni-biased public school texts became the subject of a 'textbook controversy' between 2000–2005 in Gilgit, leading to the most potent Shia movement against the Pakistani state in recent history, and one that offers an important lens for understanding the negotiation of religious identity in contemporary Pakistan. Chapter 4 continues the attention on sectarianization in educational spaces, illuminating how sectarian discord is felt, reproduced, and contested in everyday life in Gilgit. Drawing upon ordinary, daily encounters between members of the two prominent sects—Sunni and Shia—in the region, I argue that a 'sectarian imaginary' has become dominant in Gilgit whereby feelings of ill-will and suspicion have become routinized and normalized. At the same time, I discuss local poetic performances and political seminars through which Gilgitis strive to create a critical public space for contesting sectarianism, and hope to promote a progressive ethos of faith and politics in their strife-torn region. Chapter 5 turns the attention to the politics of nature conservation in Gilgit-Baltistan, demonstrating how the region is produced as an eco-body on the ground through the creation of national parks and community-based conservation schemes. I demonstrate how this territorialization of nature has been successfully resisted by the agro-pastoral community of Shimshal in an epistemic–material struggle, which counters the exclusionary ideals of development through which peasants and pastoralists are relegated as backward and marginal. In Chapter 6, the final chapter, I interrogate the discourse of humanitarian empire and education—like international conservation, this is another form of international development discourse through which Gilgit-Baltistan has been represented and reshaped in recent years. Taking the immensely popular book *Three Cups of Tea* as its point of entry, I detail how the texts and practices of imperial humanitarianism in Northern Pakistan have attempted to reinvent the American military as a culturally sensitive and caring institution, thus serving to justify and extend the culture of empire and its so-called war on terror.

In analysing the micro-politics of multiple projects of rule such as mapping, surveillance, textbook representation, and imperial conservation, my purpose is to go beyond a narrative of disenfranchisement and violence to examine what other kinds of contestations affect life in 'conflict zones' and how they reshape the state and its border subjects. Simultaneously, I analyse a range of ordinary and organized cultural–political action through which agents—including state officials themselves—strive to promote a progressive vision of ethics and politics in Gilgit-Baltistan. Covering religio-political movements, literary performances, and community-based conservation initiatives, I examine how people in Gilgit-Baltistan feel their present and struggle to imagine new social futures for their region. In particular, I emphasize that citizen-subjects in Gilgit-Baltistan—from political activists and preachers to poets and pastoralists—are demanding inclusion not only in terms of political rights—an aspect that over-determines the discourse on Kashmir—but also through struggles for religious recognition and ecological sovereignty which they see as integral to a meaningful life of dignity.

NOTES

1. Kashmir is described as the 'heart of hostility' between India and Pakistan in the Washington Times article by Emily Wax, 'In Kashmir, stone throwers face off with Indian security forces', 17 July 2010.
2. My emphasis.
3. Varma (2009); my emphasis
4. On the poetics of love, knowledge, and resistance in South Asia, see Ali (2016).
5. Gaur (2008).
6. Here, it is important to recognize feminist contributions that have long emphasized the epistemic centrality of emotions. See for example, Hochschild (1983), Jagger (1989), and Ahmed (2004).
7. For example, Alavi (1990), Daechsel (2009), and Devji (2013).
8. McClintock (2009: 51); my emphasis.
9. For insightful analyses of the connections between state power, emotions, and the everyday, see Good and Good (1988), Berezin (1999), Stoler (2004), Gregg and Seigworth (2010), and Laszczkowski and Reeves (2015).
10. Jalal (1990).
11. Kabir (2009) and Ali (2014).
12. For a notable exception, see Bhan and Trisal (2017).
13. Kabir (2009).
14. Robinson (2013).
15. Bhan (2013).
16. Hoffman and Duschinski (2014).
17. Misri (2014) and Kaul (2017).
18. Zia (2016). Historical understandings of Kashmir have also been enhanced through critical scholarship in recent years. Amongst other dimensions, this work has focused on the origin of the Kashmir dispute and the question of legal accession (Lamb, 1991), the changing contours of the Kashmir policy of India and Pakistan and the popular insurgency that erupted in Indian-controlled Kashmir in 1989 (Bose, 1997; Ganguly, 1997), the pre-partition histories of political and religious dynamics in the region under Dogra and British rule (Zutshi, 2003; Rai, 2004), the fraught relationship between the Northern Areas and Kashmir (Kreutzmann, 2008), the histories of violence and dispossession in Kashmir (Schofield, 2010; Snedden, 2011), the multiple

imaginings of Kashmir in local literary and historical traditions (Zutshi, 2014), and the gendered dimensions of violence in Kashmir (Shekhawat, 2014). Basharat Peer's Curfewed Night (2010) and the edited volume by Sanjay Kak Until My Freedom Has Come (2011), are other notable texts that have contributed to a deeper understanding of everyday life and cultural politics in Kashmir.

19   Government of Pakistan and IUCN (2003).
20   Kreutzmann (1991).
21   Ali (1990).
22   Sökefeld (2005) and Bangash (2010).
23   Haroon (2007: 181).
24   The term 'intellectual silence' is used in reference to Azad Kashmir by Rifaat Hussain (2004).
25   'People of colour' is not a term I connect with or like to use, especially because it poses white as neutral, a centre that is beyond colour, as if white is not a colour like any other. 'People of colour' is normalized in US academic discourse as a self-ascribed descriptor—defined by white theory itself for the majority of the world's population. It is a throughly unintuitive term for me as someone who grew up in Pakistan, but we live under conditions of Western-centric academic discourse, in which even feminist theory has had to normalize such otherizing categories as 'people of colour' in order to articulate its critique of racial injustice and violence.

PART I

Representation and Repression

1

UNIMAGINED COMMUNITIES IN THE ECO-BODY OF THE NATION

೮೦೦೩

Within academic analyses of state-making, it has become axiomatic to argue that state power over a territory is achieved by implementing discursive techniques of legibility, uniformity, and transparency. Indeed, in James Scott's pioneering work *Seeing Like a State* (1998), the realization of the control of the state depends precisely on the visible *seeing* and objectification of spaces and subjects. Yet the case of Gilgit-Baltistan complicates this argument because the region has historically embodied an opaque, inconsistent, and distorted representation within Pakistan. This illegibility, however, cannot be interpreted as a sign of inadequate or non-existing state authority in some kind of non-state space.

To examine this paradox, this chapter explores how the border territory of Gilgit-Baltistan has been historically constructed within the representational practices of the Pakistani nation-state. The data under review concerns the 'Northern Areas', which defined the name, status, and representation of Gilgit-Baltistan from the 1947 partition till 2009. I have thus retained the region's previous name in this chapter, as I examine the multiple modes through which knowledge about the Northern Areas is regulated in sites where the nation-state is articulated and reproduced, such as textbooks, maps, and censuses. On the one hand, I show how the Northern Areas is constructed as the eco-body of the nation—a territory that is reduced to its physical environment, and epitomized as the quintessential, pictorial landscape of Pakistan. On the other hand, my analysis demonstrates how the presence of the region in discursive sites is constituted by the very absence of its political and social identity. This amounts to an effective *unseeing* that is produced through ambiguous, contradictory, and exclusionary modes of representation, which continue to dominate even after the name change to Gilgit-Baltistan. Such modes suggest that far from embodying legibility, liminal, suspended spaces like Gilgit-Baltistan occupy a structural political indeterminacy that may translate into their illegibility within national discourses. Moreover, this illegibility serves to invisibilize the region, its people, and their political marginalization from the imagination of 'Pakistan' and 'Kashmir', hence feeding into the process of rule and legitimation that has marked this region as politically unsettled in the first place.

WHAT'S IN A NAME?

Naming is a basic yet critical way of attaching meaning to a place. It is a crucial tool of state power precisely because it can be used to privilege certain meanings over others. States also claim the power to name because it reflects ownership of space and, in fact, it is the very act of naming that symbolically transforms space into place and embeds it within the territory of a state.[1] It is an effect of power that people come to internalize names as the permanent attributes of the places they denote. This naturalization of place-names obscures the fact that place-names are chosen by authorities of power, and may reflect strategic political aims linked to nation-building and state-formation.[2] The creation and naming of Pakistan's capital city of 'Islamabad' is a case in point. Islamabad literally means the abode of Islam, or the place where Islam thrives. Such a naming and thus, place-making practice reflects the attempts by the first military regime in Pakistan to entrench Islam as the dominant motif and legitimating basis for the new nation-state.

In disputed territories, the politics of nomenclature is even more consequential, and this can be understood by exploring the history and significance of the name 'Northern Areas'. Historically, the region that formed the Northern Areas was never united politically; it comprised several independent princely kingdoms such as those of Hunza, Nagar, Ishkoman, and Yasin.[3] These kingdoms paid tribute to, and recognized the sovereignty of the Maharaja of the Princely State of Jammu and Kashmir. To distinguish these principalities from the Kashmir Valley, Jammu, and Ladakh regions, they were referred to as the Northern Areas of Kashmir in official documents.[4] Under the British/Kashmiri administration, these areas were further classified into the political units of Gilgit Agency, Gilgit Wazarat, and Baltistan—administrative classifications that remained operative even after the partition of 1947 when the entire region came under Pakistani control. Between 1972 and 1974, the Pakistani government abolished the administrative units of Gilgit Agency, Gilgit Wazarat, and Baltistan, as well as the feudal estates of local kings that were contained within these units. The region was then integrated into a single political unit that was brought under the direct rule of the federal administration. This unit was renamed as the 'Federally Administered Northern Areas' (FANA), though it became commonly known as the 'Northern Areas' or the 'Northern Areas of Pakistan'.

While the enforcement of direct rule over the region paved the way for institutional domination, the naming of the region signified a form of symbolic control. Even if the name was essentially a historical leftover, its post-1970s use was blatantly and strategically possessive. The official and popular use of the name 'Northern Areas of Pakistan' made it clear that the Northern Areas were not the 'Northern Areas of Kashmir', hence changing the region into a non-negotiable place. More importantly, by reducing the region to a mere component of Pakistan, the name also denied a sense of regional identity that would be embodied by locally significant names such as 'Gilgit-Baltistan' or 'Boloristan'. By erasing this local identity while firmly embedding the region within Pakistan, the strategic naming of the region thus symbolized the state project of 'permanent possession through dispossession'.[5]

The name of Northern Areas constituted a further form of erasure because of the effect of non-specificity that it created: it seemed like a reference to a general geographical space rather than the name of a particular demarcated place. Not surprisingly, it was often interpreted as an allusion to 'areas in the north of Pakistan', or 'Northern Pakistan', instead of being recognized as an identifier for a specific administrative unit of Pakistan called the 'Northern

Areas'. Moreover, due to a similar geographical connotation, the name of the Northern Areas was also commonly misunderstood as a reference for the 'North-West Frontier Province' (NWFP)—now called Kyber-Pukhtoonkhwa—which is adjacent to the Northern Areas.[6] Furthermore, people living outside of the Northern Areas also tended to confuse the region with the geographically non-contiguous tribal region called 'Federally Administered Tribal Areas' and specifically its territory of 'Wana', presumably because the names of these regions are similar to the official name 'Federally Administered Northern Areas' and acronym 'FANA' of the Northern Areas. Together with the already vague and mystifying nature of the name 'Northern Areas', such conflations further served to obscure the existence and identity of the actual region called the Northern Areas.

The power of naming and its relationship to the identity and marginality of a place was first revealed to me during my research in the Northern Areas in August 2004. On a visit to the Gilgit Public Library, I had ended up joining a discussion that included local politicians, bureaucrats, and lawyers. Over a duration of three hours, I listened and took notes while the rest of the group discussed various forms of political injustice that were prevalent in the Northern Areas. At one point, a consensus emerged that part of the reason for the disempowerment of the region and its people was the lack of awareness of this very fact within the 'rest of Pakistan' and that the people of Pakistan needed to be made aware of the region's issues in order to exert pressure on the Pakistani government for changing the status quo. A local politician pointed out that this was a monumental task, as people in the cities of Pakistan did not even know what the Northern Areas were. He said:

> When you tell anyone in Karachi or Lahore that you are from the Northern Areas, either they don't understand what it means or they think we are from NWFP. They are so ignorant.

Responding to this comment, another politician added:

> Part of the problem is that Pakistanis are ignorant. But part of it is also that our name is *ajeeb*.[7] It does not sound like the name of a place. *Is naam nay humain benaam kar dia hai* [this name has rendered us unknown].[8]

Over the course of my extended research in the region, I realized that an overwhelming number of inhabitants of the region similarly perceived the name of the Northern Areas as personally and politically marginalizing. The renaming of the region—which eventually happened in 2009—was in response to a strong demand of several local political parties that saw it as a way of reclaiming their identity from the Pakistan state and as a necessary first step for foregrounding and resolving their political predicament.

Importantly, the crisis of naming extends beyond the name of the region itself. The top court in Gilgit-Baltistan is the 'Chief Court', which does not follow the norms and nomenclature of a 'High Court', as activists in the region have constantly emphasized. Hence, the binding consultation of the Chief Justice of the Pakistani Supreme Court with regard to the appointment of judges is not applicable to the Chief Court, with the result that a sitting Law Minister can also be appointed as a judge on contract.[9] Similarly, the demand for regional legislative powers has been evaded through a series of 'reforms' which were essentially reforms of nomenclature: the Northern Areas Advisory Council set up in 1971 became the Northern Areas Executive Council in 1994, the Northern Areas Legislative Council in 1999, and then the Northern Areas Legislative Assembly in 2007—symbolic changes that rarely devolved any real powers to the region. The current 'Gilgit-Baltistan Legislative Assembly', which came into being in 2009 is the first to be based on general elections—and certainly a major step forward in terms of local demands for democratic rights—but the reforms under which it was established do not have constitutional protection and the assembly itself is superseded by the centre-controlled 'Gilgit-Baltistan Council'. The institutional structure of Gilgit-Baltistan has been modelled partly after Azad Kashmir, and partly after a Pakistani province with the result that both in nomenclature and in actual practice, it can only be described as 'like a self-governed territory' and 'like a province', without having a well-defined status of its own.

UNIMAGINED COMMUNITIES IN NATURALIZED LANDSCAPES

Ironically, while people within Pakistan may not have been able to recognize the name of the Northern Areas or the specific place it denoted, they could nevertheless identify particular kinds of physical spaces that fall largely within the bounds of the Northern Areas—such as the valleys of Gilgit and Hunza and mountains like Nanga Parbat and K2. This is because the region has come to epitomize the 'natural beauty' of Pakistan, constituting what I call its eco-body. As such, it occupies a central place in the geographical imagination of the nation. While I question the ways of seeing which normalize particular landscapes as beautiful and others not, I do not wish to deny the picturesque qualities of the landscape of the Northern Areas per se. Rather, my concern is with exploring how a mode of inclusion based on spatial appeal has come to embody and produce a number of exclusionary effects. To explore this dynamic of inclusion and exclusion, I now turn my attention to the representation of the Northern Areas in specific texts on Pakistan.

The first book that I examine is titled *Pakistan Studies: Class X*.[10] It is a 10th-grade textbook designed for government schools in the province of Punjab, which is the most populous province of Pakistan. I have not conducted a detailed investigation of official textbooks on Pakistan Studies used in provinces other than Punjab, but a brief overview of them has given me a sense that they treat the region of the Northern Areas in ways similar to the one in Punjab that I now proceed to analyse.

The Northern Areas are conspicuous in the text by their very absence. In the entire book, there is not even a single mention of the word 'Northern Areas'. At one point, the text does state that the Karakoram Highway 'links northern areas of Pakistan with China'.[11] However, due to the lack of capitalization, one gets a sense that it is 'areas in the north of Pakistan' that are being referred to, not the specific region called Northern Areas which in fact contains the bulk of the Karakoram Highway. While the regional identity of the Northern Areas is unacknowledged, locations within the region are frequently referenced and included as parts of Pakistan. For example, a chapter titled 'The Natural Resources of Pakistan' mentions that marble is available in 'Gilgat', and that the Pakistan International Airlines (PIA) passenger and cargo services are available in 'Gilgat' and 'Skardu'. Gilgit—which is consistently misspelt as 'Gilgat'—and Skardu are the main towns of the Northern Areas, located in the districts of Gilgit and Skardu respectively. A chapter called the 'The Land of Pakistan' more explicitly refers to the Northern Areas. It has a section on the 'Physical Features' of Pakistan, which in fact, begins with a description of the 'Northern Mountain Ranges'. The part of these ranges that falls within Pakistan primarily lies in the Northern Areas, but this fact is not acknowledged, though specific valleys of the region like Gilgit and Hunza are mentioned. The Himalayan, Karakoram, and Hindukush mountains that comprise these ranges are each described at length in separate sub-sections, and mention details such as:

> ...between Karakoram mountains and Himalayas the valleys of Gilgat and Hunza are situated. The mountain peaks surrounding these areas are covered with snow throughout the year. When the summer season sets in, these valleys are full of life. The people are busy in different activities. The hill torrents flow with great force and the green grass grows everywhere.[12]

The region of the Northern Areas is thus produced as an eco-body through its romanticization as a scenic landscape, significant to the nation merely for its beautiful mountains and lush valleys. The abstract 'people' of the region appear not as living, cultural beings but almost as physical features of the land to lend an aspect of reality to the picture. We do not get any sense of the social identities of these people as they remain absent from the whole book—even from the chapter called 'The People of Pakistan and their Culture'. Of course, one can justifiably argue that government textbooks in Pakistan are generally of a very poor quality, and embody a ridiculously simplistic depiction of Pakistan. However, while all the regions of Pakistan are likely to be portrayed in selective and distorting ways, I would argue that the representations of Northern Areas are particularly invisibilizing. Moreover, they deserve attention precisely because they shape how a strategic territory is geographically and culturally mis-imagined by its school-going population. It is also important to note that the official textbook construction of the Northern Areas discussed above is not limited to one particular text. The region is similarly represented in a variety of other nation-making sites, such as in newspaper and television, and even in unofficial sites like private school textbooks and popular/academic publications. In a sense then, there is a persistent discursive structure that characterizes the production of the Northern Areas within depictions of the Pakistani nation-state. However, this discourse is not produced in the same manner in every text and context. There are certain regularly occurring tropes, but each recurrence may also produce its own forms of inclusions and exclusions.

Introduction to Pakistan Studies is a book written by Muhammad Ikram Rabbani (2003), and is primarily used by 9th–11th grade private schools in Pakistan that follow the British O-level examination system.[13] This 420-page book is one of the most widely used comprehensive texts on 'Pakistan Studies', and also one which gives the most detailed attention to the Northern Areas. However, this emphasis is ridden with ambiguities and contradictions. The Northern Areas are not included in the 'Area and Location' of Pakistan, which is the first section of a chapter titled 'Geography of Pakistan'.[14] This may be explainable by the fact that the Northern Areas are not constitutionally part of Pakistan. On the very same page, however, there is a section called 'Neighbouring Countries and Borders' which mentions Pakistan's common border with China along 'its Gilgit Agency and Baltistan'. As indicated earlier, Gilgit Agency was a colonial political unit which ceased to exist in 1972 when it was merged with surrounding territories to form the Northern Areas. Hence, while the region of the Northern Areas itself is not included in the definition of the territory of Pakistan, older names of the Northern Areas or locations within it are nevertheless incorporated into the state's territory in descriptions of the border areas of Pakistan. Likewise, while the Northern Areas remain absent from the extensive, written discussion of 'Political Divisions' that is provided in the text, they are vividly present on a map titled 'Pakistan: Political Divisions'.[15]

Similar to the official textbook discussed earlier, the major presence of the Northern Areas in this independently written textbook appears in the section on 'Physiography'. This section begins with a discussion of Pakistan's 'Northern Mountains', and talks at length about the peaks, valleys, glaciers and passes that mark the region. Unlike the previous text, however, this text recognizes that besides the physical landmarks, the north of Pakistan also comprises a *place* called the 'Northern Areas'. This place is considered so crucial for describing the physical landscape of Pakistan that it is allocated a separate sub-section, which is titled 'Importance of the Northern Areas of Pakistan (FANA).' It begins with a basic administrative definition of the Northern Areas:

The Federally Administered Northern Areas (FANA), include the territories of Gilgit and Baltistan (Ghizer, Gilgit, Diamer, Skardu, and Ghanche) situated in the extreme North of Pakistan.[16]

It is paradoxical that this definition appears in a section on 'Physiography', while the very existence of the Northern Areas remains unacknowledged in the section on the political and administrative divisions of Pakistan. Hence, it is only in the context of the physical description of Pakistan that the region is considered significant enough to be expanded upon. As the text goes on to state:

> The FANA is one of the most beautiful locations in the sub-continent. More than 100 peaks soar over 7000 meters (22,960 ft.). World's three famous mountain ranges meet in the Northern Areas. They are Himalayas, the Karakorams and the Hindukush. The whole of Northern area of Pakistan is known as paradise for mountaineers, climbers, trekkers and hikers.[17]

It is this tourist-adventurist gaze which defines the 'importance' of the Northern Areas, and now, Gilgit-Baltistan. The text also goes on to mention how the region's rivers and glaciers serve as vital sources of water. There is not even a scant mention of the region's relationship with Kashmir—not even in separate, detailed sections on 'Kashmir' that appear elsewhere in the same textbook. And this is also true for the government textbook discussed earlier. In the private school textbook, at least the nature-related glorification is specifically linked to the 'Northern Areas' which is not the case for the government textbook. However, even this recognition is short-lived: while the section titled 'Importance of Northern Areas (FANA)' recognizes the Northern Areas as a specific, bounded, administrative region of Pakistan, the very next section called 'Valleys of the Northern Areas' displaces this unique regional identity. In this section, the valleys of the Northern Areas include those that lie in the place Northern Areas—like Gilgit, Hunza, Yasin, Ishkoman, and Skardu—as well as other valleys such as Swat and Kaghan which lie in the North-West Frontier Province. This textual manifestation of the confusion between the Northern Areas and the NWFP can be linked to the geographically related mystifying names of these regions which I discussed earlier, as well as the common context of natural beauty in which both these places are often invoked.

The tendency of claiming and acclaiming the landscape of the Northern Areas while at the same time reducing its regional identity to an ambiguous or non-existent place is also prevalent in popular and academic discourse. An example of this is provided in a prominent Oxford University Press volume called *Pakistan*[18] which was published in 1997 to mark the 50th anniversary of the creation of Pakistan. This book is written for popular consumption, and features contributions from leading national and international scholars who work on Pakistani politics, culture, and history. Images of the Northern Areas are abundantly present throughout the book. In fact, even the cover page of the book displays an image from the Northern Areas—that of the magnificent Deosai peaks, as viewed from the Skardu district of the Northern Areas. Moreover, the book has a section on 'The Land and the People' which predictably begins with a fairly detailed discussion of the beautiful mountains and valleys of the Northern Areas. Yet again, these landmarks appear to be located directly in Pakistan rather than in a specific region called the Northern Areas. Moreover, while other regions of Pakistan—mainly the four provinces of Punjab, Sindh, North-West Frontier, and Balochistan—are expanded in separate sub-sections, no such section is assigned to the Northern Areas. Instead, the region is defined in the section on 'The North-West Frontier'. This is also the section in which pictures from the Northern Areas are prominently included. Hence, this text becomes yet another site where the conflation of the Northern Areas and the North-West Frontier Province is reproduced. It needs to be noted that the book does have a separate section for 'Jammu and Kashmir', but the 'Northern Areas' do not appear in this section. There is a reference to the fact that 'Dardistan and Baltistan'[19] historically formed the north of Jammu and Kashmir state,[20] but in the rest of the section's text, as well as in the images that accompany it, one gets the sense that 'Pakistani' Kashmir exclusively refers to Azad Kashmir. Here, as in the two texts that I discussed earlier, the delinking of the Northern Areas from Kashmir exists alongside, and in fact, is produced through the romanticized landscaping of the region within Pakistan. Such depictions silence the fact that the political status of the Northern Areas is inextricably linked to the disputed territory of Kashmir, and thus, marginalize the region within representations of Kashmir.

One might argue that the majority of people within Gilgit-Baltistan themselves do not prefer to be associated with Kashmir, and that they fought a war against Maharaja Hari Singh precisely to rid themselves of Kashmiri rule. However, as political activists in the region repeatedly emphasize, the issue is not whether Northern Areas/Gilgit-Baltistan is part of Kashmir but rather that the region remains internationally considered as part of the dispute of Kashmir, and its political status within Pakistan remains inextricably tied to the 'Kashmir issue'. Hence, it is important that their region and its predicament receive attention in the discourse on Pakistan as well as on Kashmir. Neither holds true in the school texts and popular books on Pakistan.

The region of the Northern Areas—and now Gilgit-Baltistan—also remains predominantly absent from depictions of the 'people' and 'culture' of Pakistan as well as of Kashmir. For example, in the edited volume just discussed, the socioeconomic and cultural profile of Pakistan is provided on the basis of specific regions. The cultural imagining of a Pakistani national and citizen is thus associated with the regional entities to which they belong, that is, the regions of Punjab, Sindh, NWFP, Balochistan, and Kashmir, which are seen as the constitutive units of Pakistan. Hence, the Punjabi lives in Punjab, the Sindhi lives in Sindh, the Balochi in Balochistan, the Pukhtoon in NWFP, and the Kashmiri in Kashmir. Even if acknowledged, other linguistic and ethnic groups that reside in these territorial units seem to get overshadowed in this homogenizing, one people–one place configuration. In the case of Northern Areas/Gilgit-Baltistan, such a configuration is made difficult because no group can be constructed as the dominant one. The cultural landscape of the region— with its diversity of people like the Shina, the Burushaski, the Wakhi, and the Balti—cannot fit into the ethnic matrix of nationalist discourses in which places are assumed to map onto a particular social identity. To be sure, there is mention of the 'longevity and tranquility' of Hunzakuts[21] and the 'ancient Greek ancestry'[22] of Baltis, but even these scarce, often essentializing references are not related to the place called the 'Northern Areas' and thus, do not convey that Baltis and Hunzakuts live in the Northern Areas. The region is effectively reduced to an unpeopled landscape, inhabited only with peaks and valleys. This produces a double exclusion: the communities of the Northern Areas remain largely unimagined within the nationalist imaginings of Pakistan and Kashmir, and simultaneously, their political dispossession is also obscured from the nation's view.

This landscape-only, no-people no-region depiction of the Northern Areas is linked to the ambiguity surrounding the political status of the region, as well as its contested and dominated status, which necessitates the erasure of its identity in nationalist discourse. At the same time, it is important to note that the practice of effacing people from depictions of a scenic Kashmiri 'wilderness' was prevalent even in Mughal times, and continued in the colonial period particularly through the writings of European travellers.[23] This practice is not even limited to Kashmir, and extends to the depiction of mountain territories in general which have always remained barred from the realm of 'culture' and 'civilization'. Even a historian like Braudel claims: 'The mountains are as a rule a world apart from civilizations, which are an urban and lowland achievement. Their history is to have none.'[24] This outside-history depiction of mountains often accompanies a picture of timeless isolation and inertia, as evident in the following representation of the Northern Areas in an academic text:

> Over many thousands of years the economy and the society of Northern Areas had changed but little. The lives and work of its people had remained isolated from the modernization of the Indus Valley. Rulers from the plains—including the British and the Chinese from across the mountains—had come and gone, but material conditions were relatively unaltered.[25]

Such representations of mountain societies as history-less, timeless, isolated, and backward are typical and symbolic of the lowland perspective from which historical and social analysis is often written.[26] Particularly in the context of the Northern Areas, this perspective runs counter to local histories of caravan trade, travel, religious conversions, and political and military struggles that have shaped the trajectory of the region as well as that of the British Empire in India. For example, rulers of Hunza and other states that today constitute the Northern Areas/Gilgit-Baltistan were key players in the Great Game. They frequently manoeuvred the British, Russian, and Chinese authorities against each other, making their territory as one 'where three empires met' and one that was central to the security and stability of the British Empire.[27]

The global NGO discourse on environmental conservation—which often reduces lived homes to nature zones—is a new form of the lowland perspective which has become dominant in the thinking about the Northern Areas in recent years. This NGO discourse further entrenches the region as an eco-body in material practice—a subject that I address at length in Chapter 5. The implication of this discourse, however, is useful to indicate here and is captured well by the following comment from Raja Hussain Khan Maqpoon, a journalist from the region:

> It is ironic that the world is more worried about the falling trees; they are sad that our white leopards are vanishing day by day; the dead bodies of our Markhor frightens them; they are going all out to preserve our ecosystem. But nobody ever thinks of the people of this land.[28]

Hence, what is common to the lowland nationalist discourse on Gilgit-Baltistan as well as the NGO-led conservation discourse on the region is the reduction of a place of people to a space of nature. My point here is not to argue against a felt attachment to nature and a place-based sense of belonging. Indeed, a real connection to specific parts of the earth and the natural world is sorely needed to counteract the managerial discourses of environmentalism that have come to dominate today.[29] What we must remain wary of, however, are the essentialist ways in which claims about regional landscapes become implicated in nationalist narratives of identity and erasure. In the textual and visual vocabulary of Pakistani nationalism, Gilgit-Baltistan has been primarily constructed as a space of nature, ecology, and beauty, thus transforming it into what I have called the eco-body of the nation. Such constructions reduce the region to a physical and geographical territory, effectively serving to depoliticize it by invisibilizing its specificities and social identities.

CONSTITUTING THE STATE AND ITS TERRITORY

Whether they strive for a provincial, supra-provincial or an independent status for Gilgit-Baltistan, local political parties across the spectrum agree on one issue: the crux of the problem is the region's ambiguous constitutional status. Hence, it is important to understand what the constitution of Pakistan says or does not say about the political status of Gilgit-Baltistan.

The constitution is often seen as a document that is created *by* a concrete entity called the state to specify how it will function and rule the society or nation. However, it is the constitutional text itself that concretizes the abstractions of the 'state' and the 'citizen', and defines the nature and extent of the state's power over citizens. In this sense, the constitution effectively constitutes the state rather than vice versa.

The definition of state territory is inscribed in the constitution of a country, as the formal, legal definition of the dominion of a state. The 1973 Constitution of Pakistan[30] hence begins with identifying 'the Republic and its territories'.[31] The four provinces of Pakistan are included (Balochistan, North-West Frontier, Punjab, and Sindh), along with the capital city of Islamabad, and the Federally Administered Tribal Areas. Additionally, Pakistan also comprises 'such States and territories as are or may be included in Pakistan, whether by accession or otherwise'.[32] The implicit reference in this vague clause is obviously to the disputed region of Jammu and Kashmir, including the region of Gilgit-Baltistan. Since Pakistan's official position is that the region is disputed, and its territorial future must be decided by a UN-led plebiscite, the territory defined by the constitution cannot openly include even the one-third part of Kashmir that is under the control of the Pakistan state, that is, Azad Kashmir and Gilgit-Baltistan. The sentence from the constitution quoted above ensures that the Pakistan government can constitutionally defend its control of regions belonging to Jammu and Kashmir, but it is ambiguous enough for the state to declare that Gilgit-Baltistan is not 'constitutionally' part of Pakistan yet, hence enabling it to remain in compliance of UN resolutions as well as to continue denying constitutional rights to the people of the region.

The only explicit reference to the territorial control of Jammu and Kashmir is provided in Article 257 of the 1973 Constitution, which states:

> When the people of the State of Jammu and Kashmir decide to accede to Pakistan, the relationship between Pakistan and the State shall be determined in accordance with the wishes of the people of that State.[33]

The hypocrisy of Pakistan's official line on Kashmir is clearly revealed in this article. Through a clever use of words, it effectively deprives the people of Jammu and Kashmir from exercising their right to self-determination. Their wishes are to be respected only if they decide to join Pakistan presumably through a plebiscite that would be conducted by the UN. Hence, one way of reading this article is that Pakistan would abide by the UN resolution, insofar as the eventual vote is in its favor. The only choice granted to the inhabitants of Kashmir is in deciding what administrative form their territory will take when it becomes part of Pakistan. And, until they make this choice, they are not 'part' of the Pakistan state even if they are directly controlled by it.

The content of the Pakistani constitution has tremendous implications for the status of Gilgit-Baltistan. If the region is not constitutionally part of Pakistan, then the state is not bound to give any citizenship rights to the people inhabiting the region. In fact, in several court cases pertaining to the status of Gilgit-Baltistan, the Federal Government has openly justified the denial of fundamental rights to the region and its people on the basis that the region is not part of Pakistan. Hence, while the 1973 constitution of Pakistan might construct an ostensibly democratic state, it leaves enough room for the state to continue its executive rule in Gilgit-Baltistan.

As suggested earlier, a constitution is fundamental to the discourse and practice of the state as it structures and legitimizes the institutional apparatus of the state. Hence, it embodies a discursive practice that is productive of material power. But this power does not always work in favor of the state. By specifying what the contours and limits of official rule would be, the constitution imposes legal restrictions on what can be done by agents in the name of the state. While the 'legal' is itself a creation of power and those who exercise power can manipulate self-authorized legal checks in their favor, the constitution—and law in general—can nevertheless provide a space for subjects to enforce their rights, and hence, exercise power. To some extent, then, the state can be bound by what it states, within the arena of the state itself.

The state institution of the judiciary is one key site where such checks on the State can be negotiated. In the context of Gilgit-Baltistan, the Supreme Court of Pakistan has adjudicated various cases in relation to the political status of the region, and passed decisions that have played a fundamental role in pressuring the Pakistan government to establish a democratic process in the region. A landmark verdict came on 28 May 1999, when the Supreme Court decided against the Federal Government in the constitutional petition of 'Al-Jehad Trust versus the Federal Government of Pakistan'. It directed the Pakistani government to 'make necessary amendments in the Constitution' and 'initiate appropriate administrative/legislative measures within a period of six months' for the enforcement of 'Fundamental Rights' in the Northern Areas.[34] According to the constitution of Pakistan, these fundamental rights include the right to freedom of speech and expression, right to equality before law, right to vote, right to be governed by chosen representatives, and the right to have access to an appellate court of justice.[35] The representatives of the Federal Government had argued that since the region is not constitutionally part of Pakistan, but a 'sensitive' part of the disputed territory of Jammu and Kashmir, its political destiny needs to be settled according to the awaited UN-led plebiscite, not by the Pakistan government, and certainly not by the Supreme Court. However, deciding in favor of the plaintiffs, the then Chief Justice of Pakistan, Ajmal Mian, held that while the Northern Areas may not be constitutionally part of Pakistan, they are nevertheless under the 'de jure' and 'de facto' control of the Pakistan government.[36] As such, the latter is bound to extend constitutionally guaranteed citizenship rights to the people of the Northern Areas, particularly since most Pakistani statutes have already been made applicable to the region. This Supreme Court decision was widely seen in the region as a critical step towards regional political justice. Following this decision, sections of the 1973 Pakistani Constitution guaranteeing fundamental civil and human rights were extended to the Northern Areas through an amendment to the Northern Areas Council Legal Framework Order of 1994.[37] A number of 'packages' for increasing the region's legislative, financial, administrative, and judicial powers have since been announced by successive Pakistani governments.

The Supreme Court case also underscores the complexity and heterogeneity of state discourse and practice pertaining to the region. As is evident from the court case, institutions of the Pakistani state have often taken a contradictory stance on the political status of Gilgit-Baltistan. However, such differences cannot be simplistically interpreted to mean that one institution of the state is championing the rights of the region while the other is trampling on them and that therefore, there is no project of rule that unites the two. The positive move by the Supreme Court needs to be seen in light of the March 1993 ruling of the Azad Kashmir High Court, in which the Court declared that the Northern Areas are a part of Azad Kashmir and not of Pakistan, and accordingly directed its government to assume charge of the region.[38] The apprehensive Pakistan government appealed this decision in the Supreme Court of Pakistan. In its September 1994 verdict, the Supreme Court implicitly reaffirmed the rule of the Pakistan state over the Northern Areas by declaring that the Northern Areas were part of the disputed 'Jammu and Kashmir' but not of Azad Kashmir.

Given this context, the recent willingness of the Pakistani Supreme Court—and subsequently of the Pakistan government—to acknowledge the citizenship rights of Gilgit-Baltistanis can be seen as a continuing strategic effort of the Pakistan state to delegitimize the claims on Gilgit-Baltistan by Azad Kashmir, and also, of course, by India. Simultaneously, it is also a means to contain popular resentment and resistance against the Pakistan state, particularly by nationalists—as anti-establishment political activists are called in the region—and by secessionist movements like the Balawaristan National Front (BNF). For these critical progressives, the denial of constitutionally guaranteed rights is deeply problematic, given Pakistani control of regional resources and the sacrifice of regional soldiers for internal and external Pakistani wars. They are well aware that this denial is a historical outcome of the state's self-serving desire to keep Gilgit-Baltistan connected to the Kashmir dispute, so as to gain a majority Muslim vote in the case of a plebiscite. This calculation is both outdated and hypocritical—Azad Kashmir has enjoyed far more democratic freedoms despite similar concerns regarding a Kashmir plebiscite. The status quo simultaneously demonstrates the overconfidence of the state in the region's loyalty, and its abuse of the certainty of that loyalty. It is for this reason that the lack of a constitutional status is not just seen as a matter of *political deprivation* by local residents but also as the quintessential expression of *emotional deception*. To quote the founding leader of BNF, Nawaz Khan Naji:

They rule us and fleece us and *manipulate our love of Pakistan* for supranational geo-political ends but won't give us the constitutional status we deserve.[39]

As I argued in the Introduction, such feelings of betrayed love and insincerity demonstrate the centrality of emotions in defining the regional experience of the Pakistani state. While analyses of nations/states have often emphasized how state processes are formed through emotions of 'political love' that draw upon familial and romantic rhetoric,[40] what we see in Gilgit-Baltistan is that state rule in realpolitik is perceived in precisely the opposite terms—on a manipulated love that is rooted in apathy, abuse, and deception.

CARTOGRAPHIC ANXIETIES

In July 2004, the Pakistan government organized golden jubilee celebrations to mark the first ascent of K2, which is Pakistan's highest and the world's second highest mountain. Grand festivities were arranged across three weeks, for which numerous state bureaucrats and international dignitaries flew into the district of Skardu. A journalist, Israr Mohammad, who belongs to the region and was covering these celebrations, related to me the confusion of foreign visitors who had obtained copies of Pakistan's map only to discover that the region of 'Northern Areas' was nowhere to be found. In an attempt to point out the cartographic location of K2 to one of these visitors, my friend discovered much to his own astonishment that while some parts of the Northern Areas were shown as part of Pakistan, the regions of K2 and Skardu were excluded from it and instead depicted as part of the 'Disputed Territory of Jammu and Kashmir'. Recounting this experience, Israr sarcastically and indignantly commented:

This is the height of injustice and exploitation. The Pakistani government claims that our beautiful mountains and valleys are the glory of Pakistan. Yet, not only has it denied us our fundamental rights, it has even denied us on the map. *As if we don't exist.*[41]

Maps—like flags—are totemic symbols of the nation that bind the national community together, and allow the nation to be articulated in the first place.[42] They are powerful texts that orient how the nation imagines the territory of the state. In the South Asian context, maps have played a particularly significant role in shaping state-formation and interstate relations. As Razvi has pointed out,

> The Radcliffe Line, which covers most of Pakistan's borders with India, was drawn on a map in the first instance. The line was then re-laid on the ground by the survey teams of India and Pakistan. No cadastral or aerial survey preceded the Radcliffe decisions, which were taken only with reference to the guiding principles contained in the Partition Plan of 3 June 1947, and on the basis of existing reports.[43]

Moreover, the Sino-Indian war of 1962 stemmed partly from the hostilities which emerged in response to the publication of Chinese maps that depicted the Aksai Chin frontier of disputed Kashmir as part of Chinese territory. Similarly, the Sino-Pakistan Agreement of 1963 which delineated the border between Pakistan and China stemmed from Pakistani protests against the publication of Chinese maps that claimed control of some parts of the Northern Areas. Hence, the significance of maps is not only limited to a symbolic-material structuring of national thought but also extends to the formation and defence of the very territory of the state.

Before examining the cartographic representations of the Northern Areas, I wish to clarify that I have not researched the circuits through which cartographic knowledge is produced in Pakistan, and I cannot and do not wish to establish definite relationships between political intentionality and the production of Pakistani maps. My concern is with exploring the 'truth effects' of the knowledge that is conveyed in maps, both of its more emphatic utterances, and also of its equally emphatic silences'.[44] I am concerned with investigating how these truth effects might reveal and realize state power in the region.

One would expect the politically critical region of Kashmir to have a particularly clear representation on the maps of both India and Pakistan. The Indian map fulfills this expectation: it incorporates the entire former

Princely State of Jammu and Kashmir—including the region of Northern Areas — as part of its territory. This depiction represents India's official claim that Kashmir is its integral part, instead of the reality of a disputed Kashmir that has regions under control of the Pakistan state. The Pakistani map, on the other hand, embodies a curious image of Kashmir. The Pakistan state officially considers Kashmir as 'Disputed Territory', the future of which will be decided on the basis of a UN-backed plebiscite. But on the map, all of Kashmir does not appear as 'disputed'. Ironically, there are a number of maps of Pakistan that circulate within the country, all portraying different versions of Kashmir and especially, of the Northern Areas.

Map 1.1 provides a section from the official map of Pakistan that was published by the Survey of Pakistan in 1995, and is included in the *Census Report of 1998*.[45]

Conforming to the definition of Pakistani territory in the constitution, the map neither has a space marked as the 'Northern Areas', nor one categorized as 'Azad Kashmir', though both these components of Pakistan-ruled Kashmir are practically treated and controlled as administrative districts of Pakistan. There is just a blanket category called 'Jammu and Kashmir (Disputed Territory)', which has an un-delineated eastern boundary labelled as 'Frontier Undefined'. The Line of Control (LoC) which divides Indian-controlled Kashmir from the Pakistan-controlled one is not marked, as it would symbolically map the reality of Indian-held Kashmir, and undermine Pakistan's official claim to the entire territory of Kashmir.[46]

Interestingly though, the region identified as disputed Kashmir does not include all of Pakistan-administered Kashmir. It leaves out the colonial administrative unit of 'Gilgit Agency' that forms a sub-region of present-day Northern Areas. The Gilgit Agency covers districts such as Gilgit and Ghizer which constitute key administrative units of the Northern Areas, and now of Gilgit-Baltistan. Technically, the Agency itself does not exist as an 'administrative district' anymore as it was combined with the adjoining territories of Gilgit Wazarat and Baltistan to constitute the 'Northern Areas' in 1972. While the space of these latter territories is unmarked and is included within that of Jammu and Kashmir, that of the defunct Gilgit Agency retains its label and is firmly mapped within Pakistan. It is clearly *separated* from 'Jammu and Kashmir'. At the same time though, the colour of both the 'Gilgit Agency'

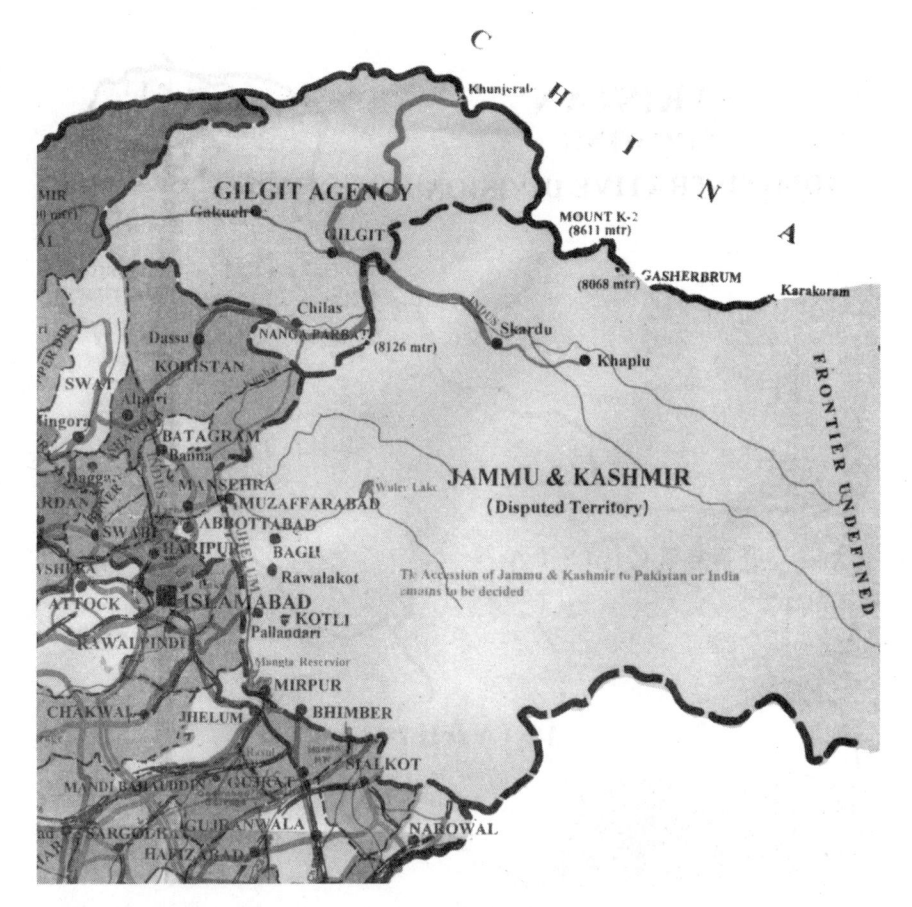

MAP 1.1 Section from 'Pakistan: Showing Administrative Districts'
Source: Survey of Pakistan, 1995.
Note: Map drawn from primary source. It is not to scale and does not represent authentic international boundaries.

and 'Jammu and Kashmir (Disputed Territory)' is the same—light green—which cannot be considered a coincidence as no other territory of Pakistan is shaded in this colour. Even in the abridged version of the map (Map 1.2) that appears right below the original map, both these regions are the only two on the map to be vertically lined, and that too in the same colour, indicating a clear connection. There is a boundary between them though, that marks them as distinct units. Hence, the colours connect but the lines divide.

PAKISTAN SHOWING ADMINISTRATIVE DIVISION

MAP 1.2 'Pakistan: Showing Administrative Division'
Source: Survey of Pakistan (1995).
Note: Map drawn from primary source. It is not to scale and does not represent authentic international boundaries.

Such cartographic manoeuvres may reflect incompetence and oversight, but are more reflective of how the vagueness of the Pakistani state in relation to Northern Areas/Gilgit-Baltistan finds an intriguing visual manifestation. These manoeuvres fundamentally redesign the landscapes of the Northern Areas, Kashmir, and Pakistan. The administrative territory of the 'Northern Areas' does not appear as such on the map, as it is not named, and its space is divided up so that most of it is included in Pakistan while the rest (including K2) appears as part of disputed Kashmir. This ambiguous and distorted presence makes it difficult to locate the Northern Areas on the map. They are neither included within Pakistan nor excluded from it. Rather, a creative and political use of lines, labels, and colours invisibilizes their very existence and identity. At the same time, their relationship with Kashmir is rendered ambiguous as they are simultaneously linked and delinked from Kashmir.

According to Wirsing (1991), this ambivalence of the Pakistani state reflects a 'calculated ambiguity' towards Pakistan-administered Kashmir where the state manages an impression of indecision and openness of the region as disputed while simultaneously enforcing deep political control on the ground. In the case of the Northern Areas in particular, the delinking of the Northern Areas from Kashmir came out most strongly during the rule of General Zia when three members from Northern Areas were also given an observer status in his appointed, national legislative body. The depiction of Gilgit Agency as part of Pakistan also occurred only in the mid-1980s as before that, the entire space of the Northern Areas (Gilgit Agency, Gilgit Wazarat, and Baltistan) was depicted as part of the 'Jammu and Kashmir (Disputed Territory)' in official maps.[47] It was with the publication of the first atlas of Pakistan in 1985 that Gilgit Agency was removed from 'Disputed Territory' and included as part of Pakistan, though not as a province.[48] Because of the conflict over Siachin which had barely emerged a year before, Baltistan was left 'disputed'.[49] Even if partial, this delinking eliminated some of the ambiguity surrounding Pakistan's relationship with the Gilgit territory, and can be linked to the post-1972 attempts of the Pakistan state to consolidate its hold over the region for frontier stability and strategic military interests—particularly in the wake of the loss of East Pakistan in 1971.[50]

The delinking also comes across more strongly than the linkage between the Northern Areas and Kashmir, as lines are more fundamental to maps than colours. Despite this 'colouring' of the Northern Areas–Kashmir connection, the message is clear: the Gilgit Agency, and by implication the Northern Areas, are part of Pakistan, not of disputed Kashmir. The official map of Pakistan hence becomes a 'model for, rather than a model of' what it purports to represent.[51] Instead of mapping the spatial and political reality of Kashmir, it constructs an imagined Pakistani state which manages to appropriate the space of the Northern Areas, while simultaneously obscuring its identity and political status.

Since the official map of Pakistan does not acknowledge the existence of the Northern Areas, it is not surprising that an official, publicly available map of the region itself is also lacking. The closest map of the 'Northern Areas' is a map produced by the Survey of Pakistan in 1995, which is titled 'Gilgit Agency and Jammu & Kashmir'. The map is too large to be accommodated in this text, but a few points are worth noting. The very title of the map suggests that there is a connection between these political units, but the 'and' separates the two and does not explain what the connection really is. This map is compatible with the more abstract map shown in Map 1.1, as the same green colour is used for both the Gilgit Agency and Jammu and Kashmir, while still dividing them into distinct political entities. The only difference is that in this detailed map, Gilgit Wazarat and Baltistan are labelled and visibly included as part of the territory of Jammu and Kashmir. Hence, in this map, it is even clearer that some territories that belong to the Northern Areas are being counted as part of disputed Kashmir, but the major portion of the region is being mapped within Pakistan.

Oddly enough, the official maps of Pakistan differ from those that are included in sites such as private school textbooks and travel guides, though they still remain broadly confined to the official, nationalist frame. As a case in point, see Map 1.3 which is taken from a textbook titled *A Geography of Pakistan: Environment People and Economy*, which is commonly used by 9th–11th grade students in the private, British O-level schooling system in Pakistan.

In this map, the label of 'Gilgit Agency' is replaced with that of 'Northern Areas', which is more accurate as the political unit of Gilgit Agency ceased to exist in 1972. However, while the name makes more sense, the lines remain inaccurate as some parts of the Northern Areas like Baltistan (though not labelled) are still mapped in 'Jammu and Kashmir (Disputed Area)'. Since textbooks for geography or Pakistan Studies are often not in colour print, the limited connection that is officially suggested between Gilgit Agency and Jammu and Kashmir (through a shared colour) does not come across in this map. Hence, while the reality of a place administratively classified

UNIMAGINED COMMUNITIES IN THE ECO-BODY OF THE NATION ⊗ 55

MAP 1.3 Section of 'Pakistan: Political Divisions'
Source: A Geography of Pakistan: Environment People and Economy, 1991.
Note: Map drawn from primary source. It is not to scale and does not represent authentic international boundaries.

as 'Northern Areas' is now acknowledged, the area bound by it remains inaccurate, and the connection to Kashmir is completely erased.

The last illustration (Map 1.4) that I want to discuss is taken from the prominent academic/popular book called *Pakistan* which I discussed earlier in relation to the textual construction of the Northern Areas.[52]

This map is one of the very few maps that I found which depicted the whole space of Northern Areas as part of disputed Kashmir. But the map contains different misrepresentations that are even more exclusionary than the ones in the official map. Pakistan-controlled Kashmir is an empty, unmarked space, literally. It incorporates the 'cease-fire line' that divides Pakistan-ruled Kashmir (coloured white) from Indian-ruled Kashmir (coloured grey), and

MAP 1.4 Map of Pakistan used in the book *Pakistan*
Source: Husain (1997).
Note: Map drawn from primary source. It is not to scale and does not represent authentic international boundaries.

labels mainly the Indian part as 'Jammu & Kashmir (Disputed Territory)'. Moreover, Pakistan-ruled Kashmir is accurately depicted as including the space covered by 'Azad Kashmir', as well as the 'Northern Areas', though neither of them is labelled as such and the division between the two is not depicted. But interestingly, while no landmark of Azad Kashmir (such as the key city of Muzzafarabad) is identified, the territory of the Northern Areas is marked with three labels—the main town of Gilgit, the mountain peaks of Rakaposhi and K2, and a supposed region labelled as 'Tribal Territory' (in capital letters). This label does not make any sense in relation to the Northern Areas, as in the context of Pakistan, 'tribal territory' commonly denotes the region of FATA that is located between the province formerly known as the North-West Frontier Province and Pakistan's border with Afghanistan.[53] Hence, while this map draws the lines such that the territory of the Northern Areas is included as part of Pakistani Kashmir, we still do not see the connection between the Northern

Areas and Kashmir because the region is neither represented with the colonial name ('Gilgit Agency') nor the postcolonial one ('Northern Areas'). Moreover, the silence perpetuated by the absence of appropriate labels is made worse by the presence of the misleading label of 'Tribal Territory' that is marked around Gilgit. Through further identification of the Rakaposhi and K2 peaks, this map represents and reinforces the nationalist tendency of signifying the region of the Northern Areas in terms of its picturesque value for the nation-state.

It is evident, then, that instead of occupying a standardized place on Pakistani maps, the Northern Areas have an opaque and distorted presence which is produced through various techniques of what Harley calls 'cartographic censorship' and 'cartographic silence' (2001). The presences and absences on these maps are significant because they produce a particular imagining of the geographies of Pakistan and Kashmir. Maps are important ideological tools because they are used in a variety of organizational contexts, such as in schools, government departments, and business offices. Hence, in everyday life, they often come to be internalized as social facts that depict what Pakistan is, instead of being considered as social constructions that represent a particular way of seeing and unseeing the territorial boundaries and divisions of Pakistan.

THE CLASSIFIED NATURE OF CENSUS CLASSIFICATIONS

While representations through maps are powerful because they abstract, simplify, and summarize the territory of the nation-state, those in census documents are significant because they provide elaborate information about this territory. Along with presenting a 'general description of the country', the *1998 Census Report of Pakistan* provides a plethora of figures and statistics on a wide range of topics, such as population size and distribution, house construction and facilities, employment and migration, and education and health. The *Census Report of Pakistan* may thus be seen as an all-encompassing text that represents and legitimizes the official description of Pakistan, making obvious what the geographical, administrative, economic and socio-cultural composition of Pakistan is. As Cohn (1987) has argued, the introduction of the census in British India led to a political process of classification that objectified the culture and society of India, making obvious to the British as well as to the Indians what 'India' was. The census not only helps to shape the national imagination but also serves to solidify totalizing identities such as those based on 'race' and 'caste', provides comprehensive quantitative data that can be instrumental for administrative control by the state, and plays a crucial role in allowing people to make claims on the state.

According to the preface of the *1998 Census Report*, 'the census was undertaken ... throughout the country including ... Northern Areas and Azad Kashmir'. However, while the Northern Areas were extensively surveyed, the district and division-level census reports of the Northern Areas are kept confidential and are extremely difficult for the public to access. In the overall *Census Report of Pakistan* too, the representations of the Northern Areas are replete with silences, ambiguities, and contradictions.

Like the constitution, the census also describes the territory of Pakistan as comprising the four provinces (Punjab, Sindh, North-West Frontier Province, and Balochistan), the federal capital of Islamabad, and the Federally Administered Tribal Areas. However, these 'administrative units' identified by the text of the report[54] are not consistent with those depicted in the map of Pakistan, which is provided in the report (Map 1.1). As discussed earlier, the map additionally includes the colonial administrative entity of 'Gilgit Agency' as part of Pakistan. Hence, the census makes a contradictory statement: it visually depicts the territory of the Northern Areas within Pakistan but does not claim it as part of the country in the written description.

Even within the written text, the Northern Areas are represented in contradictory ways. On the first page of the census report, an explicit description of the territory of Pakistan is provided under the section titled 'General Description of the Country'. As mentioned earlier, only the four provinces, Islamabad, and FATA are described as being part of Pakistan. Right after that, however, and just like the private school textbook discussed earlier, the existence of the Northern Areas within the state of Pakistan is implicitly acknowledged when the boundaries of the state are described:

> It is bounded on the north and north-west by Afghanistan, on the east and south-east by India, on the south by the Arabian Sea, and on the west by Iran. The Peoples Republic of China lies in the north and north-east *alongside*

Gilgit and Baltistan, while close across the northern borders is the Central Asian State of Tajikistan.[55]

Hence, we see the unity of the official construction of the Northern Areas—as embodied by the census—and the supposedly unofficial representation of the Northern Areas as depicted in Muhammad Rabbani's textbook for Pakistan Studies that I discussed earlier. In both these texts, spaces within the Northern Areas are implied as part of Pakistan when the borders of the state are described, but the spatial unit of the 'Northern Areas' is not included when the territory of the state is described.

As discussed earlier, the space of the Northern Areas is given prime focus when the geographical beauty of the country needs to be described. Accordingly, the census makes prominent reference to the physical features of the territory defined by the Northern Areas. For example, a section on the topography of Pakistan that begins on the first page of the census has a dedicated sub-section called the 'Northern Mountains'. This section includes the following description:

> Trans-Himalayas or the Karakoram ranges in the extreme north rise to an average height of 6,100 meters. Godwin Austen (K2) is the second highest peak in the world (8,610 meters) located in the Karakoram. A number of glaciers cover these ranges. Siachen, Hispar, Biafo, Baltoro, and Batura are some of the important glaciers.

These glaciers are located in the Northern Areas, but this fact is never mentioned. Later, a section on 'Important and Historical Places' states:

> Pakistan offers to its visitors ... un-spoilt natural beauty, boasting the densest concentration of high mountains in the world like mountain ranges of Karakoram, Hindu Khush and Himalayas with world renowned highest peak K2... and picturesque valleys like Kaghan, Swat, Gilgit and Chitral.[56]

Kaghan, Swat, and Chitral valleys do not lie in the Northern Areas, and are allocated separate sub-sections which provide details about their location, as well as general tourism-related information. No such description is provided about Gilgit valley, which lies in the Northern Areas, and is as popular a tourist site as the other valleys, if not more. Perhaps this is just a coincidence, but it is nevertheless striking that 'beautiful' sites of Pakistan located outside of the Northern Areas are expanded upon, and situated within a specific regional context, whereas the scenery of the Northern Areas is appropriated as that 'of Pakistan'.

The only landmark of the Northern Areas that is elaborated upon in a separate section is the Karakoram Highway, which is a 1300 kilometre-road that runs through the Northern Areas, connecting Pakistan's capital city of Islamabad to Kashgar in China's Xinjiang province. The section states that the Karakoram Highway is:

> The greatest wonder of modern Pakistan and one of the most spectacular roads in the world. It is an engineering marvel which connects Pakistan to China, twisting through three great mountain ranges [of] the Himalayas, Karakoram, and Pamirs, following one of the ancient silk routes along the valleys of Indus, Gilgit, and Hunza rivers .[57]

This is yet another example which shows how the space of the Northern Areas is appropriated for the production of the eco-body of the nation-state, while the identity of the region is erased. The fact that the Karakoram Highway is the only feature of the Northern Areas that is detailed, also suggests how the highway has become a prominent marker for the region, so much so that it has come to *stand for* the Northern Areas. As Haines has argued:

> The Northern Areas is the Karakoram Highway, in tourist discourse. The people and the places are things to encounter along the way, not really worthy of visiting in and of themselves. The landscape is de-peopled. The attraction, and selling point, are the highway, the deep river gorges, the glaciers, and of course, the mountain peaks.[58]

In the rest of the *Census Report of Pakistan*, even the most fundamental 'census' statistics about the region such as the size of its area and population are not provided. This is odd, given that in the preface of the census, the 'Northern Areas' are specifically mentioned as being included in the census-taking process. It is not clear what data was collected from the region, as there is no evidence of it in the entire census report.[59] Hence, an acknowledgement of the presence of the 'Northern Areas' creeps into the beginning of the report, only to be subsequently negated. The section on migration does acknowledge the existence of the Northern Areas, when people specify 'NA' (Northern Areas) or 'AK' (Azad Kashmir) as their 'place of previous residence'.[60] But the 'present residence' only includes the four provinces and the capital city of Islamabad, suggesting that migration data was not collected *within* the Northern Areas. Hence, the only way in which the people of the Northern Areas are represented in the overall census is when they have migrated to a region which is officially part of Pakistan. They are given a place only when they are out-of-place.

REPRESENTATION AND THE STATE

The official Pakistani constitution, census, and the map embody discursive practices that, in different ways, articulate the form and content of the nation-state. They offer key sites for understanding how the apparently simple and obvious 'fact' of defining the territorial structure of the state is actually a deeply political exercise that naturalizes a particular way of perceiving the nation-state, and legitimizes its claims for sovereignty over a physical and social space. Thus, such sites are not objective representations of a fixed, concrete structure called the state; rather they constitute forms of knowledge that help to produce the state itself in its formal, official garb. By emphasizing the constructed nature of the state, I do not mean to deny the existence of what Abrams calls the state-system, 'a palpable nexus of practice and institutional structure centered in government'.[61] I intend to emphasize, as Abrams does, the state-idea—'an ideological artifact attributing unity, morality and independence to the disunited, amoral and dependent workings of the practice of government.'[62]

Timothy Mitchell has argued that the 'state-system' and the 'state-idea' mutually constitute each other and are 'two aspects of the same process'.[63] This process involves mundane material techniques of disciplinary power—including map-making and census-taking—that produce 'spatial organization, temporal arrangement, functional specification, supervision and surveillance, and representation'.[64] Such techniques create the effect of an abstract totality called the state, which seemingly stands apart from society.

At the same time, however, the 'state' is not merely an effect of power. It is a crucible for the confluence, concentration, and contestation of power relations. As Foucault has argued, 'power relations have been progressively governmentalized, that is to say, elaborated, rationalized, and centralized in the form of, or under auspices of, state institutions' and that 'in a certain way all other forms of power relation must refer to it [the state]'.[65] This suggests that the state-system itself is the key arena for the deployment of disciplinary techniques that, according to Mitchell, create the state effect. Though specific to the 'state', this argument echoes Foucault's broader thesis that 'knowledge is produced within the matrix of power and that power operates through the deployment of knowledge'.[66]

James Scott, in his defining book *Seeing Like a State* (1998), argues that the legibility of spaces and subjects through practices such as mapping and census-taking is one of the preconditions for the modern state's exercise of power. An illegible society, he says, is 'a hindrance to any effective intervention by the state, whether the purpose of that intervention is plunder or public welfare'.[67] Moreover, Timothy Mitchell has compellingly demonstrated how the map and the census were part of novel disciplinary methods of order, that, through transparency and objectification, enabled Egypt to become 'readable' for the colonial state and thus facilitated surveillance and control.[68] Similarly, Benedict Anderson has argued that the map and census aided first the colonial and later the postcolonial states in Asia and Africa, by classifying, standardizing, and solidifying spatial as well as social identities that created a 'human landscape of perfect visibility' for state control.[69]

As the analysis so far has demonstrated, state rule in the Northern Areas does not follow this normative theoretical template of legibility and control. Indeed, my analysis shows that the *illegibility* of the Northern Areas helps in sustaining the image of the region as unpeopled—as only a landscape that constitutes the eco-body of the nation. If the depiction of the region has not been standardized and solidified, it does not mean that the region occupies some kind of far-from-centre, stateless space of independence. The region, in fact, suffers from authoritarian forms of state domination, as I elaborate in the next section.

TERRITORIALIZING A DISPUTED TERRITORY

At different times in history, the areas that now form Gilgit-Baltistan have come under the influence of the Scythians, the Huns, the Kushans, and the Tibetans. By the nineteenth century, several local princely kingdoms had emerged and come to dominate the different valleys of the region. During British rule, the territory that today forms Gilgit-Baltistan was of special strategic significance as it marked the northern frontier of the empire and became the site of the Anglo-Russian 'Great Game' for control over Central Asia. Through military and diplomatic campaigns that formed part of an imperialist 'forward policy', the British managed to establish, in 1877, a political unit around Gilgit called the Gilgit Agency. The Agency became a permanent base only in 1889 and included the crucial local states of Hunza and Nagar. The British were able to conquer these territories through the active support of the Dogra rulers of Jammu, who had established the princely state of Jammu and Kashmir through the Treaty of Amritsar in 1846, and had managed to annex Gilgit to their state in 1860.[70] However, this northern region of the British Empire remained a fluid frontier zone with multiple intersecting systems of authority and alliance, rather than a borderland with firmly established boundary lines.[71] In fact, after the establishment of the Gilgit Agency, the region became doubly classified as a dominion of the state of Kashmir as well as that of the British Empire. It therefore came to be supervised partly by the British Political Agent and partly by the Kashmiri governor, though the administrative control of both was quite weak as the local princely kings continued to have autonomous jurisdiction over their areas.[72]

To expand and consolidate their control over frontier affairs, the British in 1935 leased the Gilgit Wazarat from the Maharaja of Jammu and Kashmir for a period of 60 years. The historical reasons for linking Gilgit-Baltistan to the Kashmir dispute are related to this question of plebiscite. At the time of partition, it was felt that in the event of a plebiscite in disputed Kashmir, the people of the region would most likely opt to join Pakistan due to a shared Muslim identity, hence swaying Kashmir's vote in Pakistan's favor. Thus, the relationship of the then Northern Areas to Kashmir needs to be maintained and, as such, they cannot be officially classified as part of Pakistan. Second, a formal incorporation of the region would imply an acceptance of the Line of Control and a renunciation of Pakistan's claims over Indian-held Kashmir. Hence, it was doubly strategic to keep the region of the Northern Areas 'disputed'.

The link of the Northern Areas with Kashmir has been repeatedly used by the Pakistan state to justify the denial of political rights to the inhabitants of the region. State representatives have claimed that any change in the region's status would amount to a violation of international agreements on Kashmir.[73] Yet, as activists in Gilgit-Baltistan have consistently pointed out, such a fear has hardly stopped the Pakistan state from granting rights to Azad Kashmir, which operates as a semi-autonomous state within Pakistan. Adult franchise was extended to Azad Kashmir in 1970, but was not implemented in Gilgit-Baltistan till almost forty years later, in 2009. Since 1974, Azad Kashmir has also had its own constitution, legislative assembly, elected Prime Minister, and independent judiciary.[74] Gilgit-Baltistan, on the other hand, remains in a constitutional limbo. The difference in state policy between Azad Kashmir and Gilgit-Baltistan has meant that people in Gilgit-Baltistan often perceive their region as doubly victimized within the dispute of Kashmir—a 'Kashmir within Kashmir', as one resident called it. The differential treatment is also made sense of locally through a number of explanations: that Gilgit-Baltistan is kept exceptionally suppressed because it is a Shia-majority region unlike Azad Kashmir, and that Gilgit-Baltistan had already acquiesced and expressed loyalty to Pakistan and thus, was not deemed to need appeasement through rights that would weaken federal and military control. As Robinson (2013) has pointed out, Azad Kashmir was also able to obtain more rights as a distinct regional polity due to the sustained efforts of its political leadership in limiting state control from Pakistan.

In the aftermath of the 1947 partition, the political arrangement that came to be placed in the region today called Gilgit-Baltistan was one that worked well for the Pakistani government as well as for the local ruling elites; the latter were given full freedom to continue their feudal rule, while the former was not compelled to grant any rights to a pacified populace. The fact that the region was internationally considered 'disputed territory' was useful in further absolving the Pakistani state from any democratic responsibility towards the people of Gilgit-Baltistan. Simultaneously, and precisely because of the region's relationship with the Kashmir dispute, the Pakistan state began to implement coercive policies of territorialization that helped to strengthen its control over the space as well as the subjects of the region.

Between 1947 and 1972, successive Pakistani governments continued the policies that existed during the colonial regime: indirect rule was perpetuated through a Pakistani Political Agent in place of a British one, while the local monarchs continued to squeeze labour, produce, and taxes from their subjects. In some ways, the rule of the Pakistan state was even worse, as the Political Agent implemented much despised policies. These included, first, the continuing of the Frontier Crimes Regulation (FCR) that gave discretionary law-enforcing powers to state officials in the region. Subsequently, the Pakistani government abolished the State Subject Rule—a law put in place by the Dogra state which had regulated and prevented non-locals from claiming local citizenship and property rights. According to several local inhabitants, the ending of this rule eased the process of land control and demographic change in the region. Between 1972 and 1974, the Pakistani state sought to obtain more direct control of the region for securing its northern boundaries. Popular resentment was tamed by abolishing the FCR, as well as the *rajgiri* (principality) and *jagirdari* (feudal) system of local rulers.[75] The territories that were previously divided into autonomous states and political districts were now combined and brought under the direct purview of the federal administration.

These moves were accompanied by road-building projects—most prominently the Karakoram Highway—to 'advance the conquest of physical distance, the extension of central control, and economic and political integration'.[76] The construction of roads also served Pakistan's defence needs by providing a direct route to its ally China that would be crucial against potential aggression from India. The roads have also paved the way for a more entrenched role of the military-intelligence regime in defining the political and social landscape of the region—a subject that I elaborate in the next chapter.

Even within the territories that form part of Pakistani Kashmir, there is a clear difference between the administrative mechanisms that have been used to govern Azad Kashmir, versus those that have been implemented in Gilgit-Baltistan. While Azad Kashmir has an autonomous status with its own President, Prime Minister, Parliament, and Supreme Court, Gilgit-Baltistan has only recently been given a province-like status. Till 2009, it was administered directly by the Federal Ministry of Kashmir Affairs and Northern Areas (KANA), which is based in the capital city of Islamabad. Since October 1994, party-based elections have been held for a local assembly that was first called the Northern Areas Executive Council and later the Northern Areas Legislative Council, but it was not granted any significant powers of legislation and administration. Moreover, it was headed by an un-elected chief executive—usually a non-local—who was only answerable to the un-elected Minister of Kashmir Affairs and Northern Areas. The irony of the situation is captured well by a local poet, Ahmed Din, who said to me in 2003:

> In democracy, we have two bureaucrats under a political representative; here, we have two bureaucrats above a political representative.

Meanwhile, the broader regional status of Gilgit-Baltistan has remained undefined. Till the 1980s, the Northern Areas were administered by a federal organ called the Ministry of Kashmir Affairs. However, the name of this Ministry was later changed to the Ministry of Kashmir Affairs and Northern Areas and is today the Ministry of Kashmir Affairs & Gilgit-Baltistan. Despite this apparent separation of the Northern Areas from Kashmir, the people of the region were classified as 'Kashmiri Mohajirs' (migrants) on the national ID cards issued to them by the Pakistan state—a move that was later rescinded in response to local protests. Similarly, as I noted in the discussion of the Supreme Court case earlier, the Pakistani government has claimed the region as part of disputed Kashmir, when defending its record of not granting democratic rights to the region. Thus, official policies on Gilgit-Baltistan have remained ambiguous and contradictory regarding whether the region is part of Kashmir or separate from it.

This ambivalent and liminal political status of the Northern Areas/Gilgit-Baltistan is not only linked to the territorial history of the Kashmir dispute but—as highlighted in the Introduction—also to the cultural anxieties that the region poses for the Pakistani state. It is an ethnically heterogeneous, Shia-majority unit which challenges the homogenizing, Sunni-Islamist narrative of Pakistani nationalism. Such complex political and cultural anxieties posed by this border territory have translated into realities of deep-rooted military control, and together these unspoken anxieties and realities have come to ensure a sustained erasure of meaningful discourse on the region. The silencing of the region has thus become structural—and like other structural silences—need not require a conspiracy, nor even a political consensus, for its continuation.[77]

EXPERIENCING ILLEGIBILITY

The silencing illegibility of the Northern Areas is a cause of immense resentment in the region. People have been outraged by the representational and political oblivion in which they have found themselves since partition, for it reflects a betrayal of their historical choice and struggle to be part of Pakistan, and also demonstrates the callous arrogance and impunity with which they have been ruled by the Pakistan state. Some characterize the Pakistan state as downright ridiculous for not claiming the land that it controls—like India has done—but rendering it 'disputed' and 'undefined' as if it makes strategic sense.

Prior to 2009, the invisibility of the Northern Areas in the cognitive map of Pakistan also affected people in the region at a most personal level. When people from Northern Areas studied or worked elsewhere—and there is a strong historical trend of out-migrations particularly in the winter months—they felt an acute crisis of identity, as they were unable to identify themselves in terms that were recognized by other Pakistanis. Saying 'Northern Areas' unsurprisingly drew blank stares, as it sounded like a general geographical region, not the actual name for an administrative territory in Pakistan. A village name or other meaningful regional names that denote place of origin—such as Shigar, Haramosh, Darel, Astore, Gojal—were equally unknown. Most people ended up saying they were from Gilgit or Hunza, as these might sound more familiar and make more sense than the cryptic label of 'Northern Areas'. But when asked where Gilgit or Hunza was, people would have to say *shumali ilaqajaat* (Northern Areas) and get trapped again. Very often, the follow-up question they would get was: 'Oh is that ____', where the ____ could be NWFP, FATA, Waziristan, or any other place in Northern

Pakistan that might have recently been in the news, but had nothing to do with the Northern Areas.

To circumvent the issue of clarifying what exactly the Northern Areas is, one NGO worker, Qurban, who belongs to Gilgit and whom I met in Islamabad, simply used to say that he was from Peshawar, the key city in the province of Khyber-Pukhtoonkhwa. As he put it:

> People are likely to think I am somewhere from around there either way, even if I say Gilgit, Hunza, Skardu, or the Northern Areas, which are far from Peshawar and have nothing to do with it. But Peshawar is readily understood.

A student in Karachi, Gohar, had a more innovative solution, and expressed how he avoided any association with the northern parts of Pakistan, given the post–war-on-terror context where a particular, demeaning attitude towards the 'north' prevails. Before the name change in 2009, I met him by chance at a library in Karachi, and guessing that he is from the Northern Areas, asked where he was from. Much to my amusement, he said, 'Central Asia'. I was even more curious then, and probed further about where in Central Asia he came from. He hesitatingly replied, 'Hunza'. When I responded with, 'Oh wonderful, I have been there quite a few times', he was both surprised and relieved. Later on, when I asked him why he had introduced himself to me as someone from Central Asia, he explained:

> You know, I have just adopted that as my identity because when I say Hunza, people ask what is it, where is it, is it a village, and so on. When I say Northern Areas, they think I am from FATA. I don't want to explain all the time, and these days, people make bad impressions of you when they find out you are from the north of Pakistan. People think we are all *jaahil* [ignorant] and dangerous up there, but I am sorry to say, it is the Pakistani mentality here that is *jaahil*. So it's better to say Central Asian. By saying Central Asian, people know you are foreign and might give you more respect. It is also true, we do have much in common with Central Asian mountain culture.

Hence, as one way to deal with the invisibility of the Northern Areas, people from the region themselves invisibilized their link with it in their interactions with Pakistanis. Within the region itself, the lack of Northern Areas' spatial and political identity has always been the subject of intense popular discussion. In particular, the absurdity of their placelessness has been the topic of many stories as well as jokes that people like to tell about their ambiguous political status. For example, an ex-Major, Karamat Khan, once related to me in a group discussion:

> I think that God had complete plans to send the October 2005 earthquake to the Northern Areas. But when His Lt. General came down to earth, he simply couldn't find the region![78]

The implication that even God was confused by state practices of illegibility drew an ironic laughter from the group. The confusion, indeed, went deep. Many humorous narratives in Gilgit, for example, highlight how government officials were themselves confused by the illegibility that state discourse had helped to produce. One popular narrative that was repeated to me several times goes something like this:

> A delegation from the Northern Areas went to Prime Minister Junejo in 1986 to demand constitutional rights, and especially the right to representation in Parliament. He said, 'What rights? Of course, you have rights. How can you not have rights?' The delegation responded, 'That's exactly our point. How can we not have rights?' Apparently, he too had confused the Northern Areas with NWFP. What hope do we have, if even our Prime Minister does not know about our status!

Another incident that circulates in Gilgit is as follows:

> Once a district commissioner from down country was appointed to Gilgit. Can you believe that he landed in Peshawar, thinking that Gilgit was right next to it? Those who are sent to rule us don't even know where we are located.

Yet another experience was related to me by a Skardu-based member of the then Northern Areas Legislative Assembly (NALA), Riaz Habib:

In 2000, I was part of an NALC delegation that went to meet the law minister for demanding an expansion of the powers granted to the NALC. He was a very nice man, who promised us that he would look into the matter. Then, he asked me, 'What is Chitral's height?' I gave him the answer. And then he asked me what hotel would I recommend in Chitral. At that point, I politely told him that Chitral is not part of the Northern Areas.

Such narratives were related to me with a sense of amusement, but also with undertones of cynical bitterness. It often seemed to me that the humor or sarcasm with which people commented on their political illegibility, offered a way to hide their anger, or deal with it. While the narratives might be performed as jokes, they reflected harsh truths about the marginalization of the region as well as the sheer Pakistani ignorance of this condition. The 'ignorant government official', in fact, has become a dominant trope through which the Pakistani state is described in the region. Capturing the ignorance of the state is a key way in which Gilgitis express the hopelessness of their situation, but also one through which they poke fun at the state, and critique it. Through jokes, my interviewees highlighted how the Northern Areas was itself treated as a joke by the Pakistan state.

The ignorance of the Pakistani state is even contrasted with the knowledge through which the British colonial state ruled the region. As Tariq Zafar, a veteran writer from Gilgit, said to me:

The *angrez afsar* [British officer] always had a pen and paper with him, and was interested in local languages and customs. His key purpose was to safeguard British interests but at least he tried to understand the region. And now we have Pakistani officials, most of whom are ignorant and incompetent.

Thus, while practices of legibility that produced local knowledge were fundamental to the realization of colonial power, they also embodied a political recognition and cultural interest, which—at least in retrospect—is deemed positive by formerly colonized subjects. One of the main grievances against the Pakistan state is precisely that it does not *know*, or *value* the place under its control, making its rule less legitimate. This compels us to rethink the relationship between knowledge and power. Knowledge has perhaps been viewed too narrowly, as merely the field through which governmentality is produced,[79] but especially if it is non-Orientalizing, knowledge also plays a more affirming role by producing value and validation for subjects of power. In some ways, at least, it is better to be seen by the nation and state, than remain unseen altogether.

CONCLUSION

The representational illegibility of the Northern Areas till 2009 did not merely reflect an official ambiguity. Rather, it helped to realize the structure of silence that the contested and militarized status of the region necessitates. Illegibility helps to sustain state power through techniques of pictorial but people-less valorization, naming, and ambiguous mapping, which erase the identity of the region and obscure its social condition. Thus, the role of representation in the state's project of rule must not be seen as subservient to 'actual', 'real', and 'material' practices of repression and territorialization. Rather, representational devices themselves need to be seen as repressive, territorializing practices because they help to claim and acclaim rule over spaces and subjects. As such, state territoriality and rule are not only about controlling space and converting it into a legible place but also about using representation to appropriate space, while reducing a specific controlled place to an illegible, almost non-existent space. We might therefore adapt the legibility thesis of state-formation to argue that illegibility can be far more effective in realizing power, particularly in disputed border zones like the Northern Areas.

Ultimately, the discourse of rule that defines the subjection of the Northern Areas has neither been based on cultural veneration—as for example, demonstrated by the construction of Manchukuo's 'peopled places' as sites of 'primitive authenticity'[80]—nor on denigration as evidenced, for example, by the depiction of the Meratus as 'disorderly primitives' and 'immoral pagans'.[81] Rather, power/knowledge practices have appropriated and eulogized the physical landscape of the Northern Areas, transforming it into the eco-body of the nation, and through it, simultaneously, invisibilizing the identity of the region and its people. Hence, the Northern Areas have been given a *space*, but not a *place*, through silencing representations which are 'active performances in terms of their social and political impact and their effects on consciousness'.[82] The power of these silencing representations suggests that we need to investigate not only how states 'state'[83] but also how they do not state, or cannot state, and regulate and dominate precisely by not stating.

The silencing representations of Gilgit-Baltistan within national discourses exist alongside other practices of the state that silence voices and politics in the region. It is to such practices of the military-intelligence establishment in Gilgit-Baltistan that I now turn towards in the following chapter.

NOTES

1. Carter (1987).
2. Cohen and Kliot (1992).
3. Dani (2001).
4. This nomenclature continued to operate at least till 1950. See the Ministry of States and Frontier Regions document transferring authority of the 'Northern Areas of Kashmir' from the Government of NWFP to the Ministry of Kashmir Affairs (No.D. 3739-B/50, 23 June 1950).
5. Carter (1987: xxiv).
6. Like the Northern Areas, this province was also renamed in 2010.
7. This Urdu word can be translated to mean 'strange', and 'difficult to comprehend'.
8. I have also come across this inability to recognize the name and hence the place of Northern Areas in my personal interactions with friends and family members. For example, when I used to tell them that my research is based on the Northern Areas, they often assumed that I was referring to places in the North-West of the country, such as the province of NWFP, or the tribal territories of FATA or Wana. Else, they would ask, 'What do you mean by the Northern Areas?'
9. As an example of such an appointment in 2013, http://tribune.com.pk/story/525548/prime-ministers-summary-g-b-law-minister-appointed-chief-court-judge/
10. Rizvi et al. (2003). 'Pakistan Studies' is a compulsory subject in government schools and colleges in Pakistan.
11. Ibid., p. 139.

12 Ibid., pp. 87–88.
13 This system is managed by the Universities of London and Cambridge in the United Kingdom.
14 Ibid., p.165.
15 Ibid., p. 183.
16 Ibid., p. 192.
17 Ibid., pp. 192–193.
18 Husain (1997).
19 Dardistan and Baltistan are historical names of regions that today form part of Gilgit-Baltistan.
20 Ibid., p. 143.
21 Ibid., p. 93.
22 Ibid., p. 142.
23 Rai (2004).
24 Braudel (1972: 34).
25 Ispahani (1989: 185).
26 Stellrecht (1997).
27 Hussain (2015).
28 Mehkri (2001).
29 Kingsnorth (2012).
30 Pakistan has had three constitutions. The 1973 constitution is the one that is currently in force, with various amendments over the years by successive military and civilian regimes.
31 Qazi (2003: 3).
32 Qazi (2003: 3).
33 Qazi (2003: 150).
34 Mian (1999).
35 Qazi (2003).
36 Mian (1999).
37 Notification No. SRO 1169(1)/99 dated 28 October, 1999. Source: IUCN (2003).
38 I am grateful to Cabeiri Robinson for this insight.
39 Khan (2002); my emphasis.
40 Anderson (1991) and Berezin (1999).
41 My emphasis.
42 Durkheim (1976) and Ibrahim (2004).
43 Razvi (1971: 7).
44 Harley (2001: 107).
45 The maps in this chapter could not be printed in this book in colour. The original maps in their actual form and colour have been made available at delusionalstates.weebly.com.

46 The Line of Control was legitimated by the UN in July 1949.
47 Rahman and Mahmood (2000).
48 Wirsing (1985).
49 Siachin is a glacier in disputed Kashmir, which Pakistan and India have fought over since 1984. It is considered to be the highest battleground in the world, where many soldiers from both sides have lost their lives due to the inhuman conditions in which they are forced to live.
50 Wirsing (1985).
51 Winichakul (1994:130).
52 Husain (1997).
53 This area is marked in the abridged version of the official map of Pakistan, shown in Map 3.
54 Ibid., p. 14.
55 *Census Report* (1998: 1); my emphasis.
56 Ibid., p. 73.
57 Ibid., p. 81.
58 Haines (2000: 196).
59 One possible explanation would be that since census data is categorized by 'administrative units', providing information about the Northern Areas would necessitate classifying it as an administrative region of Pakistan, hence negating the official definition of Pakistani territory provided both in the text of the census as well as in the constitution. Also, of course, more-than-basic data is collected from the region but is deemed to be 'sensitive' and hence excluded for strategic and political interests.
60 There is a single column for 'AK/NA' which suggests a relationship between these two areas.
61 Abrams (1988: 58).
62 Abrams (1988: 81).
63 Mitchell (1999: 77).
64 Mitchell (1999: 95).
65 Foucault (1983: 224).
66 Ray (2000: 62).
67 Scott (1998: 78).
68 Mitchell (1988).
69 Anderson (1991: 185)
70 For a detailed discussion of Dogra and British struggles over the northern frontier of the subcontinent, see Schofield (2010) and Sökefeld (2017).
71 Razvi (1971) and Haines (2012).
72 The Gilgit *Wazarat* that came under the rule of the Maharaja of Kashmir comprised the Gilgit *tahsil*, the Bunji *tahsil*, and the Astor *niabat*, whereas

the British political agent oversaw the Gilgit agency—including the political districts of Yasin, Ghizer, Ishkoman, Pubial, the states of Hunza, and Nagar—and the Chilas sub-agency (Lentz, 1997). See also Stellrecht (1997).

73 Mian (1999).
74 Much of Azad Kashmir's parliamentary independence, however, is curtailed by the Azad Jammu and Kashmir Council which is dominated by the federal government in Islamabad, and retains the supreme authority over the affairs of the region. See Human Rights Watch (2006).
75 See Notifications REG-MISC-23/1972 dated 12 October 1972 and REG-HC. NTF-32/72 dated 1 November 1972 (Source: IUCN, 2004).
76 Ispahani (1989: 193).
77 Trouillot (1995: 99).
78 The October 2005 earthquake devastated Azad Kashmir and parts of the NWFP, but very marginally affected the Northern Areas.
79 Foucault (1980).
80 Duara (2003).
81 Tsing (1993).
82 Harley (2001: 87).
83 Corrigan and Sayer (1985) and Roseberry (1994).

2

LOYALTY, SUSPICION, SACRIFICE

୫୦୦୫

Feeling and Force under Militarism

In this chapter, I interrogate the working of military relations of force as they are institutionalized in state structures and experienced in everyday life in Giigıt-Baltistan. My aim is to go beyond a conceptualization of the military that views it merely as a state apparatus of repression where power lies in the monopoly of violence.[1] To make sense of the military-intelligence regime's hegemonic rule in Gilgit-Baltistan, I adopt a more grounded and processual approach which investigates how the Pakistani military and intelligence agencies occupy space, bodies, and resources, while also dominating discourses, emotions, and subjectivities.[2]

Militarization fundamentally structures state, economy, and society in Gilgit. It is critically linked to livelihoods and cultural orientations, shaping local understandings of family, region, and nation as well as people's identities and aspirations.[3] Central to the working of military power in Gilgit-Baltistan, I argue, is the process of emotional regulation, whereby structures of rule produce and work through arrangements of feeling. The cultivation of certain emotional dispositions by the military-intelligence regime creates a *political economy of feelings*, which buttresses Pakistan's political economy of defence.[4] Regional employment in the Pakistani military creates *loyal subjects* who revere the military and the military-state, producing the conditions of possibility for continued military authoritarianism in the region. At the same time, the working of the intelligence agencies actively creates *suspicious subjects*—instead of being a response to them—entrenching Pakistan as a delusional state in which military power is reinforced through the use of surveillance and calculated disorder along sectarian lines. Loyalty and suspicion thus constitute forms of emotional regulation that are paradoxical but not contradictory: the former integrates people into the nation and accomplishes rule by creating consent, while the latter services state power by emotionally disintegrating the region through suspicion, and hindering the possibilities of local collective action. Nevertheless, militarization is also a site of negotiation.[5] Thus, I highlight historical and everyday moments that reveal how the military-intelligence hegemony in Gilgit-Baltistan is continually fraught with tension and contestation.

MILITARIZING PAKISTAN

Studies of the military in Pakistan have focused on the issues of martial rule and civil–military relations,[6] arms procurement,[7] the extensive military capital that is hidden from public view,[8] as well as the army's historical relationship with the United States.[9] While these studies contribute immensely to our understanding of military dominance in Pakistan, what is missing from them is a focus on the ethnographic experience of military power. Instead of emphasizing the organization and activities of the military in Pakistan, or its relationship with civilian governments, I wish to attend here to the cultural–political discourses of rule, practices of domination, and emotional subjectivities through which military power works in a specific regional context of Pakistan.

Militarization as a state-formative process is neither limited to the armed forces nor to war situations. Rather, it represents a cultural and political-economic process through which military structures and ethos become deeply embedded in state and society. De Mel argues that 'a militarized society is one in which the military has taken ascendancy over civilian institutions, and is predominantly and visibly relied upon to police and regulate civilian movement, solve political problems, and defend and expand boundaries in the name of national security'.[10] While this definition applies well to countries like Sri Lanka and Pakistan, one might erringly conclude that national society in the United States is not militarized. I would argue, however, that militarization need not involve direct and visible dominance of the government by the armed forces. Rather, as has been argued for the US, the political and economic dominance of the military can be represented by the powerful role of military–industrial corporations in creating what Mills has called a 'permanent war economy' as well as in covertly shaping public policy.[11] What defines the hegemony of the military over state and society is an investment in perpetuating a cultural ethos of militarism, in which military ideals are valorized and hyper-masculinist and violent solutions to conflict favoured.[12]

In the US, this gradual militarization has meant that a 'military definition of reality' has become the common sense for the nation.[13] In this naturalized vision of reality, the meaning of 'national security' is monopolized to promote a political economy that is centrally dependent on military institutions, armaments, and warfare. This political economy is underpinned discursively by 'a shift in general societal beliefs and values in ways necessary to legitimate the use of force, the organization of large standing armies and their leaders, and the higher taxes or tributes used to pay for them'.[14] It is further sustained through what I would call an investment in delusion—a logic of threat, fear, hatred, jingoistic patriotism, and defense against internal and external Others. This discourse helps to justify and provoke more conflict, which only serves to prove the existence of the threat and bolster the need for more militarization.

In Pakistan, such an enabling discourse of delusion is provided primarily by a military-shaped nationalism in which India is constructed as an aggressive other that constantly threatens the existence of the country. This is not to suggest that the Indian state has not been hostile but, rather, that the military-dominated state in Pakistan has cultivated an extreme fear of India to the exclusion of other national needs, and also pursued aggression towards India as a means to legitimize itself and its hawkish policies. Additionally, the military also claims to provide internal stability by protecting the nation from corrupt politicians.[15] It constructs itself as an agent of cleansing discipline and security, erasing its own role in perpetuating profound violence, inequality, and religious extremism to sustain its own interests.[16] 'National security' in Pakistan has thus been reduced to the creation and maintenance of a strong and dominating military, supposedly providing internal and external protection through high defence spending, an arms build-up, and a direct role in government. For its survival, the nation is asked to prioritize the needs of military personnel, giving them privileged access to state land and resources.[17] However, what lies under the guise of 'national security' is a project of rule that has produced a military-dominated state, instead of one that facilitates democratic participation, political negotiation of resources, and rule of law. This state of affairs has been achieved through the collusion and tacit approval of elites and political groups who have been patronized as beneficiaries in a military-dominated system.[18]

The delusional, militarized states in the US and Pakistan are also deeply connected, as the perpetuation of a military-state in Pakistan is fundamentally tied to US patronage of the Pakistan army. Since World War II, the US security agenda has entailed the backing of authoritarian regimes in developing countries, particularly military ones that tend to support and gain from empire. Democratic governments tend to be less conducive to domination, and might even question the imperialist policies of the US. During the Cold War project of maintaining American hegemony, Pakistan was especially pursued as a client regime that could play a central role in defending capitalist ideology and Western oil interests in the Middle East.[19] In return for compliance and the use of Pakistan as an army base for American military needs, the US has extended significant military aid, armaments, and training to the Pakistan army. It has sometimes knowingly ignored and at many times actively supported the army's repeated use of internal and external violence, and derailment of the democratic process. Support from the US has been critical in strengthening the Pakistan army's sense of superiority and invincibility, with the result that the army has increasingly resorted to the autonomous execution of Pakistan's foreign policy, and particularly of military strategies in Afghanistan and Kashmir. Indeed, in pursuing destructive policies of military interventionism, the state of Pakistan has become a mirror image of its imperial master.

It is essential, therefore, to understand militarization at the nation and state levels in Pakistan as part of the global US-dominated process of empire-making and militarization, in which the international production and trade in arms feeds off, and builds upon national security regimes. The US military-industrial complex in particular manoeuvres political decisions in the US towards hawkish goals, and ensures support to military client regimes abroad to sustain military consumerism as well as US imperialism. Such short-sighted and destructive American foreign policies have enhanced the power of client militaries in states like Pakistan, where the army has come to dominate both politically and economically, and created extensive business interests of its own which further perpetuate the military's political predatoriness.[20]

THE GARRISON REGION

While Pakistan in general is dominated by the army and has, therefore, been described as a garrison state,[21] it is in a strategic and politically suppressed region like Gilgit-Baltistan where its garrison tendencies are especially manifested and entrenched.

Until 2004, a visitor to Gilgit-Baltistan may not have found any overt signs of military dominance in Gilgit, the key administrative centre of this region and the place where I conducted the bulk of my fieldwork. It was the magnificent landscape that met the eye, inspiring an overwhelming sense of awe—a feeling that I still remember from my first trip to the Gilgit-Hunza region in 1996. By 2006, the feeling one got was one of fear and nostalgia. Although I had traveled to Gilgit-Baltistan several times during these ten years and even stayed there for extended periods, it was in 2006 that the change seemed drastic. Numerous checkpoints guarded by military and paramilitary units had been set up after the sectarian clashes of 2005—the subject of the next chapter—and Gilgit now appeared to be a high-security zone instead of a tourist gateway. No matter how long I stayed in Gilgit, crossing a checkpoint always remained an unsettling experience of force.

Even before the coming of such palpable markers of military power as checkpoints, however, Gilgit was still defined by a militarized landscape. Driving from the airport towards Jutial, in a short span of time, one would pass the premises of the Force Command Northern Areas (FCNA), Controller of Military Accounts, Army Public School, Askari Bakery, and Helicopter Chowk.[22] Since I myself partly grew up in the 'Cantt' area of Lahore and studied in the military-controlled elite area called 'Defence', the existence of military memorials and buildings had become a normalized feature of my spatial experience of the city. Hence, initially, I considered the military presence to represent nothing out of the ordinary in Gilgit—indicating my own internalization of military symbols, which are extraordinarily pervasive in Pakistan. However, in 2006, the establishment of multiple checkpoints in Gilgit heightened the visibility of other military spaces as well. If Gilgit resembled a big cantonment before, now it looked like a fortified army base.

The military dominates both the state and the capital in Gilgit-Baltistan, reigning over economic, strategic, and administrative matters. Road-building and maintenance is a monumental service industry in the mountainous terrain of the region, and is controlled by the military-run Frontier Works Organization (FWO). The main telecommunications infrastructure is under another army-controlled body called the Special Communications Organization (SCO), which is the sole provider of domestic telephone lines in Gilgit-Baltistan.[23] Most significantly, the military exerts tremendous political control through its direct intervention in the administration of Gilgit-Baltistan. While multiple authorities govern the administration, it is the FCNA—the Gilgit-based headquarters of the Pakistan army—that is considered the key institution spearheading the overall control of the region. The Commander of the FCNA holds the position of Major-General in the Pakistan Army, and works directly under the 10 Corps—the crucible of army power based in Rawalpindi.

Amongst other tasks, the FCNA is responsible for supervising the Frontier Corps, the Rangers, and until the last 2000s, the Field Monitoring Coordination Cell (FMCC) and the District Monitoring Teams (DMTs) which were also known as Army Monitoring Teams. These teams were introduced all over Pakistan by General Mushrraf after he seized power through a military coup in 1999. The role of these teams entailed the monitoring of the civil administration, which in practice meant that military personnel were appointed to supervise individual government departments within each district of Pakistan. Such practices effectively paved the way for an invasive role of the army in the day-to-day governance of the country.[24] These teams continued in Gilgit-Baltistan till June 2009, even though they were discontinued in the rest of Pakistan within one or two years of their formation.

The direct army 'monitoring' that was undertaken in Gilgit-Baltistan from 2000–2009 through the FMCC and its DMTs was the source of intense local resentment. I was frequently told that it is these very institutional structures that directly enabled *fauj ki hukomat* or army rule in what was then called the Northern Areas. The FMCC effectively controlled the use of the Annual Development Programme (ADP) budget in Gilgit-Baltistan, selecting which development schemes would be approved, and who would be hired to execute these schemes. For example, the Northern Areas Public Works Department (NWPWD) was the biggest recipient of the ADP funds in the region, and under the army's monitoring regime, the appointment of Project Directors for various development projects under NAPWD had to be approved by a Major/Colonel at the FMCC. Speaking about the role of the FMCC, a down-country bureaucrat, Muhammad Aslam, posted in Gilgit acknowledged to me:

> The civil administration was largely ineffective in all bigger matters. Posting and transfer above Grade 17 simply could not happen without the approval of the army.

For local government servants—those who are ethnically from the region of Gilgit-Baltistan itself—such army interference could be even more gnawing. They resented how army 'approvals' for government projects often translated into the selection of down-country employees, instead of qualified people from the local populace. This reinforced the already strong perception in Gilgit-Baltistan that employment opportunities in the region are not only controlled unfairly by the army but also predominately reserved for non-locals, particularly from Punjab and Khyber-Pukhtoonkhwa. For example, I was often told how the Frontier Works Organization, the Frontier Constabulary, and the Special Communications Organization are military organizations that control key economic services in Gilgit-Baltistan and draw heavily from the region's budget, yet most of their employees are 'outsiders'. Hence, local grievances about the 'non-local' aspects of Gilgit-Baltistan's political administration are often linked to the dominant presence and control of the army.

An argument that is frequently given by the military establishment for the preferential treatment to non-locals in the civilian or military bodies is that there is 'lack of local expertise'. However, as a Gilgiti engineer, Barkat Jan, responds:

First of all, there are many locals who are well qualified. But how will we ever get experience if we are never given jobs even in our own region? People here, in the mountains, have faced a lot of hardship to get good education and training. Many of us have worked for the local government in a junior capacity as well. Plus, we have the advantage that we know the region better, and have a higher sense of accountability as we have to continue living here. Those who come from outside will just come, make money, and leave. At the least, there should be some partnership. The government just wants to perpetuate non-local rule in Gilgit-Baltistan. They want to keep us subservient, they don't want us to ever get ahead.

Military authoritarianism has, to some extent, been curtailed in Gilgit-Baltistan since the re-emergence of formal democratic rule in Pakistan in 2008, following nine years of direct military rule. But the curtailment has come as a result of political struggle. In February 2008, when the Chief of Army Staff, General Ashfaq Kayani, ordered the withdrawal of military officers from Pakistan's civilian administration, a colonel was posted as an executive engineer to the Northern Areas Public Works Department the very next day—signaling that the status quo in Gilgit need not change. However, media protests by Gilgiti progressive journalists brought pressure on the newly inducted Pakistan People's Party (PPP) government and successfully resulted in the cancellation of the colonel's appointment. A year later, the Army Monitoring Teams were officially disbanded in Gilgit-Baltistan and the PPP civilian government passed the Gilgit-Baltistan Empowerment and Self-Governance Order. Following the first regional elections in November 2009 and the establishment of a province-like setup for Gilgit-Baltistan, the direct interference of the army in the daily administration of government has been further reduced. However, the role of the military in the political economy of the region remains crucial, particularly through the Frontier Works Organization which, as mentioned earlier, maintains control of road-building in Gilgit-Baltistan. Locals deem the organization as a source of incompetence as well as injustice. The critique of the FWO—and by implication, the army—became particularly sharp in the wake of the 2010 Attabad lake disaster in Hunza, which destroyed several kilometers of the most critical road in the region, the Karakoram Highway, drowning large tracts of village land and disrupting the lives of thousands.[25] According to my interviewees, the FWO used its military-backed power to ensure that the contract for reconstruction did not go to a Chinese road firm that was already active in the region for the widening of the KKH. They feel that the destruction caused by the lake was amplified because of the non-serious attitude of the FWO—or 'Funds Wasting Organization' as it has come to be called by some activists in the region. In 2011, the FWO obtained a three-year contract for making a spillway and for rebuilding the affected road, despite protests from civilians as well as from some members of the Gilgit-Baltistan Legislative Assembly. As one of the affected residents from Gulmit village said to me, 'We can challenge our political leaders, but it is impossible to challenge the power of an army organization.'

OF DESIRE AND HONOUR

While the role of the army in the regional administration of Gilgit-Baltistan is a source of widespread resentment, the Pakistan army is simultaneously an object of intense desire as well. This is because the army has historically provided one of the key avenues of employment for locals, with the result that there is a strong tradition of military service in the region. The employment of Gilgit-Baltistani men in the military dates back to colonial times. At the end of the nineteenth century, the British established a unit of civil levies in the Gilgit Agency, which was transformed into the Fighting Levies in 1903, and then into the Gilgit Scouts in 1913. Indeed, military employment was the first formalized source of wage labor in Gilgit-Baltistan, providing a dominant source of income in the form of active service as well as that of pensions.[26]

Employment in the Gilgit Scouts was socially desirable not only because of its financial rewards but also due to the prestige and privilege associated with working for a mighty foreign power and particularly its security forces. The British commandants of the Gilgit Agency tended to induct men from influential local families into the Gilgit Scouts, a practice that added to the Scouts' authority and appeal. As Jamil Khan, a senior journalist, described:

> The Gilgit Scouts had both *rowb* [power] and *izzat* [honour] because they represented a salaried class, and had regiments, garrisons, medals—all of

which attracted the imagination of people. In fact, soldiers of the Gilgit Scouts were regarded as the most eligible bachelors.

This revered and glamorous status of the military continues today, even as other forms of paid work have emerged. The opportunities for military employment have also expanded, with the increase in the paramilitary forces from Gilgit-Baltistan and the possibilities of employment in army regiments outside the Northern Light Infantry (NLI).[27]

Most importantly, there are concrete perks and benefits associated with military service that heighten its appeal for many families. As a number of women informed me, the children of army personnel pay Rs 300–450 in the local Army Public School—considered one of the best in Gilgit—whereas a civilian child has to pay between Rs 1,100–1,350.[28] The former does not have to pay a security fee, and their school pick up and drop off is free. Two teachers of the Army Public School also mentioned that teachers cannot fail an army child. In the realm of healthcare as well, subsidized treatment is available to soldiers and their families. Put simply, families who have a member employed by the military are more privileged citizens, particularly in a context where education and health are the two most critical concerns and sources of expenditure.

Given the glory associated with military participation since British times, and the economic opportunities and benefits provided by military service, it is not surprising that almost every person I met in Gilgit-Baltistan during my fieldwork had a relative who once served or continues to serve in the army. Tales of army service, honours, and courage frequently came up in my conversations and interviews, particularly when people introduced their families to me. For many families who have a strong tradition of military service, both military conquest and military sacrifice (*shahadat*) are described as the highest form of service to the nation. As the retired Colonel Ghulamdin told me in an interview:

> In 1948, my father conquered Targabal fort in Dras. And recently in the Kargil conflict, my younger brother commanded a battalion in the same sector of Kargil. This is a huge honour for us. We can say with pride that we are true Pakistanis.

Hence, the military is not just a form of employment; for many in the region, it is part of family history, identity, and honour. This political economy of feeling and familial connection reinforces their loyalty to the Pakistan Army, as well as their emotional bond with the nation. It is the production of such loyal subjects, as well as the status, opportunities, and privileges generated by army service, which play a critical yet under-recognized role in producing the hegemony of the military in the region. In a context where the military is a key source of employment and by the nature of its service, an object of pride and respect, the possibilities of political assertion and contestation of military dominance become severely limited.

It is not just out of economic need and feelings of desire and allegiance that young men might join the army. Though I was not able to investigate this aspect in detail, I did come across two cases where the men had joined the army because they were doing badly at school, or had quit it altogether. Their parents or relatives reasoned that joining the army was a better option than sitting idle at home. There are also cases of soldiers who want to leave the army within months of joining, but all those who go through the initial Pakistan Military Academy (PMA) training sign a bond which prevents them from leaving till they reach a higher rank which might take several years. To leave before this point, soldiers need to pay a sizeable amount of money depending on the nature of their service—amounts that parents in Gilgit-Baltistan can scarcely afford. This contractual bond is yet another factor that adds to the hold of the military on the male labour of the region.

Increasingly, however, many young men do not look at the army with the same source of prestige and honour as their parents' generation did. Some question, and fear, the kind of social values that a culture of military service propagates. For example, Aftab, a university student, said to me:

> If you kill 100 people and come back, you become a *ghazi*.[29] If you kill 100 people and you die, then you are a *shaheed*.[30] Is this something to glorify?

Whether looked upon with pride or resentment, the reality remains that a dominant tradition of military service in Gilgit-Baltistan has entailed a high number of deaths of local soldiers during external as well as internal army operations in Pakistan. The possibility of becoming a *shaheed* can be a source of pride and honour, but also one of anxiety and loss for many in the region. The Kargil episode of 1999 is a tragic case in point, where the martyrdom of Gilgit-Baltistan's soldiers while fighting against India engulfed the region in simultaneous pride and suffering, and also—importantly—an exceptional bitterness towards the high command of the Pakistan Army. An in-depth analysis of the episode is much needed, and could be the topic of a separate chapter. Here, I shall just attempt to sketch an outline of the conflict, as well as its specific implications for Gilgit-Baltistan.

KARGIL

Between May and July 1999, Pakistan and India were embroiled in the worst armed conflict since the 1965 war, once again over the disputed territory of Kashmir. The encounter came to be known as the Kargil conflict or the Kargil war, as it was fought in the high-mountain district of Kargil in Indian-ruled Kashmir. The conflict was all the more frightening since the long-term rivals had become nuclear powers barely a year before.

The strategic goal of Kargil for Pakistan—specifically its Army that had conceived the plan—was to cross over the Line of Control into Indian-ruled Kashmir, and then block India's land route to Siachin so that supplies to the Indian army stationed there could be interrupted. To achieve this goal, the Pakistan Army launched a ground attack using its paramilitary troops—primarily the Northern Lights Infantry which at that time was entirely composed of soldiers from Gilgit-Baltistan. Moreover, these NLI fighters were deployed in the garb of *mujahideen* to enable plausible deniability—Pakistan could claim that independent Kashmiri freedom-fighters had launched the struggle—and consequently India would not have an excuse to declare war on Pakistan. To give credence to this *mujahideen* effect, Kashmiri and Pakistani *jihadis* were also engaged under the direction of the army.

The NLI soldiers quickly made progress towards their assigned task, but when they called for support and supplies, no help was forthcoming. Pakistan was officially claiming that it was the *mujahideen* who were fighting and hence, refrained from giving any ground or aerial support as that would reveal its own involvement. Indeed, people in Skardu movingly speak about how even the food needs of the soldiers had not been planned for and, hence, local families organized to provide food to their *jawans* (young soldiers). India, on the other hand, was fully equipped to respond to an infiltration of the territory hitherto under its control, and soon resorted to aerial bombing to quell the offensive. Left in the lurch in an already difficult terrain, the NLI began to incur a heavy loss of life, and more than 200,000 civilians on either side of the border were forced to become refugees for several months. Pakistan was eventually forced to retreat due to the failure of its operation as well as direct pressure from Washington.

The military strategy of Pakistan was ill-conceived, and bound to fail—army-backed soldiers could gain ground, but without *any* support, they could never hold the ground in the face of the massive and fully engaged Indian military. Second, the operation was deemed irresponsible by the international community at large, and shattered the diplomatic gains that Pakistan had made from the Nawaz Sharif–Vajpayee bus diplomacy barely three months prior to Kargil. When prospects of peace between the democratic forces of India and Pakistan looked bright, and were being worked upon, an offensive Pakistani military operation appeared to be a deliberate attempt to spike aggression by the Pakistan army under General Musharraf. On the domestic front as well, much conflict arose between General Musharraf and the then Prime Minister, Nawaz Sharif, as the latter claimed that he neither was fully informed about the Kargil operation nor gave his consent. Indeed, the fallout between the two over Kargil became one of the major reasons behind General Musharraf's coup barely three months later, in October 1999.

Apart from the civilians who suffered on both sides, the victims of the Kargil tragedy on the Pakistani side also included the soldiers of Gilgit-Baltistan whose bodies were used as fodder in a grandiose and reckless military plan. There was widespread discontent in Gilgit-Baltistan at the way in which NLI soldiers were left to tackle the might of the Indian army alone. However, the region erupted in total outrage when the Pakistani government even refused to accept the bodies of the martyrs of Kargil, in order to perpetuate the myth that only *mujahideen* were involved. Angry processions were taken out by political parties and ordinary people, but they were crushed and several protestors were detained. It was only after India decided to honour the Pakistani soldiers by giving them proper Muslim burials that the Pakistan government was shamed into accepting the martyred bodies. The landscape of Gilgit-Baltistan continues to bear the memory of this martyrdom, as countless graves of the Kargil *shaheed* dot the region, each made visible by a white flag. The death toll from the conflict on the Pakistan side is estimated to be between 800–1,000, while in Gilgit-Baltistan alone the official count provided by the Ex-Soldier's Board is 561 martyrs.

To diffuse local rage and make up for its callous abuse, the Pakistan Army undertook a number of appeasement and control measures. For example, the Nishan-e-Haider was given for the first time to a martyr from Gilgit-Baltistan—the NLI soldier Lalak Jan—who was a resident of Ghizer district in Gilgit-Baltistan. This honour also represented a grudging acknowledgement of the Pakistan state's central role in the Kargil 'insurgency'. More significantly, a long-standing demand of the NLI was accepted and the hitherto paramilitary organization was converted into a full-fledged regiment of the Pakistan Army. This heightened the status and privileges accorded to soldiers from Gilgit-Baltistan but, simultaneously, also embodied a form of discipline as a regiment would entail a mix of soldiers from different areas of Pakistan. Before the war, almost 100 per cent of the NLI comprised of men from Gilgit-Baltistan but, as a regiment, around half the strength now comes from outside the region. The Pakistan Army was thus able to dispel one of its chief fears after the Kargil conflict—the fear that a homogenous frontier force, when enraged, may rebel or organize against its own state.

Of course, no matter how much the loyalty and courage of soldiers is tested and exploited, the possibilities of rebellion are already limited by the material dependency and emotional attachment that participation in the military generates. Becoming a *shaheed* for the sake of defending the nation is one of the highest goals that soldiers in Pakistan are trained to aspire towards. As such, Kargil presented a unique opportunity and, ironically, at least in some part helped to re-establish the loyalty of Gilgit-Baltistani subjects to the Pakistani nation. While the families of martyrs suffered, they also learned to deal with their suffering because of the collectively recognized honour that was subsequently accorded to martyrs. Even several years after the conflict, people often mentioned their association with a Kargil *shaheed* to me with immense pride. Lalak Jan has become a symbol of regional pride, and is revered in local poetry as the one whose martyrdom finally enabled the region to get recognition within the nation-state of Pakistan. However, expressions of indignation are still present as well, particularly at the continued disregard for the promised compensation to some martyrs' families.

My interviewees, thus, often had a nuanced take on the role of the Pakistan army in the region, revealing the complexity of the political economy of feelings within which military power thrives. Illuminating a key dimension of the delusional state in Pakistan, a passionate retired military captain, Jamshed Alam, first extolled the virtues of the Pakistan Army and the bravery of Gilgit-Baltistan's soldiers to me, and then acknowledged:

> Our military psyche is that we are the best, and the *dushman* [enemy] is nothing. We have too much *guroor* [arrogance]. There is no reflection, and no public accountability. This is why we blindly thought that we would conquer Kargil.

Hence, military power is linked to the *arrogance* of the military and the resulting lack of accountability, not just to valorizing emotions of pride and loyalty. For nationalist political parties in Gilgit-Baltistan—already agitating for constitutional rights—the Kargil episode similarly epitomized the arrogance and high-handedness of the Pakistan state. Not surprisingly, their efforts as well as their popular appeal gained strength after Kargil. Unfortunately, their voices and legitimate grievances have never been heard respectfully, nor responded to diplomatically. Instead, they have been brutally crushed with repression, including bans on critical newspapers such as *Kargil*, intimidation, torture, and illegal detention of activists, and often their engineered exclusion from local elections.

Ultimately, the Kargil issue brought to the fore the ironies and contradictions within the militarized relations of rule in Gilgit-Baltistan. Gilgiti soldiers were fighting to defend a nation-state that has denied them even the most basic citizenship rights, and this denial is linked to the very dispute of Kashmir over which the Kargil war was being fought. Moreover, the same state even disowned their bodies once they were sacrificed for 'national glory'. Yet the bond of loyalty and the power of martyrdom is such that soldiers continue their service with dedication and courage. Moments of martyrdom, however, are not always moments of commemoration. They may also create a space for questioning whether a martyr's death could have been avoided.

SACRIFICE, SUFFERING, AND 'INTERNAL SECURITY'

One morning, in August 2006, the dead body of Captain Zameer Abbas was brought back to Gilgit from Balochistan. At that time, I was a visiting faculty member at the Karakoram University in Gilgit, and was living in the university's girls hostel. Captain Abbas was amongst the 21 security personnel who had died during General-President Musharraf's military operation against the Baloch leader Nawab Akbar Bugti.[31] With everyone I met that day—students at the university, staff members at a local NGO, shopkeepers, and taxi drivers—the topic of conversation was the Captain's death. How Zameer Abbas was just 29 years old when he died. How he had got married just last month, and how his mother was now in the hospital. For several days, people were mourning the tragedy that had befallen this respected local soldier and his family.

Since I had arrived in Gilgit—barely a month before Captain Abbas's death—I had noticed that people around me were avid followers of the news, both in print and on television. Whether it was in the homes of people whom I visited for research or social purposes, or at the hostel; men and women would switch to the hourly news and critically debate it at length. As Magnus Marsden has argued more generally, debate and thoughtful reflection is central to personhood in Northern Pakistan, quite contradictory to the dominant stereotypical images of rural residents as 'simple' and unthinking (2005). But it was at the time of the Balochistan operation that I realized that people in Gilgit might have a reason to follow and debate the news beyond general interest, particularly in times of escalating 'internal security operations'. Such political events were not remote and inconsequential realities; they directly and personally affected people in Gilgit-Baltistan as the region provided the very bodies on and through which the 'national security' politics in Pakistan was being played out.

The flourishing of relatively independent, private news channels—which many have called a 'media revolution' in Pakistan—provided an added draw to the news. The power of a free media dawned on me at this particular time of my fieldwork. The state-run Pakistan Television (PTV) was remarkable in its demonization of Nawab Akbar Khan Bugti, as well as its open justification and even celebration of the army operation. Moreover, PTV pathetically insisted that things were completely 'normal' in Balochistan after the operation. On the other hand, private news channels such as ARY-World and GEO highlighted the prominent political status and legacy of Akbar Bugti, the mass unrest and condemnation that followed the operation, and the diverse views on the operation from parliamentarians in official buildings as well as people on the street. What even such independent channels did not highlight were details about the soldiers who had died in the operation, and where they came from. For this, people around me in Gilgit turned to their local cable channel.

Commentary on Zameer Abbas continued for several days in everyday conversation and local newspapers. Mixed with the grief was a seething sense of rage. When I talked to the female cook, Shahnaz, at the hostel about the operation, she said:

Killing one's own people? Where is such a principle followed? Use of force can never be a solution.

An ex-government servant, Mohammad Khan, commented:

They keep sending our men to danger zones such as Balochistan and Wana. Whereas those from other areas are sent to Lahore and Karachi.

In sheer bewilderment, people seemed to be asking: how can the Pakistani government use fighter jets and gunship helicopters to openly kill a prominent leader of an already marginalized province? Very often, a sense of resentment was followed with a sense of pride or vice versa. For example, right after criticizing the military's repeated use of local soldiers in danger zones, the same government servant Mohammad Khan said to me:

You know our soldiers are from the mountains, so they know how to fight in mountainous terrain. They are very brave and competent. Look, the *shaheed*

Captain was so young, and yet he was qualified enough to be sent to an important mission.

A similar sense of pride and veneration was expressed to me by a taxi driver, and by a student at the Karakoram University. Perhaps this sensibility is precisely what enables people to deal with military deaths. The death of a *shaheed* needs to be honoured, not questioned—it has become a structural, emotional disposition in a context where every other family has a man in the army. And yet, even a genuine sense of glory in *shahadat* for the sake of the nation can sometimes fail to give comfort to those who lose their family members in the process. A female cousin of Captain Abbas, Safia, lamented to me:

What was the point of his death? He didn't have to die…he shouldn't have died. The women suffer when their men go away in the army, and they suffer when their men die for the army.

The gendered aspect of this anguished suffering was also brought home to me a year after Captain Abbas's death, at the time of the Lal Masjid (Red Mosque) operation in July 2007.[32] Once again, people around me in Gilgit seemed to be watching the news with more than a general interest. I was having lunch with Sitara, a 26-year old friend who was an administrative assistant at a local NGO. We were sitting in the cafeteria of the NGO when I noticed that she was pale with anxiety, and unable to eat. When I asked why, she explained:

You know my brother-in-law, Safdar bhai, did not call last night. He is part of the battalion that is fighting against the Lal Masjid clerics. There was no light in our house yesterday, so we could not even watch the news. And today, a TV channel said that six soldiers have died, but they did not reveal the identity of these soldiers. Before I came to the office, I could not breathe and my throat was dry. I felt more sick thinking what my sister must be going through. She is in the village these days. The phone is not working there, so Safdar bhai calls me and I communicate the news to my sister through a neighbor. My sister could not even keep calling me for information, because otherwise my mobile would be busy when Safdar bhai tried to call. A while ago, finally, Safdar bhai called and he said he was fine. It was such a relief for all of us, but I still feel tense. Who knows, when...I just keep looking at the phone.

PARANOIA AND THE STATE

The anxiety and anguish linked to military employment that I have highlighted above is heightened many times over by the repressive role of the intelligence agencies in the region. *Yahan har doosra banda jasoos hai*—every other person here is a spy—is one phrase that was repeated to me countless times during my research stays in Gilgit. Initially, I thought that my friends and colleagues were either paranoid, or exaggerating the role of the intelligence agencies so that I would be extra-cautious in my research. However, I gradually discovered that while not every other person may be a spy, the presence and control of intelligence agencies in Gilgit-Baltistan was indeed quite exceptional, and that this pervasiveness had become a social fact in Gilgit-Baltistan, firmly rooted in people's experience.

Intelligence agencies are generally quite powerful in Pakistan, often described as forming a 'state within a state' due to their apparent independence from the Ministry of Interior as well as the Ministry of Defence. It is also widely recognized that the largest intelligence agency of Pakistan, the Inter-Services Intelligence (ISI), has played a decisive role in electoral rigging, and in the production of religious militants for Pakistan-sponsored movements in Afghanistan and Kashmir.[33] However, the role of agencies in the micro-politics of government remains an under-studied area of analysis.[34] The secrecy and repression that shrouds intelligence activity is an obvious barrier to such an analysis. Nevertheless, my field research revealed aspects of the local experience of agencies that can help to illuminate their complex role in shaping the social fabric of the Pakistani state as well as the Gilgit-Baltistani region.

If military domination in Gilgit-Baltistan has translated into a garrison state, the work of the intelligence agencies, in addition, has created what I call a *delusional state* that both creates and feeds on paranoia, suspicion, and surveillance. Agencies in Gilgit-Baltistan have been able to expand their already unchecked powers in extraordinary ways, as the structure of national political representation and accountability that is at least formally present in the provinces is absent in this strategic territory. Further, agencies have used the disputed, border status of the region, along with the spectre of its always-suspected Shia populace as grounds for spreading their reach. As a result, there are known to be at least eight different intelligence units operating in the small vicinity of Gilgit, with spies employed all across Gilgit-Baltistan.

I did not have to ask about the 'role of the intelligence agencies' in my interviews—it would inevitably come up by itself whenever I asked about the political and administrative issues that affect the region. My interviewees—across class, sect, and other social locations—pointed out that the agencies are fundamental to the working of the military establishment in Gilgit-Baltistan. They closely monitor and shape the dynamics of the local administration. The decision to induct, promote, and dismiss government servants is often critically dependent on the extensive dossiers that the agencies maintain through their network of hired informers. These dossiers detail the views expressed, and activities undertaken by potential or existing government employees in private or public. This is to test whether any action could be interpreted as a sign of critique or dissent, and hence, a source of suspicion. Such dossiers are also maintained for journalists, teachers, and political activists to keep them in check. As part of this reconnaissance, intelligence agencies regularly tap phone lines, and intercept postal and electronic communication. They have also embedded informers as journalists in the local media to ensure the monitoring of media personnel and censorship of the news. Moreover, house searches, messages of warning, detaining people without charge, and violent interrogation techniques are routine methods of agency harassment and coercion in Gilgit-Baltistan.

During my fieldwork, several interviewees matter-of-factly mentioned that they knew a person or even a *rishtaydaar* (relative) in their village and neighborhood who worked for the agencies, or has been approached to work for them. In a casual conversation once with a taxi driver, I learned that he himself previously worked for the agencies but, since the money was not enough, he decided to take a loan to buy a car and become a taxi driver instead. The normality with which he brought up his employment for an intelligence agency was disconcerting to say the least, but after extended research in the region, I realized that the taxi driver was not an exception. In a context of widespread unemployment, many men spy to get an extra income and this has become a taken-for-granted reality in the region. The identity of intelligence agents is often known to the public at large, as has also been observed by Verkaaik in the Pakistani city of Hyderabad (2001).

Importantly, the way people accept and valorize employment in the Pakistan Army does not apply to the agencies. In fact, it would not be an exaggeration to say that intelligence agencies are the most despised element of the state establishment in Gilgit. A number of linked reasons are responsible for this sentiment.

To begin with, working for the agencies was often described as a result of a person's *majburi*—his helplessness due to economic need—and a cause for disdain as this need was being used as a weapon to create disaffection in his own community. More importantly, there is widespread bitterness in the manner in which agencies create and sustain the representation of the region as an untrustworthy, treacherous space. People are acutely aware—and painstakingly insist—that this representation has no correspondence with reality, and it is perpetuated only because it serves to justify the agencies' own survival and control.

As Ataullah, a teacher from a local government college tellingly explained:

It is not that agencies exist because we are unreliable. We are assumed to be unreliable so that agencies can exist.[35] We are the most loyal and peaceful Pakistanis. Ours is the only region that actually fought a war to become part of Pakistan—the other areas became part of Pakistan by political settlement. Our men have also given sacrifices for Pakistan in the 1965 war, in the 1971 war, and in Kargil. People from Punjab and from Azad Kashmir have been caught spying for India, but never from our region. Then why aren't we trusted? The border is an excuse, Shias are an excuse. It is because agencies run this place, and this is what they do...they suspect, and make everyone appear suspect. This is the biggest problem facing us—this suspicion, and this lack of trust. This is why we are denied any identity, any political rights.

Juxtaposing this comment with one from Sarwat Khan, a member of the Gilgit-Baltistan Legislative Assembly (GBLA), yields further insight:

A country needs intelligence agencies for its security. But more than ensuring external security, the agencies in our region create internal insecurity through suppression. They make sure that no rights are given to us, and if we ask for our legitimate rights, they make sure that our voices are crushed.

A journalist, Mehboob Shah, adds:

It is like thought control. So many of us live in fear, and are afraid to freely discuss anything in public—what if there is a spy around? Last week, when I sent a report about the region to a newspaper in down-country—under a pseudonym—I first got a threatening warning on phone, then through an agent who came to my house. They do this to remind us that they know where we live, where our families are. This *ghatiya* [debased] pressure is brutal. We have to ask: who benefits from this system? By denying us our rights, and holding us in fear and suspicion, it is the military establishment that benefits because they want to maintain their unchecked privileges.

The 'thought control' that Shah refers to is reminiscent of Foucault's thesis on panoptic surveillance, and the ways in which power in modern society functions through the internalization of the state's gaze and the self-monitoring that results from it. Foucault describes the modern surveillance machine as 'permanent in its effects, even if it is discontinuous in its action'—that it continues to work through psychic control and the threat of punishment, even in the absence of actual, physical monitoring or punishment. It thus induces 'a state of conscious and permanent visibility that assures the automatic functioning of power'.[36] The surveillance machine works by producing emotions of self-suspicion and paranoia—a kind of 'psychic panopticon' that serves to intensify state rule.[37]

As the views expressed by my research subjects illustrate, suspicion is also integral to the operation of political power in Gilgit-Baltistan because people are *assumed* to be suspect *by definition*, and this presumed suspicion has translated into a regime of monitoring and intimidation by a military-intelligence establishment for whom the suspicion serves as a convenient rationale for maintaining its own political and economic authority. If there is any expression of critique or dissent at the abuses of this establishment, it is treated as a threat, and as evidence of a disloyalty that is already presumed. The endemic nature of suspicion and surveillance, in fact, produces such an absurd level of delusion that state paranoia thrives even in the absence of specific expressions of protest. For example, in 2011, a group of special, disabled children from Gilgit-Baltistan visited India with their teacher to participate in a sports tournament. For months after they had returned, the teacher as well as the local non-profit that facilitated the trip were repeatedly visited by the local intelligence agents to reveal the 'real reasons' for the trip. The nationalistic paranoia characterizing Pakistani-India relations has not even spared animals. According to the Pakistani English daily *The Express Tribune*, Pakistani wildlife authorities captured an Indian monkey for crossing the border in December 2011, while in May 2010, a Pakistani pigeon was held in armed guard by Indian police.[38]

Suspicion thus creates corrosive patterns of behaviour and social interaction, serving to legitimize extraordinary political actions. It is integral to state nationalism, as nationalist ideologies seek to create a singular self by vehemently marginalizing and dehumanizing internal and external others which they are suspicious of. The others—be they religious, ethnic, regional, national, or racial—need to be seen with intense distrust, and hence constantly monitored, contained, or thwarted. Increasingly, the discourse of permanent threat and the availability of new technologies has led to a 'surveillance society' in which the *citizenry as a whole* is suspect, and intricately monitored in ways that are not open to public scrutiny and accountability.[39] The logics of secrecy, suspicion, and surveillance have come to define the very nature of the late modern state,[40] bolstering the militarization of citizenship that a security state already entails and together producing what I have termed the delusional state. The absurd nature and extent of this state of delusion is not limited to disputed zones like Gilgit-Baltistan, or antagonistic nations like India and Pakistan. Several scholars have documented—for countries such as the US, UK, Canada, Russia, and Germany—how undercover law enforcement has been disproportionately paranoid, its scale bordering on the ridiculous and tactics nasty and outrageous.[41]

The work of Anne McClintock is especially useful in understanding the contemporary paranoid state. Speaking of the US state and empire, McClintock writes, 'A social entity such as an organization, state, or empire can be spoken of as "paranoid" if the dominant powers governing that entity cohere as a collective community around contradictory cultural narratives, self-mythologies, practices, and identities that oscillate between delusions of inherent superiority and omnipotence, and phantasms of threat and engulfment.'[42] It is this dual nature of paranoia—hallucinations of grandeur existing alongside the dread of perpetual threat—that has the capacity to produce extraordinary forms of violence. McClintock argues that the rise of this paranoia is linked to the incessant rise of US militarism since the 1960s, which justifies itself through the social production of fear. The spectral, obscene violence embodied in the US invasions of Afghanistan and Iraq and particularly the Abu Ghraib and Guantanamo prisons thus needs to be traced to this history of paranoid militarism, instead of being seen as a spontaneous response to 9/11.

The Pakistani state is characterized by a similar, paranoid militarism—a sense of untouchability and arrogance has accompanied the tumorous growth of military-intelligence power in politics, business, and society, while delusions of internal and external threats have been propagated to justify the military-surveillance machine. There is yet another aspect of Pakistani state paranoia that is revealed most acutely in Gilgit-Baltistan. The military-intelligence regime accomplishes its rule in the region not only by rendering its citizens suspect and using this suspicion to further its control but also by promoting suspicion amongst citizens and hence disrupting local political solidarity and resistance against the military regime. Apart from suspected subjects, thus, the delusional state also produces suspicious subjects.

SUSPICIOUS SUBJECTS

The production of sectarian suspicion and tension is the most significant factor for which the role of intelligence agencies is condemned in Gilgit. Indeed, I was often told that 'agencian firqon ko larwati hain' (agencies make the different sects fight), and 'agencian fasad ki jar hain' (agencies are the root cause of conflict). Of course, theology itself fosters a sense of incommensurable values (Shaikh, 1989) and along with bigoted religious practices—such as stereotypes learned at home—creates a potential for discord between people with different religious beliefs. However, it is organized political action—not primordial belief—that has produced conditions for the creation of sectarian conflict in modern times.

In the Gilgit district of Gilgit-Baltistan, the time before the 1970s is remembered as a time of shared life-worlds, when religious identities were fluid and pluralistic. Though inter-sect skirmishes were acknowledged, people by-and-large respected and even participated in each other's religious rituals, and inter-marriage across sects was fairly common, with the result that several families in Gilgit-Baltistan today have members who belong to different sects. Such practices defy essentialist understandings of 'sectarian difference', which presumes that sectarian identity is inherently exclusionary and antagonistic, and that differences between sects naturally lead to conflict. It is the military-intelligence regime's calculated efforts at fomenting religious hate through strategies of sectarianization that have played a central role in radically altering the pluralist social textures of life in Gilgit-Baltistan.

According to my interviewees, the invasive role of intelligence agencies in Gilgit-Baltistan emerged in the early 1970s, particularly in the aftermath of a significant, secular movement that galvanized Gilgitis at the end of 1970. This movement had demanded the enactment of democratic rights in Gilgit-Baltistan, and especially the abolition of the Frontier Crimes Regulations—a British-era law that enabled autocratic rule in the region. The movement occurred in the larger context of political change in Pakistan, where a pro-democracy struggle led by Zulfiqar Bhutto was already underway. Interestingly, it was a case of military abuse and arrogance coupled with gendered humiliation that provided the immediate impetus for the first protest. The site of contention was a local public school—and we will see in subsequent chapters how politics at the schools has continued to remain a source of state-region tension in the region. A child of a non-local, military officer failed an examination at a Gilgiti school and, in response, the wife of the officer went to the school, humiliated its female principal, and ordered her to change the grade. The principal subsequently lodged a complaint with the District Commissioner (DC)—the highest bureaucratic post at the time—but instead of acknowledging her grievance, he fired her. This incident signified the impunity which characterized everyday indignities of militarism in the region. Students boycotted their classes and local Gilgiti leaders such as Jauhar Ali began to mobilize people and spearhead protests. The protestors first attacked and looted the shops that the military officer owned in Gilgit town. The office of the DC was subsequently stormed by a massive crowd of people from across sect and social class. When the DC ordered a local Gilgit Scout soldier to fire at the protestors, the soldier refused and fired in the sky instead. This strengthened the crowd, and when the authorities responded with jailing many of the protestors, people en masse broke into the jail and managed to release their compatriots. The incident shocked the Pakistani establishment which now realized that troops drawn from the local population could not be solely relied upon to enforce rule. By 1975, the Gilgit Scouts that were hitherto responsible for order in the region were disbanded, and the responsibility of local security was passed on to the Frontier Constabulary (FC) or other military or paramilitary units that employed non-local, primarily Pushtun or Punjabi soldiers.

An official document, *Report of the Committee of Gilgit-Baltistan*,[43] acknowledged the significance of the 1970 incident and recommended specific actions of appeasement that needed to be taken in response. It suggested that people of the region had to be given basic rights, so that they could be incorporated more firmly within the Pakistan state. Otherwise, they might rebel. Subsequently, the Bhutto government in 1972 abolished the FCR and began the process of abolishing the feudal kingdoms in the region—a move that fit well with Bhutto's campaign against feudalism, relieving people in the region from much hardship, while also strengthening the direct rule of the Pakistan state. Simultaneously, the military-bureaucratic state apparatus—chiefly the army, intelligence agencies, and the KANA[44] ministry—embarked upon a divisive project that aimed at creating disunity along sectarian lines, in order to thwart future expressions of regional solidarity and secular-nationalist aspiration.

This project of division firstly entailed state sponsorship of Sunni and Shia religious organizations, which were required to spur sectarian animosity as a means of deflecting political energy and agreement.[45] *Maulvis* (clerics) and government employees from both sects were paid by intelligence agencies to engage in dehumanizing tirades against sectarian others, through wall-chalking, mosque loudspeakers, and publications. While each sect was played against the other, the Sunni sect was especially patronized and the Shia community suppressed, as Shia identity has been rendered antithetical in a gradually Sunni-ized Pakistan state.[46] One of the first acts that represented this suppression was the banning of the traditional Muharram procession in 1974 in Gilgit, which generated a major sectarian clash in this Shia-majority region. In popular memory and discourse, this is the period that is routinely identified with the beginning of 'sectarian conflict'.[47] The late 1970s soon heralded the international mobilization of political Islam and creation of *jihadis* for the Cold War, alongside the national project of Islamization implemented by General Zia—both of which ultimately resulted in the Shia pogrom of 1988 that is discussed in the next chapter. More recently, in 2000, new school textbooks were introduced in Gilgit-Baltistan that were perceived by the local Shia community as having a visibly stronger Sunni orientation. This 'textbook controversy'—as it came to be called—turned into a full-blown sectarian conflict between 2004–2005, when almost a hundred people lost their lives, educational institutions were closed for half the year, and a constant curfew paralysed daily life in Gilgit. As a result of such episodes of conflict, there has been a marked increase in sectarian polarization in Gilgit, evidenced by trends such as a decrease in inter-marriage between the different Muslim sects, as well as in adjacent living in joint neighborhoods. Sectarian identity has thus become the most defining axis of difference in Gilgit today.

According to some political commentators in the region, the Pakistan army has used the Sunni–Shia conflict as an excuse to expand military presence and influence, by transferring key civilian posts to army brigadiers and deploying paramilitary forces. Hence, apart from subverting regional solidarity, sectarian conflict in Gilgit-Baltistan is further useful for the military state as it serves to produce the very 'sectarian' subject which it ascribes to the region, thus reinforcing the need for its own presence for maintaining 'law and order'. Moreover, state sectarianization in Gilgit-Baltistan has also entailed the induction of a particular kind of political leadership into the grain of government in Gilgit-Baltistan. In their everyday practices since the 1970s, state officials such as the Major General in FCNA gradually began to patronize their own sect—the Sunni sect, since barring a couple of exceptions, all were Sunni—while simultaneously playing both Shia and Sunni sects against each other. According to the government official Sajid Zafar, this involved telling

Sunnis in the region that the government belongs to them and that they can and should control the Shias, while telling Shias that they are in a majority and thus should be able to tame the Sunnis. Such discursive engagements became normalized, and ensured that the sectarian fire remained alive. It is not that all Sunni and Shia officials did this, but that a particular kind of leadership increasingly became normalized, fueling sectarian patronage as well as intersect suspicion. Beyond such official state practices as well as critical events such as the 1988 Shia pogrom and the textbook controversy of the 2000s, there are several seemingly ordinary practices through which sectarian suspicion and resentment is cultivated in Gilgit-Baltistan, in and through the military institutions of the region. I will discuss an example in Chapter 4, where I elaborate everyday forms of sectarianism.

Ironically, while the military-intelligence regime in Gilgit-Baltistan thrives on creating suspicion amongst the populace, their activities in turn create suspicion towards the regime itself, and particularly towards the intelligence agencies. Indeed, any discussion of political and religious conflict in Gilgit-Baltistan would be incomplete without someone mentioning: '*Is mein to agencion ka haath hai*' (the hand of agencies is responsible for this). Since there is an experiential awareness of the pervasiveness of intelligence agencies, they end up being the prime suspect whenever there is any incidence of conflict and violence in Gilgit-Baltistan. This suspicious—and sometimes, conspiratorial—outlook among citizens is symbolic of their subjectivity under conditions of secrecy and deception, instead of their pathology.[48]

This reverse suspicion also offers some solace, as people in Gilgit-Baltistan across sects—aware and wary of the 'hand' of intelligence agencies—have come to see sectarian conflict as being a political instead of a primordial matter. The heightened visibility and interference by intelligence organizations has thus resulted in the subversion of their own power. While the role of local *maulvis* and external players is recognized, it is the state itself, and particularly the intelligence agencies that are perceived to be the major culprits, trying to create sectarian conflict to continue a divisive project. We might say that this reverse suspicion reflects a crisis in the legitimacy of the state, quite contrary to what the discursive structure of the state-as-protector is designed to accomplish. In this sense, then, the effect of suspicion also marks the limit of power, even as it saturates the very horizon and operation of power.[49]

While the reverse suspicion might serve to denaturalize sectarianism, it does not of course entirely thwart it. As mentioned earlier, repeated occurrences of sectarian violence and discrimination have also infected social imaginaries and subjectivities such that there has been a rise in resentment between members of different sects—a topic that I investigate at length in Chapter 4. Religious sentiments form a deeply personal and sensitive aspect of a community's roots, making differences along religious lines perhaps the most volatile of all differences. It has been convenient for national and international powers to mobilize this religious potential for strategic ends, thus breeding intolerance and vicious conflict. That this strategic politics is undertaken by abusing religion, is a source of particular anguish and moral outrage in Gilgit-Baltistan. As Nawaz Jan, a government official, said to me:

> The saddest reality is that they have made us fight in the name of Allah and the Prophet. It is despicable. They have no *deen* [faith] and no *iman* [integrity].

Jan's critique and despondent anger is widely shared, but I mention Nawaz Jan in particular to highlight that the divisive role of intelligence officials is widely recognized amongst members of the local state itself. The next and final section of this chapter discusses how state bureaucrats have themselves tried to undertake critical action against intelligence-backed sectarian strife in the region, thus highlighting the tensions between various institutions of the state as well as the challenges to militarization and sectarianization that have emerged from within it.

CRITICAL STRUGGLES WITHIN THE STATE

Because of its divisive role, the 'government' in Gilgit-Baltistan is generally seen as an entity that rules through malice, manipulation, and 'dirty politics'. At the same time, however, we need to recognize that the state on the ground is hardly monolithic, represented ultimately by the actions of countless individuals from within as well as outside Gilgit-Baltistan. Hence, while I argue that the historical working of the militarized Pakistani state has been detrimental in many ways for people's sense of belonging and security in Gilgit-Baltistan, I also wish to emphasize the critical voices that exist within the government—perhaps at the margins, but significant nonetheless, for they too constitute the state.

Shiraz Qamar is a case in point. During the period of my fieldwork, Qamar was serving as a high-ranking civil bureaucrat in Gilgit-Baltistan. He seemed to be quite popular and well respected in Gilgit. In everyday conversations or interviews, Gilgitis would criticize the government for its high-handed attitude towards the region, but often end with: 'Shiraz Qamar is a good official though; we need people like him in the government'. On asking why Qamar was regarded as different from other officials, I variously heard that he was 'considerate', 'competent', 'principled', 'accessible', and someone who 'listened to the issues and tried to resolve them'. People across the social spectrum seemed to admire his personality, work ethic, and, importantly, his politics. Sadly, it was precisely because of his principled nature and politics that he was ultimately 'relieved' from his post.

Unlike many previous bureaucrats, Shiraz Qamar could not readily reconcile himself to the domineering role of the military and intelligence agencies in Gilgit-Baltistan. He was proving to be 'difficult' for the military establishment in Gilgit because he did follow an 'unspoken norm' of government in Gilgit-Baltistan—taking the consent of the FCNA military command in all matters. But it was his reluctance in maintaining the state's sectarian attitude that proved to be the major source of contention between him and the military-intelligence regime.

In 2006, Shiraz Qamar decided to take action against the leading Sunni cleric in Gilgit-Baltistan, after attending his Friday *khutba* (sermon) in which anti-Shia sentiment was being preached. Qamar felt that this was a clear violation of regulations related to loudspeaker use in mosques, and needed to be particularly curtailed in a region that had recently experienced such intense Shia–Sunni violence. The cleric's house was subsequently raided, and sophisticated weapons were discovered, which now constituted a more serious breach of anti-terror laws. However, when the civil government in Gilgit-Baltistan decided to press forward with stern action, the move was strongly resisted by the military command. It was made clear to Qamar—as it has been evident to locals for long—that the cleric was being patronized by the intelligence agencies and the army. Qamar refused to bow down, which eventually led to his transfer from the region.

Qamar's case was a publicly visible and discussed example of friction within the institutional structure of the state. Such struggles *within* the institutional edifice of the state, even if unsuccessful, revive some faith in the democratic potential of the state and serve to demonstrate to the marginalized that the state can be a source of justice instead of abuse. However, it is not easy to undo the damage caused by a sustained state investment in sponsoring and realizing religious hate. What is needed is a structural transformation of the Pakistani state, which amongst other policies would entail public accountability and effective political control of the military and intelligence agencies in the country.

CONCLUSION

In this chapter, I have explored how the military-intelligence regime in Pakistan defines state practice and everyday experience in Gilgit-Baltistan. The regime's domination of political administration in Gilgit is a form of repression that constitutes a key aspect of military power. However, to understand the hold of the military and intelligence agencies in the region, we need to attend to the emotional regulation through which their power is embedded in the Gilgiti social imaginary. I thus highlight the politics of desire and aspiration that the military engenders, as families strive to become part of its economic opportunities and privileges. The process of local employment in the military and sustained participation in security operations has produced a political economy of feelings that cultivates honour, pride, and loyalty towards the military, and hence, towards a military-state: these constitute the conditions of possibility for continued military authoritarianism in Gilgit-Baltistan. Efforts to challenge this status quo are made all the more impossible by the surveillance and hate-mongering activities of intelligence agencies, which have served to create suspicious, sectarianized subjects, thus eroding social cohesion and possibilities of political cooperation. Along with the panoptic gaze and control of the military-intelligence regime in Gilgit-Baltistan, it is this suspicion and paranoia which produces and consolidates state power in the region. And it is precisely the insidious and unaccountable practices of the intelligence agencies that nationalist–political movements in the region protest and struggle against, in their call for demilitarization. The command of the military-intelligence regime is contested through critical reflections both within and outside the state that construct the regime as a source of insecurity, injustice, and violence, particularly in the national context of rising 'security operations', which have deeply affected the lives of Gilgit-Baltistan's soldiers and their families.

Having discussed the cultural politics of militarism in Gilgit-Baltistan, I will now examine in depth the process of state sectarianization in the region, as well as the ways in which military-backed, exclusionary forms of 'Pakistani Islam' have been contested by people in Gilgit-Baltistan.

NOTES

1 Weber (1964) and Poulantzas (1973).
2 Chapter 2 was originally published as 'Grounding Militarism: Structures of Feeling and Force in Gilgit-Baltistan,' in Everyday Occupations: Experiencing Militarism in South Asia and the Middle East, 85–114, Copyright, 2013, University of Pennsylvania Press. All rights reserved.
3 Lutz (1999).
4 Jalal (1990).
5 de Mel (2007).
6 Jalal (1990), Rizvi (2000), and Shah (2014).
7 Siddiqa (2001).
8 Ibid.
9 Nawaz (2007).
10 de Mel (2007: 12).
11 Mills (1956) and Lutz (2004).
12 de Mel (2007).
13 Mills (1956: 191) quoted in Lutz (2004).
14 Lutz (2004: 320).
15 Incompetent as well as co-opted politicians have lent credibility to this discourse, leading to a widespread tendency where people in Pakistan see the military as the lesser of the two evils.
16 Nawaz (2007).
17 This has been a contentious process, of course, facing fierce resistance especially in the province of Balochistan. Nationalist parties in the province have consistently opposed the use of Baloch land as 'state land' for nuclear testing and for expanding military cantonments.
18 Siddiqa (2007).

19 Alavi (1990).
20 Siddiqa (2007).
21 Kamal (1982).
22 'Askari' is an Urdu word for 'soldier'.
23 Mobile services were introduced for the first time in the region in August 2006, also by SCO. Private mobile companies were allowed to operate a few months later.
24 HRW (2000).
25 Sökefeld (2014).
26 Stöber (2000).
27 The NLI was formed in 1971, and is the key army regiment from Gilgit-Baltistan.
28 These rates are from 2007.
29 A war hero with a special religious status.
30 A martyr with a special religious status.
31 Nawab Akbar Khan Bugti was a former chief minister of Balochistan, and was also an elected member of the National Assembly.
32 An attack by the Pakistani Army on the Red Mosque in Islamabad.
33 Abbas (2005).
34 For insightful analyses of intelligence work and power during the British Raj in India, see Bayly (1996) and Edney (1997).
35 My emphasis.
36 Foucault (1977: 201).
37 Harper (2008: 6).
38 See http://tribune.com.pk/story/17097/pigeon-held-in-india-for-spying-for-pakistan/ and http://tribune.com.pk/story/302548/pakistan-arrests-indian-monkey-for- crossing-border/.
39 Murakami Wood (2006).
40 Feldman (2008).
41 Marx (1988), Buse et al. (2000), Blum (2003), Lyon (2003), Los (2004), Murakami Wood (2006), Shorrock (2008), and Giroux (2015). The extent of political manipulation and media control that local and foreign intelligence agencies engage in can be gauged by archival documents that demonstrate the intrusive working of the CIA in Pakistan even in the 1950s.
42 McClintock (2009: 53).
43 Government of Pakistan (1971).
44 KANA stands for Kashmir Affairs and Northern Areas, now renamed as the Ministry of Kashmir Affairs and Gilgit-Baltistan after the region's name change in 2009. It is the Islamabad-based federal institution that oversees the administration of Gilgit-Baltistan.
45 Shehzad (2003) and personal interviews.
46 Qureshi (1989).
47 Sökefeld (2003).
48 West and Sanders (2003).
49 Anderson (2010).

PART II

Education and the Politics of Faith

3

CHALLENGING SCHOOL TEXTBOOKS

೫೦೦ತ

The Sectarian Making of National Islam

In May 2000, the Shia Muslims based in the Gilgit district of the then Northern Areas began to agitate against the recently changed curriculum of government schools in the region. The controversial textbooks were produced by the Punjab Textbook Board, and spanned various disciplines including Urdu, Social Studies, and Islamiat—a subject that focuses on the study of Islam, declared compulsory for all Muslim students in Pakistan under General Zia's Islamization agenda. The Islamiat texts for primary classes were deemed particularly unacceptable. Many in the Shia community felt that in these new books—written by a panel of four Sunni scholars—not only was the Shia interpretation of Islam blatantly disregarded, but the Sunni interpretation was also more starkly asserted. For example, it was argued that visual representations of performing prayers followed the Sunni style of prayer, implicitly delegitimizing the Shia way of being Muslim. Similarly, it was felt that the lives of Caliphs as well as the Prophet's Companions were extensively discussed, while those of the revered Shia Imams were barely mentioned. Such representations were deemed to undermine the faith and identity the of Shia youth. Four years after the agitation began, the 'textbook controversy'—as it came to be called—turned into a fatal conflict involving violent confrontations between state authorities and Shia protestors, the loss of around hundred lives, a climate of heightened Shia–Sunni discord, and a constant curfew that paralysed daily life in the region for eleven months. The matter was partly resolved in April 2005, when an agreement was reached to withdraw some of the controversial textbooks, and replace them with those produced by the National Book Foundation and the NWFP Textbook Board.[1]

Why did the issue of textbooks become so huge and consequential, and cause so much anguish? It generated the most potent and long-standing Shia collective mobilization against the state that Pakistan has witnessed in the last three decades and, at the same time, resulted in the worst episode of Shia–Sunni hostility in Gilgit-Baltistan's recent history. As such, it encompassed much more than what the term 'controversy' might suggest. In this chapter, I explore the nature and consequences of this critical event, and use it as a lens to examine the politics of sectarianism, education, and state-making in contemporary Gilgit-Baltistan and Pakistan.

The Islamic content of Pakistani textbooks has received much scholarly attention since 9/11, in response to national and international concerns regarding the perpetuation of religious intolerance and violence in the public school and madrasa curricula in Pakistan.[2] However, this attention has focused primarily on how non-Muslim others are portrayed in school texts, not on how differences within Islam—particularly between the Shia and Sunni interpretations—are represented in official curricula. This is ironic, since it is precisely the sectarian aspect of textbooks that has been prominently contested in Pakistani history, and recently became the source of violent conflict in Gilgit-Baltistan. Indeed, even after a five-year movement against sectarianized textbooks in Gilgit, it has been asserted that questions regarding the nature of the Muslim nation and the place of sectarian difference in it remain 'unspeakable' in Pakistan.[3] The lack of recognition of both sectarianized public education as well as the resistance to it reveals the limits of intellectual discourse on Islam, education, and sectarianism in Pakistan, as well as the particular silence on Gilgit-Baltistan within this discourse.

More generally, a standard narrative has come to dominate the studies of sectarianism in Pakistan. Most accounts dwell on factors such as the theological differences between Shia and Sunni Islam, the proliferation of madrasas since the 1970s, militant violence by sectarian parties such as Sipah-e-Sahaba Pakistan and Tehrik-e-Jaffaria Pakistan, international events like the Afghan war and the Iranian revolution, and national policies such as the Islamization agenda of General Zia.[4] While these aspects are crucial for understanding the rise of sectarianism in Pakistan, they hardly exhaust the terrain of sectarian experience and conflict. In these studies, moreover, the state is largely understood as an instrumentalist policy-maker and its role limited to considerations of law and party politics. My analysis, on the other hand, draws upon theories of state-making that focus on how the state is imagined and implemented through cultural representations and micro-practices of power and regulation.[5]

Textbook representation constitutes a key micro-practice of regulation, as it is a principal site where the imagined identity of the nation-state as well as its citizens is articulated. Textbooks not only serve to naturalize particular understandings of the nation, but also reinforce existing social inequalities such as those of class, rural/urban location, gender, ethnicity, and religion.[6] In Pakistan, representations of Islam in textbooks are fundamental to the project of state-making, as they provide a chief mechanism through which Islam is constructed as the ideological basis of the nation and the legitimating source for the state. Through these representations, the Pakistani state is naturalized as a space that is inhabited—barring a few small groups of non-Islamic minorities—by a homogenous national community organically united by the force of Islam. Textbook Islam is thus routinely constituted as a singular belief system, with no sectarian differences. While it is often claimed that this Islam emphasizes the commonalities of the various schools of thought within Islam, in actuality it is mostly the tenets of Sunni Islam—adhered to by around 75 per cent of the Muslim population in Pakistan[7]—which has come to be legitimized as correct Islam in textbook representations as well as in classroom teaching. Shia beliefs tend to be silenced in these representations, and this becomes particularly problematic and contested in Gilgit-Baltistan as around 75 per cent of the region's population follows some form of Shia Islam—almost an exact reversal of the norm in the rest of Pakistan.[8]

The Gilgiti movement against textbooks challenged this silence, raising fundamental questions pertaining to religion, nation, and citizenship in Pakistan: what a Pakistani is or should be, what a Muslim is or should be, and what are the ideals of citizenship that the Pakistani nation should aspire towards. However, the movement was not just about textbooks. It reached such explosive proportions because biased textbook content was viewed as part of a long-standing political project of state-making in the Northern Areas, in which sectarianism has been used as a tool for both religious as well as regional suppression—a theme that I began exploring in the previous chapter and will continue here.

Apart from investigating the politics of sectarianized state representations of Islam, this chapter further problematizes the role of the Pakistani state in relation to sectarian identity by interrogating practices through which the state represents minorities, labels political tensions, and implements conflict management. These provide additional means through which meaningful citizenship is denied to otherized religious groups, and sectarianism is fostered. But before analysing such divisive state policies and their impact on the nature of sectarian ties and citizenship in Gilgit-Baltistan, it is important to understand the historical meaning of Islam and Muslim culture in the specific regional context of Gilgit-Baltistan.[9]

SITUATING SECTARIANISM

In several conversations that I had with Gilgitis over the course of my research, people commented on how new the present situation of sectarian bitterness really is in the region. Particularly for those who are middle-aged and older, memories of a more harmonious past are very real and recent, and the change in sectarian relations palpable. For example, Noor Afroz, a 38-year old Shia woman from the Ampheri area of Gilgit related to me:

> I remember that when I was young, there were always women who brought fruit and juice in our *majalis* [religious gatherings] in *muharram*. Only later, when the conditions changed, did I become aware that these were Sunni women.

Similarly, Parveen Bibi, a 50-year old Sunni woman from the same neighbourhood in Gilgit said:

> It wasn't like this in previous times. We met women from other communities who were also living close by. We didn't even know who was of what sect. *We didn't think about it.*[10]

Sectarian identity did not seem to be an active category of subjectivity and thought in the Gilgiti social imaginary—especially so in the social universe of women. People in Gilgit do acknowledge that notions of sectarian difference and even revulsion existed, more in some places than others, and this has been part of Muslim history in many places. But this did not mean that sect hampered the way in which people connected with each other in practice. Debates about Shia and Sunni theology could continue—even leading to each sect acrimoniously claiming its superiority—without any actions of violence, and denial of the right to be different. A peak into the colonial record also lends credence to this, even as I recognize the contested and partial nature of the 'facts' embodied in the archive.

In 1880, Colonel John Biddulph, the first British Officer on Special Duty for the Gilgit Agency, wrote:

> The people of Chilas, who were always a less tractable race than their neighbours, make it their boast that, though travelers and traders are safe in their country, no Shiah ever escapes out of their hands...In Gilgit, at the commencement of the Sikh occupation, the greater proportion were Shiahs or Maulais,[11] and it is related that any Soonnee falling into their hands was branded with a hot iron unless he consented to become a proselyte.[12]

Having said this, Biddulph immediately recognizes:

> Wherever Soonnees and Shiahs are found living together, they seem to practice a mutual tolerance rare in other purely Mahommedan communities. Intermarriage between the sects is so common as not to excite remark... They [the Maulais]...wherever permitted, live on good terms with Soonnees and Shiahs, with whom they intermarry without restraint.[13]

Biddulph captures well the intriguing dialectic between what Gilgiti Shias and Sunnis *claim* about each other, and how they *act* towards each other. According to my interviewees as well, the *rishtaydari* (kinship ties) stemming from inter-marriage between Sunnis, Shias, and Ismailis established 'mutual tolerance' and served to cement ties across communal lines. Indeed, it is erroneous to even consider these relations as 'inter-' marriage or 'cross-'

communal because sect was not considered a defining marker of identity and community. What mattered more in terms of social identification and differentiation was affiliation with a *qoum*, an agnatic descent group that might be translated as tribe or people. Alongside the significance of *qoum* identity, there was also *ilaqiat*—a recognition of difference, and contention between people from different geographical regions. Both tribe and region were more crucial signifiers of difference as compared to sect.

Communal peace and understanding was further helped by the common body of work that people across sect drew upon for religious and ethical guidance. For example, the writings of the Persian poet–scholar, Sheikh Saadi, were deemed especially important for Muslim education, and were referenced both at home and by the local *maulvi* who taught Quran to the children in his neighbourhood. These writings were known for their moral guidance, and deemed integral to the practice of religion. In the modern school as well—introduced in the region by the British in the late nineteenth century—the possibility of conflict over what counted as legitimate religious practice was minimized as religion was not part of the subjects that were taught. Indeed, a male Gilgiti elder ruefully commented to me on how he once studied with Hindus and Sikhs without any sense of religious conflict, while the current state of intolerance is such that 'Muslims cannot study with Muslims'.[14]

Historically, the maintenance of sectarian peace was further enabled by both princely and colonial rule in the region that today forms Gilgit-Baltistan. Royal alliances as well as marriages were often 'cross-communal' and as in other monarchical regimes in princely India, the ruling families in the Northern Areas practiced a form of 'managed pluralism' in which the accommodation of different communities was considered foundational to the political and moral order.[15] For the British as well, the imperative of geopolitical security at this frontier translated into a special concern for internal peace and calm. Quite apart from practices of 'divide and conquer' along religious lines—as colonial policy elsewhere in the subcontinent often instituted—the norm at this frontier was to keep local rulers and conflict situations in check so that the overall political control of the region could be ensured.

Pluralism and coexistence was thus the norm in the mountainous region of present-day Gilgit-Baltistan, similar to what Mushirul Hasan has argued for Hindu–Muslim relations in *qasba* society in Awadh (2004). In both contexts, local relationships were considered more important than religious structures, helping to share risk, manage disputes, and co-survive. In Gilgit-Baltistan, even religious occasions were considered more cultural than sectarian; in particular, Shia mourning rituals and gatherings in *muharram* were not only respected by other groups, but also involved their participation. As Hasan has argued for colonial Awadh, one of the reasons for the trans-communal importance of *muharram* might be that 'the Karbala paradigm itself communicated profound existential truths not only to Shias but also to Sunnis and Hindus'.[16]

Hasan, however, suggests that pluralism was a mark of the gentry in Awadh, and emerged primarily from their education and self-conscious role as carriers of ethical piety. In Gilgit-Baltistan, on the other hand, a pluralistic religious sensibility can be seen as a 'pre-secular tradition'[17] which was integral to a local life-world in which sectarian identity did not disrupt social relations. Indeed, modern education in the postcolonial context of Gilgit-Baltistan has contributed to the *erosion* of inter-sect peace and social solidarity, as I discuss later in this chapter.

THE VIOLENCE OF 1988

Before discussing the conflict over school textbooks, I must highlight an earlier critical event that took place in 1988 which marked a significant turning point for inter-sect relations in the Northern Areas, and was also identified to me as a simmering cause of the textbook protests that gripped Gilgit in 2004–2005. Indeed, *atthasi ka waqia* (the incident of 1988) or *atthasi ka tension* (the tension of 1988) has become a historical reference point in people's memories, with social and political life perceived as perceptibly different before and after 1988.

Between 13–24 May 1988, a systematic pogrom was launched against the Shia population of Gilgit area by well-armed Wahabi-Sunni *lashkaris* (militants), most of whom were non-local and came from the NWFP.[18] Ostensibly, the immediate cause was a sectarian squabble over the sighting of the Eid moon, which led to the Shias celebrating Eid one day before the Sunnis. But as interviewees across sects pointed out to me, it is highly improbable that such a localized, and even commonplace argument would overnight turn into a large-scale massacre in which fully-equipped militants from outside would descend upon Gilgit, claiming to wage *jihad* on Shia *kuffar* (infidels). The estimate for the number of militants ranges from 2,500 to 40,000;[19] that the figure is in the thousands alone points to the planned nature of the violence. At least 12 Shia-dominated villages were brutally attacked, through acts of torture that were wholly new to the region—bodies were burnt, *imambargas* (Shia mosques) torched, crops destroyed, and even animals were slaughtered. Villages like Jalababad were completely ruined, and civilians in several other areas fled from their villages to seek protection. The official death toll was put at 200, but unofficial accounts estimate the number of deaths at 800.[20] Accompanying this physical annihilation was the cultural project of transforming both local Sunnis and Shias into 'proper Muslims'. The militants distributed pamphlets to local Sunnis that preached how any family relations—let alone marital ties—with Shias are un-Islamic, and how Shias must be converted and shown the 'true' path of Islam. Those who survived this period recall how Shia Muslims were forced to perform *namaz* (prayer) amongst Sunni *maulvis*, and how married Shias were forcibly divorced and then made to go through a new Sunni *nikkah* (Muslim marriage contract).

Such open and outrageous violence against the Gilgiti Shias must be understood in the context of a national and international mobilization of political Islam that continues to ravage Pakistan today. On the one hand, General Zia's Islamization agenda in the 1980s had institutionalized a conservative Sunni interpretation of Islam that sanctioned the repression of other sects,[21] while on the other hand, the US, Saudi, and Pakistani governments had actively transformed frontier Sunnis into militants for the Afghan jihad against Russia.[22] The ideological training of these *mujahideen* promoted a fanatical, militant version of Sunni Islam that was also rabidly anti-Shia. Once the Afghan war ended, the thousands of militants who were well-equipped to hate and kill in the name of Islam returned to Pakistan, and focused their *jihad* on perceived internal enemies of Islam such as the Shias.[23] In this, they found common cause with the Sipah-e-Sahaba Pakistan (SSP), the most prominent Deobandi–Sunni political party that had emerged in Pakistan in 1985. Both *mujahideen* and SSP activists were supported by a gradually Sunni-ized Pakistani state, the Wahhabi monarchy in Saudi Arabia, and by the US administration as all three states were interested in countering Shiite radicalism in the wake of the Iranian revolution.[24] And both formed the bulk of the perpetrators of the 1988 Shia massacre in Gilgit.

The 1988 violence was thus a consequence of a transnational US–Pakistan–Saudi political alliance, and of its narrow Cold War vision of achieving 'strategic' goals through the support of Islamist militancy. The blowback—in the form of sectarian violence in Pakistan—had begun way before the US suffered itself in the form of the 9/11 attacks. Emboldened by the 'success' of the Afghan jihad, Zia's military government, the ISI, and the Islamist groups could now expand their reach in Pakistan, Afghanistan, and Indian Kashmir, using militancy as a strategic tool for political power as well as for the assertion of an extremist Sunni ideology. Indeed, it is widely believed in Gilgit that the perpetrators of the 1988 violence had been specifically given the task of 'teaching a lesson' to Shias in areas where the latter had a prominent presence. Lending credence to this is the fact that earlier in the same year, state-backed violence had also occurred in Parachinar, another Shia-dominated locality in Pakistan.[25] Thus while the sectarian assault was exceptionally destructive in Gilgit, it was certainly not an isolated event.

More than the *lashkaris* and their international benefactors, Gilgiti Shias resent the Pakistan state for its role in the 1988 massacre. They hold General Zia directly responsible, arguing that the operation was in line with Zia's Islamizing agenda, and could not have taken place without the backing of his military regime. Moreover, the KANA Minister of the time, the Frontier Corps, as well as two higher-up military officials who were then posted to the Northern Areas are directly named and blamed for their involvement in the attack—to the extent that some state officials joined the *lashkaris*, instead of protecting Shia civilians. More than twenty-five years later, Gilgiti Shias still ask: how is it that the non-local *lashkaris* knew well the location and access routes of Shia-dominated villages? Why was there no curfew imposed, or any attempt made to stop the *lashkaris*?

The most devastating long-term consequence of the 1988 violence was that it introduced among Muslim communities in the Northern Areas, a vehement fear and intolerance of the other. While there were numerous cases of Gilgiti Sunnis extending protection to their Shia relatives and neighbours, several hardliner local Sunnis had also participated in the violent campaign, which severely polarized inter-community relations and generated several episodes of sectarian violence in successive years. Each group was more 'Shia' or 'Sunni' now, shunning cross-communal social interaction as well as inter-marriage. Alongside this mistrust and hostility emerged the drift towards weapons. The Shia community in particular realized its vulnerability, and felt that it had to acquire weapons for it to be perceived as a strong force, and thus for ensuring future security. The concern for self-protection and self-assertion likewise prompted other communities to purchase weapons.

A violent event such as that of 1988 can cause both structural transformation in the way communities are organized, as well as intense personal suffering. Those who lived in mixed villages and fled their homes in 1988 regret how they are not able to return home even to visit their ancestral graves. Even those who may not have directly witnessed the violence can nevertheless remember its chilling sound, because the *naaray baazi* (chanting) of the *lashkaris* was deafeningly loud. The subjective transformation and anguish caused by the traumatic violence of 1988 was particularly brought home to me one day when I attended a cultural show with two female students at the local university, KIU. Because of bad weather, the show was moved from the spacious outdoor venue of the university to an indoor hall, with the result that only 300 people could be accommodated instead of the more than 500 who had bought the ticket for the event. There was quite a ruckus outside as the men who were denied entry fought with the management, trying to force their way inside. The twenty or so women in the crowd, including myself, had comfortable seats indoors thanks to patriarchal privilege, and were sitting with a number of male acquaintances with whom we had come to the event.

The event predictably ended early, and I returned with my friends to the hostel where I was staying at the time. While all of us had felt anxious at points, one of my friends, Gulnaz, seemed overly edgy and paranoid. She felt that the hall would be burnt down and the *izzat* (honor) of women was at stake. In fact, when Gulnaz was recounting the experience to other hostel girls who had not attended the event, I felt that she presented quite an exaggerated version of the entire episode. It seemed almost comical to me. With a slight smile, I said: 'Don't you think you are reacting a bit too much? The situation was not *so* bad.' She replied: 'No *baaji*. You don't know. Anything can happen in Gilgit.' I tried to calm her down, telling her that she worries too much. Eventually, she relaxed and said:

Mein dari dari si rehti hoon [I tend to feel scared a lot]. I was eight years old when I saw the *hamla* [attack] on the Shias, in 1988. My father is in the army and was stationed in Bonji at the time. Women were in the fields without their *dupattas* [scarves], trying to hide from the chanting *lashkaris* who were destroying everything they saw...homes, fields, cattle, people. We are Ismaili and we were in a military cantonment, so we were safer and yet so vulnerable...since then, I feel nervous in public events. Anything can happen in Gilgit.

Gulnaz's comments completely threw me off. I apologized to her for being dismissive about her feelings earlier, and tried to imagine how it must have been to witness such violence at the age of eight. I had heard about the brutality that 1988 signified for the region, but had not realized the intimate ways in which the experience of sectarian violence can transform the emotional selves, minds, and bodies of the victims. I had also not realized that the stories of sectarianism were so ubiquitous. Another example is that of Amin, an Ismaili who had been engaged to a Sunni relative of his parents choosing for ten years, but could not marry her as recent inter-sect discord had made the girl's extended family disapprove of the match. Cases like those of Gulnaz and Amin illuminate how the personal and the political are intimately tied, and reflect experiences and consequences of sectarianism that are often overlooked in accounts centred on death tolls and curfews. Conflicts over sectarianized representations of Islam are similarly overlooked in these accounts, and it is to these conflicts that I now turn my attention.

THE TEXTBOOK CONTROVERSY (2000-2005)

By 2004, it had been four years since the Shia community in the Northern Areas started agitating against the controversial curriculum of public schools in Gilgit. Delegations had repeatedly appealed to the Ministry of Education as well as the Ministry of Kashmir and Northern Areas Affairs in Islamabad, only to be dismissed each time.[26] Discouraged and angered, Shia students began to boycott classes and stage rallies, and more than 300 of them went on a three-day hunger strike in Gilgit on 17 May 2004.[27] Within days, the situation gravely deteriorated as thousands took to the streets, blocking roads and bringing businesses to a halt.[28] When the prominent Shia leader Agha Ziauddin Rizvi declared 3 June as a day of protest if the government failed to resolve the syllabus issue by then, the army was called in and a curfew imposed in Gilgit town. However, street processions continued in defiance of the curfew, leading to violent clashes between the protestors and security personnel in several parts of Northern Areas.

In the following months, the situation kept worsening as the curfew continued and caused severe food shortages and transport problems, schools remained closed, and government services and businesses virtually shut down. An atmosphere of severe sectarian discord and violence engulfed the region, as the conflict between the Pakistan state and local Shia communities over the controversial syllabus spiraled into a sectarian one that pitted local Shia and Sunni communities against each other. For many belonging to the Shia and Ismaili communities, even quotidian activities like traveling in the bus became fraught with danger as busses started to get attacked and passengers—deemed to be non-Sunni based on information about names and home addresses on national ID cards—were singled out and killed. The conflict intensified even more when on 8 January 2005, Agha Ziauddin Rizvi—the imam of the central Shia mosque in Gilgit and the most vocal opponent of the controversial syllabus—was gunned down. Even as it was widely believed that the killing was an act of government intelligence agencies to discipline the Shia community, it nevertheless generated another wave of Shia–Sunni sectarian strife in the Northern Areas. More than a 100 people lost their lives in the long-drawn conflict resulting from the textbook controversy.[29] Things returned to a relative calm only in April 2005, after leaders from both sects came to a peace agreement through a *jirga*, and the government agreed to withdraw two key textbooks that had spawned the controversy.

Deep sectarian fissures, however, have taken root in the region as a result of the textbook controversy, heightening divides that previous state policies had already been generating. For example, a foreboding trend towards sect-specific, 'secular' schools has emerged, reducing opportunities for socialization and friendship between the youth of different sects. There are government-run schools such as High School Number 1 and private ones such as Aga Khan Higher Secondary that children of all communities attend. However, as several respondents pointed out, there is a growing parental preference for schools that are dominated by their own sect, or located in sect-specific neighbourhoods. As Saeeda, a Sunni woman residing in the Ampheri area of Gilgit told me:

> There is a school in Zulfiqarabad which I would like my son to attend. But that is not our territory, and I would always be scared for his safety in case the situation become tense. That is why I have enrolled him in Tameer-e-Millat which is in our area, and mostly our children go there.

Relations have even been tense among students from different Muslim communities who study in the same educational institution. As in other conflict situations, women in the Northern Areas have become particularly vulnerable because their bodies are constructed as embodiments of community honor, and become sites for enacting and reproducing community identity. Thus, for instance, when schools and colleges reopened in 2005 after remaining closed for a whole year, Shia girls in some colleges started taking a black *chaadar* (long scarf). This was a marker of Shia identity,[30] but was also practiced so that in the event of a conflict, Shia women could be singled out for protection by being distinguishable from others wearing the white college uniform. Shamim bibi, a teacher at the FG College for Women in Gilgit who pointed this out to me, noted the absurdity of a protective measure that would render women more visible for attack, and the sadness of a logic that construes some women as more worthy of protection in situations of conflict. She also commented on how disconcerting it was for her to see an educational space being visually and physically divided into black and white, and how this stark dichotomy symbolized the general deterioration of inter-sect relations in the region.

The imprint of the sectarian conflict can even be felt in the residential landscape of Gilgit. While there are neighbourhoods such as Central Gilgit where all three communities continue to reside together, other 'mixed' *mohallas* (neigbourhoods) have increasingly transformed into segregated dwellings, making it easier to identify a 'Shia' *ilaqa* (locality) from a 'Sunni' or 'Ismaili' one. The tensions of 2004–2005 strengthened this trend, as some of the remaining Sunni households living in Shia-dominated Khomer moved to the more Sunni-dominated Basin and vice versa. The towering mountains that surround the town have also been informally classified as Shia and Sunni, based on the sectarian composition of the neighbourhoods that lie underneath.

QUESTIONING THE TEXTS

The textbook movement was spearheaded by the late Agha Ziauddin Rizvi, who was the principal leader of the Shia community in the then Northern Areas. Agha Ziauddin seemed to be a popular leader for the Shias, many of whom stood by him in his call for a change in the textbooks irrespective of whether they understood or cared about the curriculum issue. Even those who disagreed with his stance on the textbooks nevertheless respected him for the sense of integrity with which he dealt with the government. He was often described to me as one who 'could not be bought' and who 'did not fawn on the Chief Secretary'.

Agha Ziauddin and other proponents of the textbook movements firstly argued that Sunni beliefs and values were deeply embedded across the various disciplines that are taught in government schools. They called for the implementation of a consensus curriculum, which would be representative of and acceptable to all sects, and teach respect for all faiths. Further, they demanded that in the absence of such a curriculum, the Islamiat curriculum should be optional for Shia students in the Northern Areas.

The specific objections to the curriculum were detailed in a document published by the Islah-e-Nisab (correction of curriculum) Committee, Northern Areas, under the aegis of the *Markazi Imamia Jam-e-Masjid* (central Shia mosque), Gilgit. In this document, the textbooks used for teaching Urdu, Islamiat, and Social Studies in classes 1 all the way through BA were meticulously analysed, and the silencing or negation of Shia beliefs and practice was identified.[31] Most of the objections relate to differences in the interpretation of Islamic history, and in the performance of Islamic ritual.

As a case in point, consider an objection to a section from *Meri Kitab* (My Book), a text used by class 1 students in the Northern Areas (Figure 3.1).

According to the Islah-e-Nisab Committee, the section is problematic because its visual depiction of the performance of *namaz* (prayer) privileges the Sunni interpretation of Islam. In Shia practice, hands are typically held loosely on the side during *namaz*, not clasped in front as shown in the image. This example was also considered problematic by several Shia respondents whom I interacted with during my fieldwork, who argued that such images routinely confuse young Shia children who are learning a different practice at home, and thus have the potential to make them *gumrah* (astray).

Another representation considered one-sided by the Islah-e-Nisab Committee is present in the official 7th grade textbook for 'Art and Drawing', which is reproduced in Figure 3.2. It contains an exercise that directs students to imitate—in sketch and color—a calligraphic text illustrating the names of the four Caliphs: Abu Bakr, Umar, Usman, and Ali. This is in line with Sunni belief in which Ali is regarded as the fourth caliph. Shia doctrine, on the other hand, reveres the *imamat* system instead in which Ali is the first Imam instead of the fourth Caliph. In the textbook, the exercise in figure 3.2 appears right after two other exercises that instruct students to calligraphically reproduce the word 'Allah' and 'Mohammad' respectively.

The exercise is particularly significant in the context of the textbook controversy, as in September 2001, a 7th grade Shia student was reportedly kicked out of a school in Gilgit for tearing the page of this exercise from his book.[32] This was the first of several incidents that prompted Shia students to boycott their classes, and mobilized the Shia community in general against the curriculum.

The exercise is both striking and disturbing, as first, it demonstrates how an already pervasive presence of religious content in supposedly secular textbooks in Pakistan extends even to the realm of drawing. Second, the exercise is accompanied by an intriguing instruction that can be translated in English as: 'If you wish, you can also sketch the names of other revered personalities apart from the ones depicted here.' This might be read as a subtle form of recognizing and permitting sectarian difference, but it is a limited one: the page neither has an example for calligraphically reproducing the names of other Muslim personalities, nor space for a sketch that students might wish to create on their own. Importantly, the Urdu instruction is such that the option to illustrate different names in

عارف کی صبح سویرے آنکھ کھلی تو مسجد سے اذان کی آواز آرہی تھی۔ موذِّن پکار رہا تھا اللہُ اکبر اللہُ اکبر۔

اذان سنتے ہی عارف کے ابو نماز کی تیاری کرنے لگے۔ نماز کے لیے کپڑوں، بدن اور جگہ کا پاک صاف ہونا ضروری ہے۔ نماز سے پہلے عارف نے اپنے ابو کی طرح وضو کیا۔ ابو اس کو اپنے ساتھ لے کر مسجد کی طرف چل دیے۔ امی نے گھر میں نماز پڑھنے کی تیاری کی۔

مسجد میں داخل ہو کر وہ ایک صف پر بیٹھ گئے۔ تھوڑی دیر بعد امام صاحب سب نمازیوں کے آگے کھڑے ہو گئے۔ نمازی ان کے پیچھے صفوں پر ترتیب سے کھڑے ہو گئے موذِّن نے تکبیر کہی۔ امام صاحب نے نماز پڑھانی شروع کر دی۔ نماز میں امیر غریب مل کر کھڑے ہوتے ہیں۔ تمام مسلمان ایک دن میں پانچ بار نماز پڑھتے ہیں۔

FIGURE 3.1 Page from Meri Kitab (My Book), Class 1
Source: Punjab Textbook Board, Lahore.

سوال نمبر 9: نصف دائرہ میں ابوبکرؓ، عمرؓ، عثمانؓ، علیؓ رضی اللہ تعالیٰ عنہم کے نام خوش خط لکھیں۔

شکل کے مطابق نصف دائرہ میں ابوبکرؓ، عمرؓ، عثمانؓ، علیؓ کے نام لکھیں۔ اور رنگ بھریں۔ ان کے علاوہ اگر آپ اور مقدس ہستیوں کے نام لکھنا چاہیں تو لکھ سکتے ہیں۔

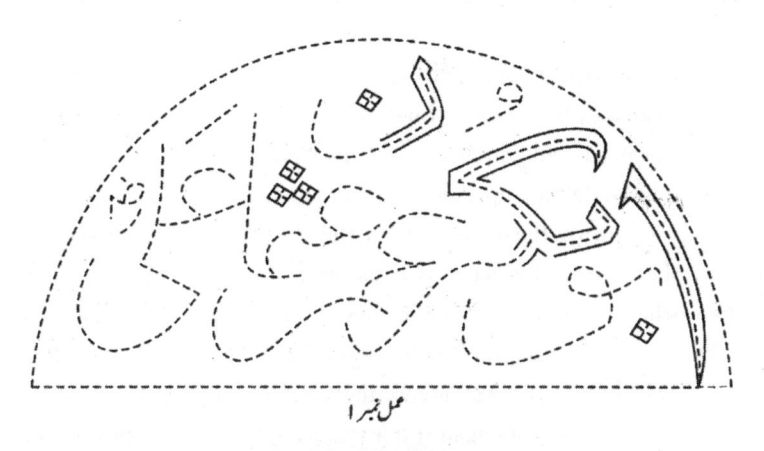

عمل نمبر ۱

عمل نمبر ۲

51

FIGURE 3.2 Page from *Art and Drawing*, Class 7
Source: Punjab Textbook Board, Lahore.

accordance with Shia thought can be availed only after the order of names in accordance with Sunni tradition has been traced.

The above exercise was also specifically pointed out to me during an interview that I conducted with a Shia religious leader in Gilgit, Haider Shah. Shah was deeply involved in the textbook movement, and continues to play a prominent role in the activities of the central Shia mosque in Gilgit. He argued:

> First of all, what is the point of putting religion in an art book? Don't we have enough of it already in the Urdu, English, Islamiat, Social Studies…basically all other books? Yes, calligraphy has an important place in Islamic history, so if desired, one could have an exercise about painting 'Allah' or 'Bismillah ir-Rahman ir-Rahim' [In the name of Allah, the Most Beneficent, the Merciful]. But why should our kids have to paint something that contradicts their religious beliefs? I am not saying that we should have a separate exercise for Shia children, where calligraphically shows the Twelve Imams. We should not have any content that represents the beliefs of a particular sect. The voice that we raised was not against one picture, it was against the one-sided representation of Islam in the entire curriculum, from class 1 till Bachelors. The curriculum has become so poisonous, fussing over rituals and losing sight of ethics. You see the main problem is that *maulvis* are writing the curriculum instead of scholars. The *maulvis* get their say because they have managed to portray and dismiss scholars as Westernized and secular. But why should the government buy into their agenda? This surely has to change.

Haider Shah's comments came as a surprise to me, as I had grown to perceive the textbook movement predominantly in terms of the assertion of a Shia 'religious' identity, instead of the 'secular' demand—and a broader progressive vision—that it evidently embodied. I realized that my own unconscious prejudice—stemming partly from the liberal -secular epistemic lens that we tend to internalize under modernity and academia— had led me to believe that a struggle about religious representation which was actively promoted, primarily by clerical figures, would be devoid of secular ground and legitimacy. I was all the more struck that this perspective of what I would call *Shia secularism* was communicated to me by a devout Shia, closely involved in running the affairs of the mosque, and that it emerged from within his understanding of religion. Ultimately, the entire encounter made me realize the profound unhelpfulness of 'religious' and 'secular' as categories of analysis and as descriptors of social reality.

It is more useful, then, to pay close attention to the terms used by the participants of the textbook movement themselves. In my interviews as well as in the documentary sources, the demand for a consensus curriculum was articulated as an *insaani* (human), *aaini* (constitutional), and *islami* (Islamic) right that is due to Shias as citizens of Pakistan.[33] The demand was further underpinned by a nationalist and developmentalist impulse, proposing that a consensus curriculum was necessary for achieving intra-Muslim unity—and specifically, Shia–Sunni solidarity—in order to ensure peace, justice, and development in Pakistan. Simultaneously, it was emphasized that people who have helped to create Pakistan and have continued to defend it have come from all sects, and hence all of them deserve recognition in the official school curricula.

The Sunni community of Gilgit, on the other hand, by and large opposed the textbook movement. A teacher, Sarfaraz Taj, objected to the tactics of the movement:

> Shia kids were often pressurized into boycotting their classes. I think that Shia elders are poisoning the minds of young kids with their propaganda.

Hajra Jabeen, a college student, was concerned about the consequences of the movement for the region:

> Look where we are now. There were open killings in Gilgit because of the textbook issue. Rangers have set up their *chowki* [checkpoint] at every corner, and even if the situation is more normal now, we'd feel scared if Rangers were to leave.

Yet another respondent, Gul Azam, questioned the very rationale of the movement:

> How can we change the curriculum and remove references to Hazrat Umar? Why do Shias hate Umar? The whole Pakistan follows this curriculum. We are Pakistani and we should not try to be different.

This comment indirectly renders the movement as anti-national, reflecting a perception that was common amongst the Sunni inhabitants of Gilgit. It is presumed that there is neither any reason nor room for religious difference within a Pakistani nation that is implicitly conceived as homogenous. The mention of hating Umar also shows that the movement was perceived as anti-Sunni.

The Shia participants took pains to dismiss the allegation that the movement was anti-Sunni and anti-Pakistan. They argued that their efforts were directed towards the freedom of religious belief that has been promised to every citizen in the constitution. However, they felt that the movement was given an anti-Sunni colour by the local administration and intelligence agencies, to mislead the Sunni community and create a sectarian rift between Sunnis and Shias in the Northern Areas.

EDUCATION, ISLAM, AND THE MAKING OF THE PAKISTANI NATION-STATE

To contextualize the controversial Islamic representations discussed above and understand why the resistance to them was perceived as 'anti-national', it is important to step back and explore how Islam and education came to be imagined and intertwined in the historical unfolding of the Pakistani state.

The question of education was a prominent concern for the leadership of the new nation-state of Pakistan, even as they grappled with urgent matters of state survival and structure. Soon after partition, at a social gathering for members of the Constituent Assembly, the 'founding father' and first Governor-General of Pakistan, Muhammad Ali Jinnah, emphasized to the attending educationists:

> Now that we have got our own state, it is up to you to establish a viable, productive, and sound system of education suited to our needs. It should reflect our history and our national ideals.[34]

That these 'national ideals' would partly be defined in terms of Muslim personhood was perhaps inevitable, given the ways in which the Muslim League had used Islam as a mobilizing device in the years leading to partition.

But the actual content of these ideals and the educational policies that would be implemented to reflect them was far from given. After all, the movement for Pakistan reflected the demand for a Muslim-majority nation, not a theocratic Islamic state.

The first education minister, Fazlur Rahman, has often been identified as the key figure—and culprit—who introduced the idea of orienting Pakistani education predominantly along Islamic lines. At his behest, the first All Pakistan Education Conference convened in 1947 passed a resolution stating that Islamic ideology would form the basis of the new national education system. A number of academics have offered compelling arguments to make sense of this deployment of Islam as educational policy, and, ultimately, as state ideology in the early days of Pakistan. Islam provided a way to distinguish Pakistan from India,[35] addressing the common anxiety of uniqueness and legitimacy amongst new nation-states. It was imagined as a source of national integration,[36] but was actually utilized more for excluding and suppressing regional identities in order to protect the growing powers of a centralizing, authoritarian state.[37] Recourse to the discourse of Islam also helped to placate the clergy and religious parties, and to undercut their critique of the predominantly secular leanings of prominent Pakistani leaders.[38]

While such analyses provide critical perspectives on how and why Islam became a salient force in the new nation-state of Pakistan, they tell us little about the actual meanings and values that Islam represented for the official proponents of 'Islamic ideology'. The speeches and writings of Fazlur Rahman are particularly insightful in this regard, and important to attend to, as he was the chief proponent of an Islamic educational system in Pakistan.

Rahman's rationale for emphasizing the place of Islam in Pakistan, and indeed, in the 'progress of humanity at large'[39] did not stem from a desire to suppress the different provinces or distinguish the new country from India. Instead, Rahman looked towards Islam to provide an alternative to the 'evils of unbridled Capitalism as well as Communism'.[40] Pakistan, he argued, could not afford to remain a 'spectator of the clash between these two systems'.[41] As he emphasized:

> Unless we offer to the world an ideology that will provide an effective answer to both Communism and Capitalism, we may not be able to keep at bay the

influences that emanate from them. It is my faith and conviction that Islam supplies the ideology we are looking for.[42]

Hence, it is against this 'background of European domination' that Rahman posits the importance of 'eastern ideals' and Islamic ideology.[43] Rahman is not vague about what this Islamic ideology would stand for in practice. Repeatedly, he identifies the 'fundamental' and 'cardinal' principles of Islam, not in terms of religious doctrine but in terms of a *social order* based on 'universal brotherhood, tolerance, and social justice'.[44] I emphasize the term *social order* because it is neither the establishment of a *Muslim nation* nor an *Islamic state*—the terms in which the debate has often been cast—that concerned this early and critical proponent of Islamic ideology. According to Rahman, what distinguished Islam was its just and egalitarian social order that 'abolished all distinctions based on caste, colour, or sex'[45] and 'guaranteed the free and unrestricted scope [to minorities] for pursuit of their religious and cultural interests'.[46]

Importantly, while this Islamic order is opposed to Western imperialism as well as to 'war and class' which are 'the twin curses of modern civilization',[47] it is nevertheless fundamentally aligned with democracy because like Islam, the authentic meaning of modern democracy is the 'attainment of the real equality of mankind'.[48] However, according to Rahman, only a procedural, market-centric democracy exists in Western countries as the 'persecution of religious and political minorities' as well as the distinction between the privileged and underprivileged is still in place.[49] An Islamic social democracy, on the other hand, would embody the democratic spirit in a more substantive sense and ensure equal rights to all citizens.

Rahman further argues that this vision of Islamic democracy has not been reflected in the practice of Islamic states since the Prophet's time, and hence the task of Pakistan is to re-establish the social order of Islam in its true spirit. In keeping with this spirit, the means to establish the social order cannot be through the 'suppression of movements like Communism' since Islam is a 'positive ideology'.[50] Rather, it is the terrain of education that has to 'play a dynamic and creative role in the *reconstruction of the social order*'[51] in Pakistan, in light of the Islamic principles of tolerance, justice, equality, and peace. This reconstruction of the social order—which Rahman sometimes calls 'world-order'—is the very *'raison d etre* of Pakistan'.[52]

This fundamental concern with *reconstruction* and *social order* is deeply striking in its emancipatory aspiration and world-historical orientation, and it was not unique to Rahman. The search for a 'new society' symbolized the affective power and purpose of anti-colonial nationalism for many leaders, beyond the imitative and derivative discourses that nationalism also represented.[53] Rahman's emphasis on reconstruction and a new order is particularly reminiscent of Muhammad Iqbal, the poet-scholar who is celebrated in Pakistan as the first to outline the vision for an independent Muslim nation in India. In his poems and lectures, Iqbal imagined a reconstructed Islam as central to the meaning of Muslim personhood and nationhood. But even for Iqbal, as for Fazlur Rahman, the role of Islam was emphasized in terms of *ethical–religious principles* of equality and justice that would help to create a tolerant social order, not in terms of a prescriptive *theological* ideology that would form the basis of nation and state. As Iqbal clarified in one of his letters:

> The aim of my Persian poems is not the advocating of Islam. In reality, I am eager to find the best social order and in this search one cannot ignore the existing social system aiming the overcoming of all differences based on race, caste and colour of skin.[54]

While Iqbal poetically defined the vision for an Islam-inspired ideal society—and this vision certainly had its parochialisms and exclusions—Fazlur Rahman had to tackle the more practical task of implementing it through a new educational framework for Pakistan. Having identified the principles of equality, justice, and tolerance as the basis of an Islamic education, Rahman proposes a number of ways for teaching such principles in schools. It is worth quoting at length here:

> Teachers...should be asked to prepare definite projects on the basis of the chief characteristics of Islamic ideology so that students in their charge may seek to embody these characteristics in their conduct during school life. Take, for example, the concept of the dignity of labour. During his lifetime,

the Prophet of Islam never considered any labour too mean for himself, though he was the unchallenged ruler of Arabia. He could have had, if he had so wished, scores of servants, yet he himself used to sweep the floor of his house and join his followers in digging trenches or performing any other kind of manual labour. There are other salient aspects of his character—his vast compassion for the poor and the suffering, his unique sense of justice, his tolerance, his uprightness of conduct—on each of which separate projects could be appropriately based, with a view to developing the ideal type of mental attitude in students. Similarly, qualities from the lives of other great prophets and teachers of the world could also be embodied in educational projects, to impart the necessary width of outlook and mental elasticity in our youth. It is thus alone that educational theory can become fruitful.[55]

Islamic ideology, then, is clearly meant to translate into exercises of positive, moral–ethical teaching and character-building instead of punitive, orthodox preaching. As Rahman clarifies, these exercises might draw inspiration from the Prophet's life but need not, and should not be limited to the Islamic world so as to encourage a broader, inclusive outlook. Labour rights have a particularly salient place in this outlook, as Rahman was deeply concerned about the unequal distribution of wealth and opportunity in society. It is thus not surprising that Rahman tends to use the terms 'Islamic ideology', 'Islamic socialism', and 'Islamic social democracy' interchangeably. Such an Islamic system cannot be achieved just through teaching humanistic principles; these need to be put into practice through political, economic, and social policies so that students do not feel conflicted between the equality that is being taught, and the inequality that they find around themselves. In this regard, Rahman places special emphasis on the need for land reforms:

> It is a welcome sign of our awakening that in some Provinces agrarian reforms are being brought about through legislation directed towards the emancipation and amelioration of large numbers of landless agricultural tenants…These agrarian reforms are the crying need of the hour and, though there will be opposition from vested interests, we must not shrink from carrying them out if we are to shape Pakistan on the basis of Islamic principles.[56]

Reading such perspectives more than half a century down the line, one is struck by the egalitarian impulse and liberatory potential that the discourse of Islam initially embodied *within* official corridors. This discourse was not without its problems, particularly since it constructed an ahistorical notion of a bounded and ever-present 'Muslim' nation that denied the syncretic religious identities and shared cultural milieus that characterized Indo-Islamic social life. Yet, arguably, the inclination towards a creative re-imagining of Islam as a modern, just, social order, combined with the rural tradition of lived Islam that emphasized morality and spiritual devotion instead of theological dogma, together provided a strong, pluralistic vision that was far more likely to define the meaning of Islam for the new nation-state of Pakistan as compared to other, more rigid interpretations. However, tragically, the discourse of a tolerant and just social order inspired by Islam soon disappeared from debates over the nature of the 'Islamic' state and education in Pakistan. Instead, aided by the silence of the Pakistani liberal elite, the rhetoric of Islam came to be used by state officials and its fundamentalist opponents alike for pushing forward a pretentious and bigoted interpretation of Islam and, by extension, of the Pakistani nation itself.

For example, as early as the 1950s, Prime Minister Liaqat Ali Khan issued an official injunction urging Muslims to fast, which helped pave the way for populist Islamist moral policing—mobs could storm restaurants that did not close during fasting hours, non-fasters could be paraded through bazaars in NWFP with the support of the local police, and the judiciary in Haripur could sentence people for eating in public.[57] In such an environment, fundamentalist parties like the Jamaat-e-Islami flexed their muscles even more. By 1953, in the name of creating an 'Islamic' nation, Pakistan had already succumbed to forms of religious terror that it now associates with the Taliban: in organized riots all over Punjab, religious parties as well as the Muslim League government collaborated in the extensive looting, arson, and murder of fellow Ahmadi Pakistani citizens.

Islam came to be used not only for brutalizing Muslim minorities to create a 'pure' nation but also as a political tool for oppressing regions like East Pakistan that demographically constituted a majority in Pakistan. During the national language controversy over Urdu and Bangla (1947–1952), elite groups at the centre insisted that Urdu was the true repository of Indian Islam, and denigrated East Pakistani-Bengali culture and language as not 'Muslim' enough due to its 'Hindu' and 'Sanskrit' influences.[58] Indeed, the state openly enlisted the support of religious parties like the JUI to promote Urdu and particular constructions of national Islam in order to suppress the culture of Bengali Muslims as well as their legitimate demands for regional rights. The insistence on the cultural, linguistic, and Islamic inferiority of the 'effeminate' Bengali became internalized as common sense in the West Pakistani mindset, and facilitated not only the systematic political and economic repression of East Pakistan by West Pakistan but also the vicious violence and rape that ensued in the 1971 Bangladeshi war of independence.[59] The most prominent, fundamentalist religious organizations involved in this violence were the paramilitary groups Al-Shams and the Jamaat-e-Islami's Al-Badr, both of which were sponsored by the Pakistani army and worked alongside it in a systematic campaign of subjugation and killing.[60] As we saw in the last chapter, this early, explicit use of religious groups to quell regional, secular-nationalist movements for political rights in East Pakistan was followed almost simultaneously in the case of the Northern Areas as well.

Such state-led brutalities against Ahmadis, Bengalis, and Gilgitis—all Muslims—testify to the violent intolerance that came to characterize the 'Islamic' state of Pakistan right from the start. Much before the rule of General Zia, the tradition of politically using Islam for claiming the centre's legitimacy and establishing its repressive authority had been set. Hence, far from constituting an integrative ethic, Islam came to represent a force of control and disintegration in which all forms of societal and regional diversity were conveniently labelled as a threat to state sovereignty, as well as to 'Islam'.[61]

It is this puritanical Islam that came to be preached in the Pakistani education system as well—one that only became worse during Zia's Islamizing regime. A particular kind of Sunni Muslim is created and privileged in textbook Islam in Pakistan. While there are many ways of being Sunni and generally of being Muslim, the textbooks emphasize a narrow and intolerant interpretation that reduces Islam to excessive ritualism, and openly demonizes non-Muslim faiths. Such a vision of Islam is conducive to and facilitated by fundamentalist groups as well as by the military establishment in Pakistan. As has been documented in various studies,[62] Pakistani school textbooks promote a militaristic interpretation of Islamic ideology as the rationale for the creation and purpose of Pakistan, while constructing Hindus and Indians as fickle others. Rubina Saigol in particular has meticulously and richly detailed how Pakistani textbooks abuse Islam to promote the ideologies of hate and violence.[63] Through school textbooks, Pakistanis are trained to be in a state of permanent enmity and preparedness against India. The heroes in the curricula tend to be the plunderers of the past or post-partition soldiers who have shown bravery in wars against India, and are idealized as defenders of the nation and of Islam alike. Such an 'Islamic' curriculum that valorizes military ethos is also a key ideological component of military hegemony in Pakistan and the delusional arrogance that it promotes. The textbooks not only embody an anti-India posture, but also an anti-minority and anti-women one, which together serve to create a bigoted, hyper-masculinist society while justifying high defence expenditures for the Pakistani state.[64] As such, these texts can be seen as forms of 'politically organized subjection'[65] and 'moral regulation'[66] through which the social identities of subjects are flattened for the creation of a sectarianized and militarized state and citizen in Pakistan.

SECTARIANISM AS SECTARIANIZATION

The embodiment and escalation of sectarianism through Sunni-biased textbooks in Gilgit must also be placed within the historical context of regional state-making and sectarianization in Gilgit-Baltistan. Sectarian difference in Gilgit-Baltistan did not always have the meaning and consequence that it carries today. As discussed in the previous chapter, a strong sense of religious difference has emerged and become politically significant precisely since the formal integration of the Northern Areas into the Pakistan state, between 1972–1974, with practices of sectarianization being deliberately adopted by the military-intelligence regime and the KANA bureaucracy to suppress secular–nationalist aspirations. Political and religious subjection are thus intimately linked in Gilgit-Baltistan, together helping to maintain territorial control over the region. This link is commonly understood as well as articulated by people in Gilgit. Irrespective of their sectarian affiliation, many locals perceive modes of inscribing Shia marginality—particularly since the 1988 riots—as part of a 'divide and conquer' state project, in which religion has become both a rationale for regional subordination as well as a tool for accomplishing it—the rationale being the threat of a Shia-majority province, and the tool being the perpetuation of religious sectarianism through various mechanisms.

Such historically shaped perceptions about the state affect the meanings that people give to any new state policy, as well as the consequences that these policies produce. This was amply demonstrated in the context of the textbook controversy. While it has been suggested and can be reasonably believed that at least part of the stronger Sunni orientation of the textbooks comes from the domination of the Punjab Textbook Board by members of the Jamaat-e-Islami, or others who profess an authoritarian Sunni sensibility,[67] many Shia protestors as well as local journalists felt that 'divide and conquer' was the key project behind the change in curriculum. How far that is true, I do not know. But it is important to note that because of historical experiences, people perceive it as such. The fact that the textbook issue did in fact end up intensifying sectarian conflict in the region made people believe all the more in an assumed intention of the state to politically suppress the region by religiously dividing it. The logic of 'divide and conquer' as an explanation for sectarian conflict in Gilgit-Baltistan is also significant because—like the memories of inter-sect harmony and acceptance—it serves to challenge arguments that explain 'sectarianism' as a natural outcome of religious differences.

The link between sectarian differences and regional politics was centred in the demands of the Shia protestors as well. When the issue of the controversial textbooks emerged, many local Shias argued that there would not have been any problem with textbooks, if, like other regions of Pakistan, Gilgit-Baltistan too had a separate textbook board to author its own curriculum.[68] If such a body existed, the local populace could have ensured that textbook representations of Islam were not biased but rather reflective of the different Muslim practices that are prevalent in the region. This perspective meant that the Shia protests against the controversial textbooks had the potential of being transformed into a cross-community political demand for the creation of a separate textbook board, hence becoming a vehicle for the assertion of regional identity and sovereignty. Such a platform for local unity and citizenship would pose a major threat to the Pakistan state, and the fear of this possibility was perhaps one of the key reasons that led the government to crack down severely on the movement against textbooks. Even before the government crackdown, however, such a platform could not materialize—partly because the Shia demand for a separate religious curriculum—even if inclusive and common—was simply unacceptable to the Sunni community, but also because many locals felt that a separate curriculum for Gilgit-Baltistan would create more divisions in an already polarized environment. Indeed, the demand for a separate curriculum was opposed within the Shia community itself, as I elaborate in the next section.

DEBATES AND DILEMMAS OF CULTURAL REPRODUCTION

Like any other community, the 'Shia community' in the Northern Areas is not a homogenous group in which all the Shias were uniformly offended by, and against the new curriculum. While grievances against Shia representation in textbooks were widely shared, many within the local Shia community—particularly older members and veteran leaders—felt that collective action calling for a replacement of the curriculum was unwise and unnecessary. At least three discernible reasons for this stance emerged during personal interviews that I conducted with Gilgit-based Shia elders.

First, it was felt that the negative impact of discriminatory textbook representations on Shias dwarfs in comparison to the widespread violence against the Shia community that has escalated all over Pakistan in recent years. As one leader, Jamal Zaidi, puts it:

> In Karachi, our doctors, engineers, and military officers are being targeted, while ordinary people continue to die in attacks on our mosques. As a minority that is facing such a systematic campaign, we need to pick our issues wisely.

According to Zaidi, several Shia leaders elsewhere in Pakistan also shared this perspective, and hence disagreed with Agha Zia on his decision to contest the textbooks. Second, the extent of danger posed by Sunni-biased representations in textbook Islam is itself considered debatable. As a prominent leader Abbas Hussain commented:

> We have always been learning Sunni thought in secular schools, but we have never lost our faith. Our faith is taught to us at home, and no one can take it away. So why should we be scared of textbooks?

Third, as Abbas Hussain further pointed out, there was a successful struggle for gaining Shia representation in textbooks elsewhere in Pakistan but far from benefiting Shia youth, it proved to be immensely detrimental:

> In President Ayub Khan's time (1960s), our people raised their voice. A *Shia Mutalibat Committee* [Shia Demands Committee] was formed and because of its efforts, a separate curriculum for Shias was eventually introduced in Prime Minister Zulfiqar Bhutto's time in the 70s. But the person who was grading the Shia section of the Islamiyat syllabus remained Sunni, so Shias were easily singled out for discrimination. In the exam that one has to take to join the Civil Service, Shia youth particularly suffered as the rate of failure increased. And so, access to government jobs decreased. It was at this point that Punjabi Shia youth told the Tehrik-e-Jafaria Pakistan:[69] we are suffering because of your policies. So finally, Shias themselves got rid of the separate curriculum that they had worked so hard to introduce.

This historical experience highlights the paradoxical dilemma in which religious minorities often find themselves when they get political and cultural recognition at the state level. Affirmation of their identity and difference is accompanied with a heightened visibility that renders them even more vulnerable to forms of discrimination. Particularly in the context of an oppressive and puritanical state, religious minorities therefore feel that it is much safer to keep a 'low profile'—a policy that often translates into internalized modes of suppressing religious identity and practice in the public sphere. Munasinghe (2002) has similarly discussed how East Indians in Trinidad 'downplay' their culture in order to claim native status. It might be the case that minority ethnic and religious groups, as well as the 'others' of hegemonic nationalism in general, need to engage in this *invisibilizing* of their own identity in order to fit in and avoid marginalization. This suggests that the 'others' of nationalism might also help to produce the homogeneity of the nation from below.

The discourse of 'keeping a low profile' is particularly prevalent amongst the Ismaili-Muslim community in Gilgit-Baltistan, which time and again has found itself caught between the Shia–Sunni conflict. However, for the Shia community in Gilgit-Baltistan, the situation is different. It might be a minority from the perspective of a Sunni-majoritarian Pakistani state, but numerically it comprises a sizeable majority of the population in Gilgit-Baltistan. In such a context, the desire, legitimacy, and possibility of the recognition of Shia religious identity takes on a different salience.

CITIZENSHIP VERSUS SECTARIANISM: COMPETING REPRESENTATIONS OF STRUGGLE

The demand for equal representation in textbook discussions of Islam can be seen as a religious right, which Shias in Gilgit claim for the simple reason that they too are Muslims, and that their children deserve to learn about their own faith whenever Islam is taught in public schools. However, as mentioned earlier, the movement participants and supporters employed the liberal discourse of citizenship to describe their struggle. They claimed that as citizens of the Pakistani state, it was their *secular*, constitutional right to have 'freedom of religion', and necessary protections as a national minority.[70]

Recourse to this vocabulary is critical and effective for two reasons. First, it constitutes a creative strategy of making a claim to citizenship rights, in a context where these have been consistently denied even in their most basic forms. In fact, it can be argued that it was precisely the historical marginalization of the region and the repression of secular–nationalist struggles within it, which paved the way for religion to emerge as an idiom of claiming citizenship and sovereignty for the Shias in the region.

Second, the discourse of rights offered a way to counter the official representations of the struggle against the controversial textbooks, in which the demand for the withdrawal of the textbooks was portrayed as part of a subversive 'sectarian agenda' by the Shia populace. Instead, the protesting

Shias constantly asserted that the issue was not a Sunni–Shia one, but one that was fundamentally tied to the state–citizen relation.[71] The discourse of constitutionally guaranteed citizenship allowed the Shias to overcome their representation as the 'others' of secular politics, and claim that their agenda was fully in line with the criteria of a modern liberal democracy—in fact, it was the Pakistan state itself which was upholding sectarian biases by privileging Sunni ideology, and promoting authoritarianism by denying legitimate regional rights to the people of the Northern Areas. Hence, the state was portrayed as the culprit because it was abusing its duty of looking after the common good of society, which is constructed as its fundamental purpose in the modern, liberal paradigm.

In contrast, the dominant way in which the textbook issue was represented in official and media discourses was through the motif of 'sectarianism'. Indeed, in the decade following the textbook controversy, the sociopolitical landscape of the Northern Areas in general often came to be characterized and explained through the paradigmatic idiom of Shia–Sunni 'sectarian conflict'. This is not to deny that inter-sect discord in multiple forms has indeed become a grave everyday reality in the region. What is problematic, however, is the way in which the depictions of the region as a sectarian mess overshadow the substantive political contestations that underlie most of the cases that are branded as instances of sectarian conflict.

The representation of state–society political conflict as inter-group religious discord is both a reminder and continuation of colonial strategies of rule. The rhetoric of Hindu–Muslim communalism was routinely employed by the British colonial state in India to reduce particular conflicts that challenged its authority to local 'religious' differences, so that it could absolve itself of responsibility, construct resistances as pathological, and then quell them under the pretext of restoring harmony.[72] The vocabulary of religion provides a particularly useful means for deflecting political contestation and reinscribing state paternalism, as it helps to recast legitimate political grievances as primordial, anti-modern demands by emotional, irrational subjects. Such an 'emotionalizing' of political issues is a key strategy of accomplishing state rule.

In present-day Gilgit-Baltistan, the discourse of 'sectarian conflict' similarly produces a depoliticizing effect: backward society is in a state of anarchy, stemming from supposedly primordial intra-Islam differences, and the innocent and caring state constantly needs to intervene to create order. If it were not for the state, the region would remain steeped in violence and, as a state official put it, 'the uncompromising attitude of ulema of both the sects' would 'destabilize the area'.[73] This was the language used in an official press release by the Northern Areas Home Department to explain the violent clashes and continuous curfews that paralysed the region in October 2005. The clashes had started after security personnel shot at students who were peacefully protesting against the death of their colleague in custody, but the incident was conveniently represented, officially and in the media, as one in which law enforcement agencies were dealing appropriately with the 'sectarian elements' afflicting the region.[74] Similarly, the discourse of sectarianism can be and has been instrumentalized by intelligence agents for covering up attacks on anti-government leaders, as these can be conveniently attributed to the workings of some Shia or Sunni fundamentalist outfit depending on the ascribed identity of the leader.

MINORITIZING THE SUBJECT

Apart from creating a depoliticized representation of conflicts in Gilgit-Baltistan, the discourse of official sectarianism also invokes a majority/minority distinction that further misrepresents the political and social realities of Gilgit-Baltistan. When one hears of Shia demands in Gilgit-Baltistan and conflict due to these demands, the internalized image that is conjured is one of a religious minority trying to scramble for rights and 'creating issues'—it is not usually known that the Shias constitute a sizeable majority in the region. Even if this is known, there is a certain way in which majoritarian politics creates a complacency that undermines the concerns of national minorities. This complacency is widely spread in society and not limited to the views and practices of members of religious parties. Hence, the majority/minority distinction itself becomes a key mode of subjection for religious groups like the Shias in Pakistan.

Let me problematize this distinction more. To begin with, the distinction assumes that homogeneous cultural groups exist which can be neatly parceled into 'majority' and 'minority'. However, culture is a messy, interactive process that is necessarily constituted through borrowings across boundaries.[75] Hence, cultural identities—whether majority or minority—cannot be construed as pure, unified, and fixed. Gilgit-Baltistan in particular has a long history of pluralist religious identities, with inter-marriages and shared participation in religious rituals being the norm instead of the exception.

Second, constructions of majority and minority privilege one particular form of identity in defining and numerically dividing a population, as if the reality of people's multiple social positions and complex subjectivities—stemming from the interacting identities of class, gender, ethnicity, religion, and language amongst others—can be simplistically reduced to a single, determining essence. Most importantly, the majority/minority distinction constitutes a critical discourse through which the hegemonies of particular collectivities are sustained, and their access to the apparatus of the state naturalized. Hegemonic power asserts itself as the legitimate authority by appealing to the logic of 'majority rule'—defined in terms of religious, ethnic, class, and other identities. Simultaneously, by constructing various others as 'minority', it renders them somehow less legitimate, as assumed deviants because they are not 'normal', and hence justifiably deprived from a recognition of identity and participation in structures of authority.[76] This utility of the majority–minority distinction in maintaining hegemonic power makes it effective for the accomplishment of state-making. Not surprisingly, then, the minority/majority distinction has been deeply embedded in legitimizing discourses of nationalism. In nationalist projects across the world, the 'imagined community'[77] of the nation was frequently constructed as one in which an imagined majority personified the nation, and a 'minority tolerated only insofar as it proved able to accommodate the demands of the fictitious majority represented by the state'.[78] The distinctiveness of the minority was 'to receive expression only in private, and destined eventually to disappear within the majority'.[79]

This disappearance within the majority has not only been achieved through the denial of equal and substantive citizenship to those labelled as 'minorities' but also the denial of their very existence via mechanisms of legal subjugation and physical violence. Such processes of minoritization can be totally disruptive of people's sense of security and belonging, as has been amply and shamefully demonstrated in the case of Ahmadi repression in Pakistan.[80] However, in some situations, the discourse of a minority status can in fact be appropriated to claim rights and protection. The problem, of course, is that even when so-called minorities achieve their objectives, just treatment is not a guarantee. On the contrary, the granting of demands can make minorities even more vulnerable to discrimination, by making them legible to state officials whose ways of thinking remain structured by the majority/minority discourse. My reference here is to my earlier discussion of the ways in which Shias in Pakistan successfully struggled for a separate curriculum, but then themselves organized to abdicate this right as their new visibility became the very source of their educational and economic subjection.

CONCLUSION

Sectarian conflict has risen drastically in recent decades in Pakistan, particularly in the wake of Zia's Islamization programme, the Iranian revolution, the Afghan war, and the US-led war on terror, all of which have fuelled the creation and sustenance of sectarian hostility and violence. The death toll between 2007 and 2013 alone is estimated to be around 2,300,[81] with Shias being subjected to a systematic assault of genocidal proportions. This genocide is enabled and made particularly pernicious by the fact that anti-Shia death squads and Sunni militants in Pakistan have proven links with, and support from the fanatically anti-Shia, Al-Qaeda.[82] These processes have surely influenced and sustained the dynamics of Shia–Sunni conflict in Gilgit-Baltistan as well. However, a closer study of sectarian conflict in Gilgit-Baltistan reveals that here the issue is fundamentally linked to the religious and geo-political anxieties that this Shia-majority contested border territory poses for the Pakistan state, as a result of which the state has established particularly harsh regimes of political and religious subjection in the region. Further, analyses of sectarianism in Pakistan have focused heavily on the politics of militant religious parties but, as the case of Gilgit-Baltistan demonstrates, we also need to be attentive to the ways in which sectarianism is both propagated and contested in the realm of cultural representations as well. It has been argued that sectarianism constitutes a key 'threat' to the Pakistani state, due to which the country remains an 'unachieved nation'.[83] Such discourses tend to render the state as a hapless victim with no causal responsibility in the matter and, moreover, risk a reproduction of the standard hegemonic narrative in which the military-dominated state claims to be striving to protect Pakistani society from extremism and sectarianism. The regional context of Gilgit-Baltistan, however, illuminates a reverse logic, as the state itself is perceived as a threat to people's identities and intra-Muslim relations in the region.

As Gilmartin and Lawrence (2000) have argued, 'seeing how [religious] identities relate to the structure of the state and to its networks of patronage is critical to understanding how identities get meaning.' We hence need to focus more on the role of the state, on the content of categories such as the 'state' and 'religious identity', and on the ways in which these categories are mutually constituted in a dialectical relation with each other. These categories are historically formed and internally contested, and, in fact, always *in the process* of making and negotiation. Instead of assuming them to be unified, already-made, and oppositional, we need to investigate how the nation-state is itself formed through the cultivation of particular religious identities, and the ways in which the latter are transformed in the process.

The textbook conflict in Gilgit offers a useful lens to interrogate this intertwining of nation and religion in contemporary Pakistan. Instead of homogenizing identity by 'managing' difference, sectarianized representations of Islam have served to aggravate inter-sect differences and conflict in Gilgit-Baltistan. Hence, it is not surprising that movements for religious assertion have taken strong root in the region in recent years.[84] For many in the Shia community of Gilgit-Baltistan, the movement for a separate Shia curriculum involved a concrete, verifiable manifestation of the state's sectarian–political agenda, around which the local Shias could mobilize and have more realistic chances of getting their voices heard as compared to mobilization around other demands. The controversy was an outlet for, and consequence of a history of political and religious suppression in Gilgit-Baltistan that has been vitally responsible for the polarization of sectarian relations in the region. The right to have representation of Shia identity in school textbooks was seen by Shia protestors—particularly by the younger generation—as a mode for securing recognition and cultural reproduction, even as veteran leaders challenged this connection. Moreover, through the idiom of religion, the

Shia subjects of Gilgit-Baltistan were also articulating a political demand for legitimate, substantive inclusion in a polity that has historically denied them even the most basic citizenship rights—partly on the very grounds of their different religious identity. Hence, asserting religious difference and getting it politically recognized in official arenas such as education becomes a potential and practical way to achieve equal treatment as citizens of the Islamic Republic of Pakistan.

Shia protestors and sympathizers of the movement against textbooks viewed their struggle in a religious idiom as well as in liberal–political terms, challenging the sense of contradiction that is usually ascribed to these forms of politics. By drawing attention to the controversial texts and also by securing an agreement with state authorities for withdrawing the texts, the movement participants challenged the universalizing project of the state to claim and establish a narrow vision of Islam as the basis for a supposedly homogenous national culture. Yet, at the same time, the movement against the textbooks produced a sharp response from the paramilitary and intelligence apparatus of the state as well as local Sunni groups, resulting in a violent conflict that severely disrupted people's lives and livelihoods. This led many across the spectrum to question whether textbooks justified such a confrontation with a repressive regime, and thus alienated them from the cause of the movement. Ironically, then, the movement helped to reproduce state power by intensifying sectarian resentment and conflict in the region, and thus obstructing possibilities of local unity for regional political empowerment. In the next chapter, I examine other, routined dimensions of sectarianism in Pakistan and analyse how sectarian resentment is both recreated and resisted in everyday social life in Gilgit.

NOTES

1 'Schools re-open today in northern Pakistan after one-year', *Pakistan Times*, 27 April 27 2005. http://pakistantimes.net/2005/04/27/national1.htm. I say 'partly' because the controversial texts numbered far more than those that were going to be replaced.
2 Nayyar and Salim (2003), Ahmad (2004), and Aziz (2004).
3 Nelson (2009: 602).
4 Malik (1996), Zaman (1998), Nasr (2000), Abou-Zahab (2002), and Rieck (2014).

5   Mitchell (1991), Steinmetz (1999), Trouillot (2001), and Sharma and Gupta (2006).
6   Apple and Christian-Smith (1991), Pigg (1992), Starrett (1998), and Saigol (2000).
7   Such figures—whether used to represent Sunnis or Shias—always need to be accompanied with words of caution: information about sects is not collected in the Pakistani census, and hence the figure quoted is a commonly used estimate. The figure is an abstraction of course, as the 'Sunni sect' or 'Shia sect' incorporates diverse and often contradictory religious perspectives. Also, many Muslims would describe themselves as Sunni or Shia in a broad cultural and social way, without adhering to particular religious beliefs and practices.
8   In Gilgit town, specifically, the Twelver Shias are perceived to be in majority, alongside a sizeable presence of Sunnis as well as Ismailis.
9   This chapter is a revised revision of an article previously published in the journal *SAMAJ*. See Ali (2008).
10 My emphasis.
11 A historical name for the Ismaili Muslims of the region.
12 Biddulph (1880: 118).
13 Biddulph (1880: 119–123).
14 The 1947 partition changed the communal dynamics, forcing the several Hindu and Sikh families settled in Gilgit to migrate to India.
15 Copland (2000).
16 Hasan (2004: 37).
17 Nandy (1988).
18 Shehzad (2003), Ahmed (2005).
19 Rieck (1995).
20 Aase (1999).
21 Weiss (1986).
22 Cooley (2000), Mamdani (2004), and Abbas (2005).
23 Abou-Zahab (2002).
24 Abbas (2005).
25 Daily Times (2005).
26 Stöber (2007).
27 'Hunger Strike', *Dawn*, 20 May 2004..
28 Syllabus Protests Paralyse Business and Traffic,' *Daily Times* 1 June 2004.
29 Abbas (2005).
30 Black is a traditionally significant color for Shias. It is especially symbolic of the practice of mourning the martyrdom of Hussain, the grandson of Prophet Mohammad.
31 Islah-e-Nisab Committee Shumali Ilaqa jaat (2003).
32 Islah-e-Nisab Committee Shumali Ilaqa jaat (2003).
33 Islah-e-Nisab Committee Shumali Ilaqa jaat (2003) and Markazi Shia Tulba Action Committee (2004).
34 Qureshi (1975: 27).
35 Jalal (1990).
36 Saigol (2003).

37 Alavi (1988).
38 Jalal (1990).
39 Rahman (1953: 21).
40 Rahman (1953: 20).
41 Ibid., p. 20.
42 Ibid
43 Ibid., p. 21.
44 Ibid., p. 28
45 Ibid., p. 31.
46 Ibid., p. 28.
47 Ibid., p. 20.
48 Ibid., p. 30.
49 Ibid., p. 30.
50 Ibid., p. 20.
51 Ibid., p. 21; my emphasis.
52 Ibid., p. 32
53 Chatterjee (1993).
54 Yuldoshev (1999).
55 Rahman (1953: 32–33).
56 Rahman (1953: 91–92).
57 Jalal (1990).
58 Toor (2012).
59 Saikia (2011).
60 Khan (2014).
61 Gilmartin (1998).
62 Aziz (1993), Saigol (1994), and Nayyar and Salim (2003).
63 Saigol (1994), Saigol (1995), and Saigol (2003).
64 Saigol (1995).
65 Abrams (1988)
66 Corrigan and Sayer (1985).
67 Shehzad (2003).
68 It is worth noting that even Azad Kashmir has a separate textbook board.
69 Founded in 1979, Tehrik-e-Jafaria Pakistan (TJP) is the foremost Shia political party in Pakistan.
70 Interestingly, these protections were first put into the Pakistani constitution precisely because of Shia mobilization for rights and representation (Rieck, 2000).
71 Even in the so-called sectarian riots that had engulfed the region in June 2004, the buildings that were burnt were prominent government buildings, not Shia or Sunni mosques.
72 Freitag (1989) and Mayaram (1997).
73 'Eight Religious Leaders Held,' *Dawn*, 16 October 2005.
74 This is not to deny that the Sunni and Shia clergy has indeed inflamed the sectarian situation in Gilgit-Baltistan on several occasions. Rather, my point is that several

recent cases of 'sectarian conflict' in Gilgit-Baltistan cannot be simplistically reduced to the rhetoric of the parochial, conflict-prone 'sectarian elements'. Moreover, it is important to recognize that state policies themselves have indirectly or directly contributed to the power of the clergy in Gilgit-Baltistan, and elsewhere in Pakistan.

75 Hall (1992) and Said (1993).
76 Anthias and Yuval-Davis (1993).
77 Anderson (1991).
78 Benbassa and Rodrigue (2000: 105).
79 Benbassa and Rodrigue (2000: 105).
80 Kennedy (1989) and Saeed (2007).
81 Rafiq (2014).
82 Ahmed (2011).
83 Jaffrelot (2002).
84 For historical perspectives on Shia identities and mobilization in South Asia, see Rieck (2014) and Jones and Qasmi (2015).

4

SECTARIAN IMAGINARIES AND POETIC PUBLICS

As demonstrated in the last chapter, the conflict around textbooks was a public confrontation that brought the tensions around faith, education, and citizenship into sharp political focus in Gilgit-Baltistan. In this chapter, I examine how sectarian discord is experienced, reproduced, and contested in less visible contexts. To begin this inquiry, I explore three episodes of everyday sectarian tension that help to illuminate the micro-politics of sectarianism in Gilgit. Drawing upon these ethnographic cases, I argue that a *sectarian imaginary*—a normalized mode of seeing and interacting with the sectarian other through the feelings of suspicion and resentment—has come to structure intra-Muslim relations in Gilgit. The concept of the sectarian imaginary draws upon Charles Taylor's concept of the social imaginary, which he describes as 'the imagination *of* society *by* society'.[1] I use the concept of the sectarian imaginary to analyse how the Shia and Sunni Muslim communities in Gilgit imagine, feel about, and relate to each other, and the subtle ways in which sectarian anxieties emerge in everyday interaction. The notion of the sectarian imaginary thus helps me to articulate the complex of subjectivities and feelings that international politics combined with national structures of rule have served to produce in Gilgit-Baltistan.

As in the case of the previous chapter, in my analysis of everyday forms of sectarianism as well, I focus specifically on spaces of secular education. While madrasa education in Pakistan is routinely criticized for producing the radicalized agents of sectarian violence,[2] the relationship between secular education and sectarianism remains largely unproblematized. Indeed, education is constructed as a key solution for combating sectarianism within popular discourse in Gilgit and elsewhere in Pakistan. This discourse assumes that school education constitutes an entirely non-sectarian milieu, and that it somehow automatically helps students to rise above parochial sectarian sentiments, thus promoting a more progressive and tolerant understanding of Islam. Ground realities in Gilgit, however, starkly contradict this assumption. My analysis of the textbook conflict in the previous chapter demonstrates the extent to which secular education is implicated in the production of sectarian tension. Beyond these eruptive incidents, and also because of them, it is important to investigate the more everyday experiences of sectarianism that have become routinized in secular educational contexts, so as to grasp the sectarian subjectivities that shape the personal as well as the political in Gilgit.

No matter how pervasive, however, sectarian imaginaries do not exhaust visions of life and possibilities of self in Gilgit-Baltistan. Religious affiliation is amongst the multiple identities that shape action, and people have shared traditions and interests that constantly disrupt sectarian divisions.[3] In Gilgit, for example, I observed that people continue to sustain traditional cross-sect kinship ties through gift giving and hospitality, while regularly asserting that sectarianism is a political ideology that 'came from outside' in the region. There is a vibrant discourse in Gilgit-Baltistan about how its citizens must strive towards religious harmony, and not succumb to the machinations of the clergy or the state. To explore such spaces of cross-sect connection and community in Gilgit, I highlight a range of discursive and performative public arenas where social actors can overcome divisions, and come together for the pursuit of common interests and progressive goals. Included in these publics are sports events such as polo matches, journalistic discourses, community development activities, political seminars by nationalist parties, and most intriguingly, poetry festivals organized by literary groups. The latter part of this chapter focuses specifically on exploring this poetic dimension.[4]

Political sociologists have often analyzed poetry as an artistic tactic that accompanies a social movement, servicing the task of collective mobilization.[5] However, the role of poetry itself as a form of social struggle and resistance has received less attention. Instead of viewing poetry as a tool or tactic, I place poetic performance at the very centre of the sociological analysis of power and protest. Poetry festivals in Gilgit go beyond the shared enjoyment and cultural refinement, as the poets of the region actively use long-standing literary traditions of Muslim humanism to struggle for a non-sectarian vision of Islam and a democratic vision of the Muslim nation based on substantive rights. Because of the significant yet under-studied role of poets in creating peace and pluralism, I devote particular attention to their activities and to what we might call the poetic public in Gilgit-Baltistan. This sphere is one of moral–intellectual struggle and political self-fashioning, where the imagining and realization of a progressive polity is made possible.[6] My analysis is focused on the endeavours of a literary collective *Halqa-e-Arbab-e-Zauq* (Halqa), which may be translated as the 'Circle of Literary Fellows'. By exploring the poetic interventions of Halqa in Gilgit, I show how the region's poets strive to nurture harmony and humanity as the essence of ethics, faith, and politics, thus helping to counter the sectarian imaginary that has come to dominate social relations in the region.

BAAT BAAT MEIN MAZHAB

Javed is a 16-year old Shia student from a village in Ghanche—one of the districts of Gilgit-Baltistan—who is enrolled at a local government school in Gilgit. When I asked him about his views on sectarianism in Gilgit, he narrated the following incident:

> Last week, there was a cricket match between class 8—in which I study—and class 7. I was balling, and it went wide. A Chilasi-Sunni boy, Kamran, who was in my team angrily said, 'His balling is atrocious, we should beat him up.' I was hurt, and dejectedly responded, 'Go ahead and beat me, if you like.' To this, Kamran responded, 'You Shia people are like this only, incompetent.' The other Shia boys in my class then came to my defence. One of them said to Kamran, 'Ok, so you really want to talk about religion? Then talk to us. He is a *pardesi* and not even *mazhabi type*.[7] How cowardly it is to scare him.' Then the situation calmed down, and we continued the game. After all, we were in the same team.

Having related this incident to me, Javed went on to explain it. In a simultaneously amused and puzzled tone, he said, 'You see even when there is no link, people have to bring religion in between from somewhere or the other! *Baat baat mein mazhab dal deytay hain* [people bring in religion in every other matter].'

Javed's narrative provides a revealing glimpse into what we might call the everyday forms of sectarianism in Gilgit. There is no involvement of organized religious groups, and no physical violence. Yet sectarian tension is created and manifested through the invocation of epithets, and an unexpected ridicule of sectarian identity. I say 'unexpected' because the denigration of Shia identity neither emerged in the context of a religious discussion nor is it based on religious differences. The taunt is instead based on a lack of worldly ability that is presumed to emerge from an inferior Shia identity, hence expanding the available rationales for sectarian othering. Consequently, even an ordinary situation of playing cricket in the playground of a secular school—a form of inter-sect social encounter that should ideally reduce prejudice and promote harmony—can lead to the reproduction of sectarian boundaries.[8]

It is interesting to note that Kamran is not told to apologize or take back what he said, but that he has cowardly picked on a target who is a foreigner—implying that Javed is not yet socialized into the Gilgiti norm of inter-sect relations where exchanging taunts as well as the ways of dealing with them might be common knowledge. In interacting with sectarian others, thus, it has been assumed that a taunt or any verbal attack of a sectarian nature must be strongly confronted. Javed's assessment of this incident is equally telling, and also resonated with my own experiences in Gilgit. As much as I would like to resist generalizations, it seemed to me that the invoking of sectarian sentiments in every other matter—*baat baat mein mazhab* as Javed aptly put it—had become a disturbingly common structural disposition in Gilgit. It is not surprising that someone like Javed would find this disposition particularly striking, as he had come to Gilgit only recently, and that too, from a rural culture which had not experienced the kind of sectarian anxiety present in Gilgit.

Even more troubling is the demonstration that the arena of secular education—often proposed as the panacea for sectarianism in local and supralocal discourse—has in fact become implicated in the production of everyday sectarian tension and distrust. One form of this implication is a spontaneous, tense exchange over sectarian identity that Javed experienced while playing cricket in his school. At other times, the altercation can stem from more organized sources, and assume larger dimensions.

FORM-ING DIFFERENCE

In 2006, a new principal at the prestigious and 'secular' Army Public School in Gilgit introduced bio-data forms for teachers and students, in which their sectarian affiliation had to be specified. School teachers had to ask students— even nursery-level ones—to find out or confirm their sectarian identity from parents, in order to fill out the forms. Not surprisingly, teachers across sects resisted this move, citing it as a 'sensitive issue'. Parents were likewise suspicious, and complained bitterly to teachers. Shia and Ismaili teachers felt particularly resentful, as the new principal was considered a zealous Sunni who would use the bio-data form as a basis for targeting non-Sunni teachers and students. One female teacher complained to a higher-up military official in Gilgit through her husband, but there was no response. Parents as well as teachers whom I interviewed felt that the decision to introduce the forms had the sanction of the military establishment in Gilgit. Despite resistance from teachers and parents, the principal refused to back down and the sect-specific data he wanted had to be collected.

According to two teachers of the school whom I interviewed, the whole process had a severely damaging impact on relations between students. Bushra, a 4th grade teacher said to me:

> In my class, I noticed that children were now more aware of each other's sect. They started to self-segregate, with Sunni ones sitting and socializing with other Sunnis, Shias with Shias, and so on. Several teachers noticed this tendency in their classrooms.

Aafreen, a senior head teacher, said:

> Young kids are so vulnerable. Some of them did not even know what sect means, and what their sect was. Because of the forms, kids started talking

about religion and sects. In fact, a class 2 boy discovered that one of his classmates was Shia and beat him up. Apparently, he had heard at home that Shia people are bad, and should be beaten up.

This particular case of a sectarian-driven physical fight between young students was repeated to me a number of times in Gilgit, as people commented with cynical dismay on the extent to which the *zehar* (poison) of sectarianism has spread in their region. I will provocatively call this incident a case of 'sectarian violence', to underscore and ask why such discursively and physically violent encounters at the micro-political, everyday level are silenced in normative analyses of sectarianism. Attention to such encounters is critical for understanding the deployment of sectarian discourse in practice, and for grasping the routine production and experience of sectarian difference. These encounters help to illuminate the very content of sectarian othering, its pervasiveness, as well as its consequences for sense of self and collectivity. Moreover, such micro-practices of sectarian hostility embody a violence of the everyday that serves to constitute the very conditions of possibility for dramatic eruptions of collective violence.[9]

At the same time, we also need to attend to the ways in which the everyday is structured. The above case is instructive in this respect as similar to the role of sectarianized textbooks discussed in the previous chapter, it demonstrates the crucial role of institutional practices in cultivating sectarian anxieties. While a sense of religious difference and bigotry might emerge in the space of the home, it has the potential of becoming more pronounced and volatile through administrative forms of classification—quite literally so in this case. These forms are reminiscent of colonial methods of categorization like the census, which objectified social identities and served to produce notions of religious difference instead of merely reflecting them.[10] If the bio-data form was indeed introduced at the behest of the military establishment, then we can view it as a disciplinary practice of the modern state that ends up giving 'socio-political significance to the fact of difference', by raising difference from 'the realm of doxa, the assumed, into the realm of notice, where disputes can occur between the orthodox and the heterodox, the normal and the strange—that is, between the values associated with what are now *recognized* as significantly different options...but were not previously seen to be so'.[11] This politicized recognition of difference has a fundamentally emotional tenor, as it is accompanied by feelings of difference and suspicion. Ironically, such forms of difference can also be produced through struggles that seem to *resist* sectarianism, as I discuss in the next section.

SECTARIANIZED EQUALITY

In July 2006, the government-run Karakorum International University (KIU)— the only university in Gilgit—held its first convocation. On this occasion, the university administration awarded an Honour Shield each to its first Dean and first Vice Chancellor (VC) for services to the university, as well as one to the most prominent mountaineer of Gilgit-Baltistan, Nazir Sabir, for his outstanding performance at an international level. Sabir is the first Pakistani to climb the Mount Everest.

Soon after the convocation, the *Aman Jirga* (Peace Jirga) of Gilgit passed a resolution that strongly condemned KIU for these honors, and argued that there were 'sectarian interests' behind the selection of recipients.[12] This was an allusion to the fact that no Shia was awarded an honour, as the first Dean and first VC were known to be Sunnis, while Nazir Sabir belonged to the Ismaili sect. The resulting controversy was covered in the local Urdu press, generating public visibility and debate. The Peace Jirga also wrote a sharply worded letter to the KIU administration, demanding an apology for its alleged discrimination.

Incidentally, I had joined KIU as a visiting lecturer on the very day that this letter was received by the KIU administration. The Vice Chancellor, who was also relatively new to the university and not local to Gilgit-Baltistan, seemed genuinely stunned and incensed. He told me that the honours were given to recognize the achievement and contribution of well-known people, and that he did not even know what the sects of the awardees were. I myself was perplexed by the situation. The Jirga's letter neither questioned the merit of the existing awardees, nor did it propose a potential Shia recipient who was overlooked and could now be awarded. It simply accused KIU of malicious intent, and claimed that the university was promoting sectarianism in the region. Addressing the Jirga's concerns would effectively require the university to first think about people's sectarian affiliation, and then consider whether they deserve an award or not. It seemed to me that such an attitude is itself a form of sectarianism—precisely what the Peace Jirga aimed to counter.

Several faculty members who belonged to the region were also disappointed by the defamation of their university, and argued that the Peace Jirga should have issued a request for information, instead of jumping to an inflammatory resolution. Yet subtly echoing the Jirga's logic, they simultaneously insisted that the university administration should try to maintain 'sectarian balance' and 'equal treatment'. This was perhaps an indirect way of suggesting that sectarian considerations did play a part in shaping the decision-making process for granting honours.

I could not ascertain whether this claim had any validity or not, but of course agreed that no sect should be discriminated against, or unduly favoured in any administrative policy undertaken by the university. However, over the course of my affiliation with KIU, and extended fieldwork in Gilgit, I realized that this was not the only meaning of 'equal treatment' for my respondents. When people—government officials, Jirga members, and faculty members amongst others—employed the language of 'sectarian balance' and 'equal treatment', what they actually meant was that sectarian considerations *should* play a role in administrative policies. If you hire a Shia and Ismaili for two new posts, for example, it is assumed that Sunnis are being discriminated against so a Sunni should also be hired. If a Sunni and Ismaili are awarded with honours, it is considered obvious that Shias are not being treated 'equally' and hence, there should be 'balance'. A supposedly liberal–democratic logic of equality is thus appealed to, but one that entails the reinforcement of sectarian thinking instead of meritocratic values. This logic holds even with different permutations, so members of each sect could and do claim discrimination whenever any university decision was undertaken that did not include one of their own. Hence, as I discovered in my time at KIU, whether someone was being given hostel space, employment, prominent responsibility such as heading an administrative committee, or an award, 'sectarian interests' were almost always assumed to be at work. The discourse has been naturalized to such a bizarre extent, that it would continue to operate even when someone from the so-called victimized sect was not available for, or had not applied for a given position. Moreover, as my field interactions and interviews demonstrated, the discourse is not limited to the space of the public university alone but rather is prevalent more generally within government institutions in Gilgit.

THE SECTARIAN IMAGINARY

The three episodes discussed above help to illuminate key facets of what we might call the *sectarian imaginary* in Gilgit. I develop this concept based on Charles Taylor's notion of the 'social imaginary' (2004). Taylor describes the social imaginary as 'the ways [in which] people imagine their social existence, how they fit together with others, how things go on between them and their fellows, the expectations that are normally met, and the deeper normative notions and images that underlie these expectations'.[13] Adapting this concept, the sectarian imaginary can be described as the ways in which people imagine their social existence and interaction in relation to sectarian identity. To be sure, I do not wish to suggest that there is something inherently problematic in sectarian identity or difference, or that both need to be overcome for the emergence of a secular–modern individual.[14] Moreover, while sectarian identities and inter-sect relations in Gilgit surely encompass multiple perspectives, affects, expectations, and possibilities, my purpose here is to point out some specific evaluative frameworks that serve to heighten sectarian tension in Gilgit. Hence, instead of focusing on the ways in which people fit together—as Taylor's conception of the social imaginary emphasizes—my use of the sectarian imaginary pertains more to the ways in which people feel that they do not fit together, and especially the emotional underpinnings of this distance.

To begin with, the sectarian imaginary in Gilgit entails a dominant tendency to view and foremost assess people as members of a sect within Islam. Second, there is the linked tendency to define and understand all sorts of non-religious matters through a sectarian lens—or *baat baat mein mazhab* in Javed's terms. Third, there are prominent feelings of suspicion between sects, and a wariness that the interests of sectarian others are being served while one's own security, status, and rights are being undermined. And finally, there is the recurring rhetoric of 'sectarian balance' and 'equal treatment' which reflects and reinscribes the previous three tendencies, while purporting to be a critique of sectarianism. These four dispositions form part of a sectarian imaginary that imbues social life in Gilgit, resulting in the production of sectarian distrust and tension.

The notion of a sectarian imaginary is useful in comprehending how sectarianism is locally understood, lived, and felt. The dominant ways of thinking that it entails and authorizes highlight the paranoid subjectivities and emotional ill will which lie at the heart of sectarianism in Gilgit. Gilgitis themselves recognize this paranoid condition, describing it as one characterized by *taasub*. *Taasub* is commonly translated as prejudice but, in the Gilgit context, it also denotes sentiments of suspicion, anxiety, and resentment. In everyday talk, people in Gilgit commonly comment and worry about the extent to which *taasub* has spread, and how it hinders political unity as well as economic progress. Indeed, *taasub* has become the popular local idiom for describing sectarianism, instead of the more literal term of *firqavariat* which means conflict based on sectarian difference.

The frequency with which every other matter becomes imbued with a sectarian character in Gilgit is an uncomfortable and complex social reality to recognize. It also risks complicity with the statist construction of Gilgit-Baltistan, which is centred precisely on representing the region as a sectarian mess, where primordial intra-Islam differences are too strong to be managed without the coercive control of the state. Hence, instead of naturalizing sectarian paranoia as evidence of parochial religious sentiments, we need to ask: where do sectarian imaginaries and paranoid sensibilities come from? Sometimes, the immediate cause is apparent, as in the case of sectarian bio-data forms in the Army Public School. However, beyond interrogating the immediate scenario, such forces of feeling need to be understood in relation to structures of rule. Thus, we need to situate everyday sectarianism in Gilgit within the context of delusional political rule that Gilgitis inhabit, and which I discussed at length in Chapters 2 and 3.

State practices of sectarianization—including the sponsoring of sectarian organizations, organized violence against Shias, and biased textbooks—have all served to polarize Shia–Sunni relations in Gilgit over the last four decades. As Gilgiti Shias have suffered most from Sunni political and cultural hegemony, their sense of victimization tends to be more acute than that of other sects. It is an outcome of their historically institutionalized marginalization that

Shias in Gilgit now make claims to 'sectarian balance' which is indirectly a demand for inclusion through a logic of affirmative action. This context needs to be kept in mind, for example, why the Peace Jirga in Gilgit criticized the Karakoram International University for not choosing a Shia figure as one of the three awardees for its Honour Shield. Who deserved the award has become a secondary concern in a charged context of sectarianized decision-making, in which a Sunni affiliation and ideology has become privileged in regional and national state institutions, and other Muslim identities have become marginalized or suppressed. Such sect-based discrimination needs to be openly acknowledged and formally addressed. In the absence of a process of redress and democratic institution-building, the discourse of sectarian balance and equal treatment tends to become an anti-democratic political tool of entitlement in the hands of each sect in Gilgit. Hence, it ends up promoting a culture of sectarian prejudice and favoritism, instead of rectifying it.

Sectarianized sentiments also disrupt the capacity for political solidarity and resistance in this strategic, border region. These sentiments are thus both a product of, and productive of, state power, embodying not just the micro-politics of sectarianism but of state-making itself. State power 'works through the way it forcibly organizes, and divides subjectivities and thereby produces and reproduces quite material forms of sociality'.[15] Analyses of inter-community conflict, more generally, need to attend to such forms of sociality—specifically the everyday emotions, imaginaries, and enactments of resentment—as situated in and shaped by larger processes of state-making, and as practices of emotional regulation themselves that constitute everyday forms of state power.

CULTURAL RHYTHMS AND CIVIC FORUMS

Despite their pervasive presence, sectarianized sentiments in Gilgit-Baltistan are constantly overcome through the shared cultural rhythms of music, dance, and sport that are keenly appreciated across the different communities of the region. Hence, in analyses of Gilgiti social imaginaries, we must also attend to such spheres of sociality. Polo might sound like an odd choice, but it is nevertheless a significant sphere to recognize as it constitutes the most popular form of sport and entertainment in the region. While the selections of players can sometimes become a sectarianized matter, the polo teams in general, in Gilgit, have players from different sects, while the audience is also drawn from all the sects. This alone serves as an integrative function, as it helps to constitute a sense of shared public community through the performance of a collective activity.[16] Polo matches tend to form an exclusively male public arena, however, though younger girls and non-local women may be present.[17]

During my fieldwork, I had the occasion to attend a polo match in Gilgit that is held annually as part of the Silk Route Festival. The audience numbered at least 500, if not more, ranging from ordinary Gilgitis to prominent government bureaucrats. The crowd enthusiastically voiced its support or disappointment, depending on the ups and downs of the game. The match took place against the backdrop of towering mountains, accompanied by an instrument-only musical performance by the *Dom* or *Bericho*.[18] Using the traditional instruments of *surnai* (pipe), *dadang* (drums), and *damal* (tabla), the musicians played slow-paced, suspenseful tunes reflecting the tense moments of the game, and joyful, euphoric ones when a goal was scored. In fact, each player had a distinct *hareep* (tune) that was played, if and when he scored a goal. The match was even preceded by music, and accompanied with traditional dances from the different regions of Gilgit-Baltistan (Figure 4.1) These dances are similar in their rhythm and soulful movements, yet distinct in their specific bodily gestures. For example, a dancer from Diamer might initiate a dance with leisurely steps while a Gilgiti dancer might energetically hop from side to side before slowing down. The dancers move with a sensual grace that is uniquely captivating, and thoroughly enjoyed by the audience who express their delight by clapping, praising, hanging rupee notes on the sides of a dancer's cap, or joining in the dance. Overall, the blending of sport, music, and dance creates a phenomenal sense of immersive, aesthetic experience that enables a presence-of-togetherness, the celebration of historical tradition, and an ambience of shared pleasure and joyful fulfillment.

The appreciation for music and movement runs so deep in Gilgit that every other public event—from the final day of an NGO conference to a book launch at a college—tends to end in song and dance. On one occasion during my fieldwork, I was conducting a focus group with women in a local village

FIGURE 4.1 Dancers and musicians perform before the polo match at the Silk Route Festival, Gilgit, 2006
Source: Author.

located eight hours away from Gilgit, and it was suggested to me that we end the session with singing and dancing. I enthusiastically agreed, and soon realized that when social norms are relaxed, women are as entranced by music and dance as the men in the region.

During my fieldwork in 2006—barely a year after the textbook tensions had subsided—it seemed to me that Gilgitis were consciously striving to counter the air of sectarian discord with cultural events that involved music, dance, and sport. For example, a group of civil society members had organized an art exhibition and musical performance—which they called 'Torch'—for the explicit purpose of rebuilding inter-community ties. At the event, children from a local, cross-sect school also read self-authored poems on the theme of peace, and performed a skit highlighting how their education was affected during the textbook tensions. On another occasion, a different group of Gilgitis organized a volleyball tournament in order to bring youth from different sects together. Sadly, the event became overshadowed by the sectarian imaginary, as the umpire was accused of being biased towards a particular sect, and the match ended in a scuffle. Efforts towards creating peace are thus not always successful, but it is significant that artistic and civil-society segments of Gilgitis keep working towards enhanced interaction and understanding.

Sectarianism in Gilgit-Baltistan is also curbed through the shared concerns and positive values that are promoted through local journalistic and development work. Print journalism in Gilgit-Baltistan—which is almost entirely in the Urdu language —tends to be more socially engaged and progressive as compared to national Urdu papers in Pakistan. The landscape of local print journalism is unusually prolific, including popular daily newspapers such as *K2*; weekly papers such as *Baad-e-Shumaal*, *Naqqara*, *Sadaa-e-Gilgit*, *Chataan*, *Bedaar*, and *Waadi*; monthly magazines like *Boloristan*; and quarterly magazines such as *Jamhoor*. The sectarian affiliation of a newspaper owner might be widely known, but the flavour of the papers is generally non-sectarian. There are also publications like *Bang-e-Sahar* and *Shaoor* that are published by Karachi-based Gilgit-Baltistani residents, and available in the towns of Gilgit and Skardu. *Shaoor*—which means 'awareness' or 'knowledge'—is published annually by the Gilgit-Baltistan Students Association at Karachi University. On the cover of each issue, the magazine describes itself as *arz-e-shumaal kay roshan khayal tulba ka tarjuman*—'the voice of Northern Areas' progressive students'. Articles in the magazine are grouped under the categories of education, history, science and society, tourism and the economy, personalities, current affairs, and literature. The magazine also includes information about job openings, and reports on political and NGO seminars conducted in Gilgit. To give a sense of the progressive bent of the magazine, an editorial in one of its early issues entailed a fascinating examination of the causes of *gair hamwar taraqqi* (uneven development), pointing out factors such as structural adjustment programmes, *sarfi saqafat* (consumer culture), and *siyasat bezari* (depoliticization).[19]

Alongside progressive publications exist several civic associations—such as the Bolor Research Forum and Bolor Thinkers Forum—that regularly organize seminars on the politics, history, and society of Gilgit-Baltistan. More recently, the Internet has become an important space for extending the discursive public sphere in the region, and includes local initiatives such as the popular news and analysis blog *Pamir Times*.

The vibrant culture of critical discourse in Gilgit-Baltistan reflects the importance of intellectual–political inquiry and engagement in the region. This culture has been sustained despite the harassment that journalists routinely face from the military–intelligence establishment, as well as from political and religious organizations in the region. For example, a monthly magazine, *Kargil*, was launched in 2000, soon after the Kargil operation of 1999 that I discussed in Chapter 2. It critiqued General Musharraf's operation, paid tribute to the Northern Areas soldiers who died as a result of it, discussed the problems faced by the families of the soldiers, and demanded a commission to inquire into the conflict. The magazine was subsequently banned, and its editor arrested for instigating the public against the President.

The gendered nature of the Gilgiti public sphere also needs to be acknowledged, as it highlights the limits of progressive arenas. Local women are marginally present in the newspapers and magazines that I have discussed above. However, women are quite prominent in the non-governmental and university spaces in Gilgit. They are also increasingly visible in the political arena. The 33-member Gilgit-Baltistan Legislative Assembly has six reserved seats for women, and in the elections of 2009 female candidates also competed for three general seats.

Non-governmental organizations more generally constitute an important part of the critical and engaged public in Gilgit-Baltistan. International NGOs became prominent in the region after the Karakoram Highway facilitated access to the region in 1979, beginning most notably with the rural support programmes, schools, and health services created by the Aga Khan Development Network (AKDN).[20] The role of NGOs is often seen in negative terms in the region, as the emphasis on foreign-funded development projects is deemed to contribute to depoliticization—a lack of engagement in the political process and future of the region, through, for example, collective action and social movements. This critique is borne out by evidence elsewhere in the world as well.[21] Secondly, NGO work has often led to the commodification of social justice issues. This means that the core ethical and political concerns of a society are transformed into a business that is addressed based on the availability of funds, instead of being recognized as matters of collective rights and responsibilities that must be ensured for all by the state and society. Finally, a journalist from the region, Jan Faraz, pointed out to me how the high salaries paid to development professionals served to create a class society in the region while also changing youth aspirations. Earlier, the youth of the region regarded teaching as an honourable profession; now, vocations such as teaching, journalism, and activism are often perceived as lowly concerns while development is considered a lucrative career.

At the same time, however, NGO discourses and projects such as those on 'gender mainstreaming', 'governance', and 'capacity-building' have their positive dimension as well. Particularly in the context of a politically and socially marginalized area such as Gilgit-Baltistan, several NGOs have initiated important projects focused on the upliftment of the region, introduced a progressive language that has raised public consciousness about civic rights, and also enhanced people's ability to organize for these rights.

SECULAR-NATIONALIST PARTY ACTIVISM

I now turn my attention to political efforts against sectarianism and dispossession in Gilgit, as embodied in the activism of *qaum parast tanzeemain*—local, secular-nationalist parties with leftist leanings. The 'nationalists'—as they are called in Gilgit-Baltistan—include those groups who struggle for more substantive regional rights within the sovereign nation-state of Pakistan, as well as those who have more separatist leanings. The nationalist parties have been mobilizing for social and political change in the region for many decades, stressing social justice over sectarianism, and debate over dogma. Their activities form a key part of the progressive public arena in Gilgit-Baltistan.

The landscape of political movements and parties in Gilgit-Baltistan can be described as flourishing. Apart from prominent national parties such as the PPP, PML (N), and Jamaat-e-Islami (JI), and sect-specific parties such as the SSP and the Tehrik-e-Jafaria Pakistan (TJP), the local political scene is dotted with more than a dozen home-grown secular–nationalist parties and coalitions, such as the Boloristan Labor Party, the Progressive Youth Front, Gilgit Baltistan Democratic Alliance (GBDA), the Gilgit-Baltistan National Alliance (GBNA), Karakoram National Movement (KNM), and the Balawaristan National Front (BNF).[22] These parties are cross-sectarian and cross-ethnic in their leadership and membership base.

Secular–nationalist movements first emerged in Gilgit-Baltistan in the 1960s. At the time, their struggles were directed against the authoritarianism of local *mirs* as well as against the Pakistani government. Most of the activists of the time trace their political consciousness to their university life in Karachi, where multiple political and student movements were struggling to shape the nature of the new nation-state of Pakistan. After the abolition of princely states in 1972, local movements lost some of their appeal to Pakistani parties such as the PPP, and also to the fact that a key target of their activities—the princely state—was now disbanded. However, the emergence of state practices of sectarianization in the 1970s revived the impetus for local political mobilization. Thus, while state-backed sectarianism did in fact damage the regional social fabric by breeding a culture of suspicion and intolerance, ironically, it simultaneously fuelled local secular–national movements that sought to resist the state project of rule. In effect, the process of state sectarianization led both to heightened sectarianism as well heightened secular nationalism in Gilgit-Baltistan.

The Shia pogrom of 1988 not only marked a turning point in inter-sect relations in Gilgit-Baltistan but also in the landscape of political movements in the region. The Balawaristan National Front (BNF), for example, is a prominent secular nationalist party in Gilgit-Baltistan that is demanding a sovereign and independent state for the region. While it was formally established in 1992, its founding leader Nawaz Khan Naji as well as one of its ex-party leaders Abdul Hamid Khan trace their political awakening to the sectarian violence of 1988. At its first *ijlas* (conference), BNF launched a 'Berozgar Action Committee' (Unemployment Action Committee) to tackle unemployment in the region, and importantly this first conference was held in Jalalabad—the worst affected Shia village during the 1988 sectarian violence. This was significant as the nationalists wanted to recognize 1988, and yet go beyond it. They wanted to emphasize that the Shias of Jalalabad were not just 'Shias'—they were displaced people who were economically affected by the 1988 massacre as their homes and livelihoods were completely destroyed due to state-backed sectarian violence. Simultaneously, the mobilization around unemployment emphasized that lack of economic security is a common concern for people in Gilgit-Baltistan and hence, should be the main agenda that people in the region should rally around.

While such efforts serve to steer the region towards the path of social and political justice, the actual support for nationalist parties in the region remains limited. This is partly because critical political activity is seen as a source of inviting trouble from the military–intelligence regime. Further, nationalist political activists have often been prevented from taking part in local elections, and hence their influence on voters is hard to gauge. However, even if the votes for or actual membership in nationalist parties might be small, this does not mean that these parties are marginal to political action in Gilgit. On the contrary, these parties are quite active and visible in the local scene. They routinely organize seminars and strikes against ongoing political injustices in the region, and give statements on current events that make headlines in the local newspapers. I found it telling that Gilgitis often made it a point to clarify to me that they were not affiliated with any nationalist party, and that generally, nationalist parties did not have much local support. Yet this statement would be followed up with an expression of *hamdardi* with these groups.

Hamdardi is often translated as 'sympathy' but its literal meaning is 'shared emotion and pain' which is a more appropriate translation in this context. When Gilgitis say that they have *hamdardi* with nationalists, they are not suggesting that they merely sympathize with the nationalist cause, or pity the nationalist's suffering. Rather, the sentiment of *hamdardi* reflects a recognition of the shared grievances and pain that unite the party activist with a lay person. On one occasion I was planning to attend a political seminar by a nationalist group, and an ex-government servant, Jamil Khan, said to me:

> My heart really desires to go and at least hear what they say, because they are speaking the truth. Even if nothing comes out of their activities. But the agencies monitor these events, and note down who comes to them. As a

recently retired person, I cannot really take part in these activities. But one day I might. I want to speak up.

More generally, there is an implicit appreciation for the work of nationalists, and I was often told to meet nationalist leaders because of their *gehri soch* (deep thought) on the predicament of the region. I was amazed that it was often the self-described 'apolitical' Gilgiti—usually working in a government office, NGO, bank, or the university—who was most interested in my research, and actually pointed me to nationalist magazines and seminars that might be useful for my work.

To give a sense of the discursive arena constructed by nationalist activism, I will now review one particular seminar that I attended in Gilgit during my fieldwork. In July 2007, the Gilgit-Baltistan Democratic Alliance organized a seminar on the 'National Question of Gilgit-Baltistan'. This was the fourth in a series of political events organized by the alliance. The earlier three were centred on the 'Bhasha Dam', the 'Karachi Agreement of 1949', and the 'Naming of the Northern Areas', and were held in Diamer, Skardu, and Ghizar districts of the then Northern Areas respectively.

The seminar on the 'National Question' was held at a hotel in Gilgit, and was attended by around hundred people—all men—and myself. One or two representatives from each of the seven parties belonging to the GBDA spoke at the seminar. Over the three hours that the seminar lasted, the various speakers addressed a key concern: what is the relationship of Gilgit-Baltistan to Pakistan, and what kind of a political set-up is desirable for the future? There were many common strands in the speeches, such as a retelling of the Gilgit war of independence and the subsequent denial of constitutional status. Likewise, common demands were raised across speeches, such as the demand for regional autonomy.

But what I found particularly fascinating about the seminar was the degree of discussion, debate, and disagreement that it entailed. On the historical and future boundaries of Gilgit-Baltistan, for example, a representative of the Balwaristan National Front argued that Kargil, Ladakah, and Chitral were historically part of Gilgit-Baltistan—or Balwaristan as they have renamed it— and hence the nationalist struggle is also about regaining this lost territory. The vice-president of the GBDA, on the other hand, argued that instead of creating new borders to replace arbitrary, colonial ones, we need to push for open borders that permit freedom of travel and trade. Similarly, an audience member belonging to the Shia Tulba Action Committee (Shia Students Action Committee) requested to speak, and contended that society in Gilgit-Baltistan is deeply religious but their religious values are being ignored by the secularist tendencies of nationalist organizations. This is why these organizations lack popular appeal, he said. To this, a number of GDBA members clarified that their use of 'secular' does not mean 'without religion'; rather, it entails the freedom of religion for all beliefs. It was argued that it is precisely religion raised to the level of state that has caused sectarian division and conflict in the region, and that the protection of religious values is ensured precisely by not embroiling religion with politics. Yet another point of difference was raised when the Chairman of the Northern Areas Transport Union—also speaking from the audience—mentioned that the 'special' constitution-less status of Northern Areas means that a 20 lakh luxury car is available for 2 lakhs to people, as at the time, there was no custom tax imposed in the region. He asserted that this affordability is the 'constitution' that poor people want, and that the political constitution is perhaps important only to MNAs (Members of the National Assembly). Having a proper constitution would reduce this affordability, and 'we will have to return to tractors'. In response, a member of the GBDA argued that access to consumer goods should not justify acceptance of political violence, and that progress is indicated by the recognition of people's dignity.

None of the issues regarding the 'national question' in Gilgit-Baltistan were resolved in the seminar. Instead, the seminar was a forum that facilitated a debate on key issues, instead of proposing and imposing already-formed positions. Cultivating such a culture of dialogue is a key mode of political engagement and pedagogy by nationalist parties in Gilgit-Baltistan. The discursive openness in their events enables a participatory civic–political space, in which people can air their grievances as well as their different visions for the region's future while learning from the opinions and experiences of others. Such a space, therefore, promotes critical reflection and engagement, while also fostering a sense of collectivity and agentive capacity. In the remaining chapter, I show how poetic events similarly expand such a space for civic togetherness, reflection, and transformation in Gilgit-Baltistan.

POETRY AND PUBLIC PROTEST

Poetry—like other oral genres such as folktales, songs, and proverbs—fundamentally shapes the consciousness and psychic selves of people.[23] However, it has often been seen merely in terms of folk wisdom or private, individual expression, thus under-recognizing its role in social interaction and political life. In her brilliant analysis of the place of poetry in Bedouin society, Abu-Lughod (1986) demonstrates how the Bedouins understand, employ, and value poetry as an expressive medium that moves people and thus has the power to change their minds and actions. Not surprisingly, then, poetry has regularly been used for conflict mediation in Yemeni tribal contexts.[24] This centrality of oral communication—and especially poetry—in the public spheres of many non-Western contexts requires us to rethink the emphasis on text and on the literate domain of formal education that dominates studies of the public sphere.[25]

The role of the literary-poetic in political and social transformation has a long history in South Asia. Dharwadker (2010) argues that South Asian nations are in essence 'literary nations', whereby the articulation of national feeling and reformist thought in the literary imagination prefigured, and made possible the realization of the nation in the political realm. This connection is perhaps most visible in the case of Pakistan, where the reformist poet–writer Muhammad Iqbal is revered as the figure who 'dreamed' of Pakistan—and hence, as the one who sowed the seeds of Pakistani nationalism. South Asia, of course, is not unique in its poetic-national culture, as poetry has also helped to articulate collective understandings of the nation in other contexts such as in Yemen and Nicaragua.[26]

In Gilgit, contemporary critical poetry contests the meaning of the nation, instead of accomplishing it. It provides a glimpse of postcolonial nationalism from the vantage point of regional cultural production, while also constituting an expression of critical political subjectivity in a sectarianized, disenfranchised context. Hence, if the printed word provided the technical means for imagining and representing the nation as an 'imagined community',[27] it is the oral word that is helping to critically re-imagine this community in the region of Gilgit-Baltistan.

It is also important to situate the life of poetry in Gilgit-Baltistan in the context of long-standing traditions of Muslim literary humanism in Central and South Asia.[28] In these shared traditions that nevertheless vary with linguistic and regional context, poetry encompasses far more than what the English term 'poetry' has come to denote in the West today—reduced as it often is to a privatized, individualized sense of solitary writing. Poetry in the context of Muslim literary humanism is better described as *poetic knowledge*, as the poetic word was deemed a multidimensional knowledge form intimately connected to notions of the intellect, to practices of self and moral formation, as well as to the domains of spirituality, art, music, and communal storytelling. Such poetic knowledge traditions may hence be understood as constituting a way of being and as ethical–political philosophy that is integral to the formation of public sentiment. The very Arabic–Urdu word *shair*—which in popular use denotes a poetic couplet—affirms this connection between poetry and knowledge: the foundational meaning of this word in Arabic is 'to know', and it is etymologically linked to the word *shaoor* which means 'consciousness'. Poetic thought was thus considered integral to ethical, aesthetic, worldly, and spiritual education. For South Asia in general, such traditions of poetic knowledge must be placed not only in a vernacular context but also in a supra-social, spirito-poetic, transcendental context where *ishq* (love) and *insaaniyat* (humanism) serve as meta-concepts for life, understanding, and critique.

Unlike many heavily urbanized areas of present-day Pakistan, poetry recitation continues to hold a prominent place in the social life of Gilgit-Baltistan. Whether at casual gatherings, cultural celebrations, NGO conferences, or political seminars, participants are likely to quote couplets in Urdu or in one of their local languages. *Mushairas*, or gatherings dedicated to poetry recitation, are often organized in people's homes, at hotels, and in public spaces, and are much valued as a source of pleasure and intellectual stimulation. While *mushairas* have been part of the Indo-Persian cultural landscape at least since the sixteenth century,[29] poetic performances have a particularly central place in the cultural and spiritual life of Muslims in Northern Pakistan. The ability to use words for poetic, playful, and creative expression is considered the hallmark of intellect, and both the production and reception of poetic performances is deemed integral to Muslim personhood.[30] In Gilgit, I was often told that poetry is truly the *rooh ki giza* or nourishment for the soul. Local poetry that has been put to music is also very popular in Gilgit-Baltistan, and is enjoyed both through recordings and in live performances. Hence, a 'cultural of poetry' infuses social life in Northern Pakistan, similar to what has been claimed for other contexts such as Arab culture.[31]

Poetic expression has been particularly encouraged in Gilgit-Baltistan by the literary organization *Halqa-e-Arbab-e-Zauq*, or Halqa in short. Founded in 1939, Halqa is a prominent Urdu literary forum that promotes literature and poetry through publications and *mushairas*. The Gilgit chapter of Halqa was established in 1987, at the initiative of a retired army major from 'down'—the term most commonly used for Pakistani regions located south of Gilgit-Baltistan—who himself was a poet, and was at the time posted in the education department in Gilgit. However, the seeds of a literary organization in Gilgit were already sown in the form of the Karakoram Writers Forum, a local initiative that preceded the formation of Halqa.

The role of Halqa in the sub-continent is often contrasted with that of the Progressive Writers Movement, another eminent literary organization that was founded before the partition of 1947. While Halqa is largely seen as embodying a non-political and individualistic modernism that does 'art for art's sake', the Progressives are seen as a political movement that espouses realism and engages in 'art for life's sake'.[32] While the divide was certainly never this neat, the overall connotation seems to be that unlike the Progressives, the Halqa lacked social responsibility and a commitment towards collective social change.

My research in Gilgit-Baltistan firmly challenges this interpretation, as the Halqa chapter in Gilgit has consistently used the medium of poetry to contest political dispossession and sectarian hostility in the region. Although the current Halqa chapter in Gilgit may formally have nothing to do with the historical Halqa of the subcontinent, it is nonetheless significant that the banner of Halqa—with its known history and mainstream appeal all over Pakistan—is what unites and facilitates the contemporary poets of Gilgit in their efforts to organize for progressive social change. While the traditional themes of dealing with the self, love, and separation are present, it is the concern with political and social transformation that dominates the work of the key movers of Halqa. In my individual interviews with Halqa poets in Gilgit, it became even clearer to me that what motivates their poetry is a concern with promoting a progressive vision of humanity and harmony as the essence of faith and politics.

My first encounter with Halqa was at a *mushaira* that was held at the Karakoram International University in Gilgit, as part of the Pakistan Independence Day celebrations in August 2006. Jointly organized by KIU and Halqa, the four-hour *mushaira* featured the most distinguished poets from Gilgit-Baltistan, as well as a few renowned ones from other parts of Pakistan. It took place in the university garden, in the late evening, against the backdrop of a mountain lit up with *charagan* (firelights) by KIU faculty members. No fee was charged for attendance. There were around 400 people present, all men except for six women: three female poets on stage who were from down-Pakistan, and three women in the audience including myself. We could be there because we taught at the university, and were also non-local. The vast majority of male attendees belonged to the town of Gilgit and nearby areas, and came predominantly from an oral culture—which mainstream language would call 'illiterate'. The rest were students at KIU.

Like several others, I too was completely enthralled by the poetic performances at the *mushaira*. In an Urdu that was both simple and eloquent, and a recitation that was deeply moving, the region's poets attempted to stimulate the audience with their reflections on politics, society, and love. Barring a few couplets, most of the poetry that was recited at the *mushaira* was in Urdu. When I talked with KIU students and faculty members after the *mushaira*, they expressed how they valued the poetry for the beauty of words and of thought, and especially for the *dard* and *josh*—compassion and fervor—that it embodied. The performance was thus valued for the way in which it appealed to, and nourished the creative, intellectual, and emotional sensibilities of the listeners.

Several poets powerfully captured the political dispossession of Gilgit-Baltistan, and criticized the attitude of the Pakistani government towards the region—this, ironically at a festival that was meant to celebrate the independence day of Pakistan. Sectarian prejudice was likewise a prominent theme, with many verses criticizing the role of orthodox clerics in propagating sectarian hatred. I found it striking that critical poetry pertaining to faith and politics tended to attract the strongest applause from the audience. This applause may be viewed as an endorsement of how the sentiments expressed by the poets echoed the feelings of audience members. In the next section, I discuss the main concerns that animate the genre of Gilgiti progressive poetry, and discuss a few of its verses that I heard in Gilgit—some at the *mushaira* and some in personal interviews with local poets.

RE-IMAGINING MUSLIM ETHICS AND POLITICS

The key theme that dominates Halqa's progressive poetry is a contemplation of Muslim nationhood. Halqa poets critique the meaning of Muslim nationhood in contemporary Pakistan by exposing the inhuman values and exploitative practices that both Pakistani *Islam* and the Pakistani *nation-state* have come to embody in Gilgit-Baltistan. According to these poets, Muslim nationhood has neither lived up to the ethical values of Islam nor to the legal norms of democratic citizenship. The former is evident in the prejudice and hatred that dominates inter-sect relations within Islam, while the latter is exemplified by the absence of a constitutional place and proper political and legal rights for Gilgit-Baltistan in Pakistan. Critiquing such conditions of sectarian prejudice and regional non-citizenship, Halqa poets urge the *ameer-e-waqt* or 'Ruler of the Time' to reform state policy, while imploring Muslims to live with respect and humanity towards each other.

Consider, for example, the following verses that condemn the authoritarian policies of the Pakistan state in Gilgit-Baltistan:[33]

> *Zuban ko mein nay bhi ab be-lagaam chor diya*
> *Amir-e-waqt! Tira ehtraam chor diya*
> *Gila baja hai ke aiy doston! Nahin hai baja?*
> *Nisf sadi se hamain kyon gulaam chor diya*
> *Abhi tak hain qawaneen Dogron kay yahan*
> *Wo khud to chal diye apna nizaam chor diya*

I've let my tongue lose from now on
Ruler of the Time! I've stopped respecting you from now on
Am I right in complaining, or no my friends?
Half a century, and we are still in chains
The laws of Dogras[34] still prevail here
They have long gone, but their system remains

—Anwar Jami

Na mera jism apna hai khuda-vanda na jaan meri
Ye meri zindagi kia hai badi kia nekiyaan meri

Vahan Kashmiriyon pe zulm gairon nay kia lekin
Yahan apnon nay looti hain sada aazaadiyan meri
Amir-e-waqt se keh do mujhay aain de varna
Kisi din ley ke dubein gi usay mehrumian meri

Neither my body belongs to me nor my soul, oh God
What is the meaning of my life, my sins, my kindnesses
Others have committed atrocities, there in Kashmir
Here, always, my own have robbed me of liberties
Tell the Ruler of the Time to give me a constitution or else
Some day he will be drowned by my rightlessness

—Shams Zaman

The sentiment in the above verses is angry and rebellious. The disenfranchisement of Gilgit-Baltistan is paralleled with the historical conditions of Kashmir—when the Dogra rulers of Jammu and Kashmir marginalized Muslim subjects through their Hindu-dominated modes of sovereignty—as well as to the present conditions of Indian-ruled Kashmir where a military occupation continues to oppress Kashmiri Muslims.[35] The irony and tragedy is critical here; what is being highlighted is that fighting to join a *Muslim nation* like Pakistan—as Gilgitis did at the time of partition—has made no difference to their present predicament where their 'own' (Muslims) have been responsible for injustice and subjugation.

Along with exposing this hollowness of the Muslim nation, Halqa poetry also emphasizes the poet's understanding of what it means to be a Muslim, and how his interpretation embraces difference and respect instead of the prejudice and othering that has come to dominate understandings of the Muslim faith:

Mein dastaar-e-fazeelat maangta hoon
Vo kehtay hain tumhara sar nahin hai
Sabhi momin hain mere deen-e-haq main
Koi mushriq koi kafir nahin hai

I ask for the crown of goodness
They tell me I don't possess a head

In my true faith everyone is a believer
I see no one as polytheist, no one as non-believer
—Ali Manzoor

Taasub say bhara paigaam ye hai
Bahao khoon dars-e-aam ye hai
Musalmanon ka jab anjaam ye hai
Mein kafir hoon agar Islam yeh hai

It is a message overflowing with prejudice
'Shed blood!' is being commonly preached
When this is the meaning of being Muslim
I am a non-believer if this is Islam
—Shams Zaman

Both Manzoor's and Zaman's verses may be seen as constituting a moral discourse that nurtures a pluralistic vision of Islam—one that has always been present in the history and practice of Muslims in Gilgit-Baltistan—in place of the more insular one that has recently become ascendant in Pakistan and Gilgit-Baltistan.[36] We might be compelled to see this as an 'alternative' discourse as compared to 'mainstream Islam', but such a characterization would belie how dominant and widespread the traditions of spirito-poetic, literary humanism have always been in Pakistan and, indeed, in South Asia. The tenor of these contemporary verses is also often didactic, instead of embodying lyrical allegory and aesthetic experimentation. According to the poet Shams Zaman, it is important to be 'direct' when faced with the kind of political and religious inhumanism that has come to prevail in Gilgit, so that the true values of Islam and democratic equality may be cultivated.

Like Urdu poetry elsewhere, Gilgiti poetry also has a fair share of verses that mock the hypocrisies of the *vaez, mullah, zahid,* or *sheikh*—titles for pious men, preachers, and religious leaders in Islam. Such mockery is usually done in a witty and playful manner, within the limits prescribed by convention. However, Gilgiti poets seem to be extending this genre by directly accusing the *vaez* for spreading hate.[37] For example, the verse below critiques how preachers in Gilgit promote *taasub*—the sectarian prejudice and resentment that I discussed earlier in this chapter:

Vaez ko muhabbat ki fiza raas nahin hai
Anjam-e-taasub ka bhi ehsaas nahin hai
Hoon kaar-e-muhabbat mein hi masroof main itna
Nafrat ke liye vaqt mere paas nahin hai

The Preacher and Love are unknown to each other
He is oblivious to where his prejudice leads him
And I am so busy doing the deeds of love
That I possess no time for hate

—Dost Faqir

Another verse exposes the patron–client relation that exists between state officials and clerics in Gilgit-Baltistan and Pakistan. The poet suggests that instead of religious guidance, the purpose of the clergy has become one of promoting sectarian conflict at the orders of the ruler, reflecting the widely held local belief that state officials in the region have used sectarian differences for disrupting local political solidarity.

Kuch hain mazhab ke junoon mein garq kuch zaaton mein hain
Dushmanan-e-qaum har su mukhtalif ghaaton mein hain
Ik bahana hai rasai ka amir-e-shehr tak
Hum ko apas mein lara kar khud mulaqaaton mein hain

Some are absorbed in the madness of religion, some are drowned in castes
Enemies of the nation are everywhere hiding in their trenches[38]
It is only an excuse to get to the ruler of the city
They make us fight, so that they can sit in meetings with him

—Anwar Jami

In personal interviews, Gilgiti poets spoke to me about sectarian hate and political–religious violence with a profound sense of anguish. Indeed, it is this grief and pain that compels them to write poetry. One poet, Dost Faqir, commented to me that 'the path of poetry ultimately meets the path of

God', and that he writes poetry as a form of *ibadat* (worship) and *insaaniyat* (humanism). Other poets shared similar sentiments. The emphasis on the poetic expression of piety and the values of *insaaniyat* is indeed central to folk and Sufi traditions of Islam more generally, and yet remains understudied in anthropological studies of Islam that tend to dwell on *muharram* rituals and *dargah* practices, or more recently, on the pious embodiments in Muslim reform movements.[39] An examination of the poetic thought and activism of Gilgiti poets thus enriches the anthropology of Islam by offering a different lens on Muslim identity, reform, and piety in contemporary Muslim societies.

The poetry of Halqa also demonstrates how the Islamicizing politics of the state and religious parties in Pakistan is grappled with and contested by Muslim subjects, instead of being unthinkingly accepted.[40] Yet Gilgiti poetic performances are not just 'everyday' forms of resistance as linguistic expressive traditions have often been seen. Even if they are embedded in the rhythms of everyday life, they are neither ordinary nor hidden. Such performances constitute a critical public arena and 'cultural intervention', in which 'the capacity for change may be highlighted and made manifest to the community'.[41] While Gilgiti poetry might convey a sense of disillusionment and bitterness, it rarely resorts to pessimism and cynicism. And this is one of its main strengths as a force of socio-political change. Gilgiti poets actively seeks to reflect and reshape the political consciousness and the moral imagination of the public, thus helping to create the conditions for peaceful coexistence and democratic development in Gilgit-Baltistan.

The work of Halqa in Gilgit can therefore be conceptualized as a form of social struggle and collective action that is as concrete as a movement. Indeed, even though Halqa is a non-governmental *tanzeem* (organization), some poets of the organization themselves perceive it as a *tehreek* (movement). As a senior official of the organization Shams Zaman said to me:

We have to create religious harmony and local unity to ensure peace. We have worked harder for the promotion of tolerance and peace, than for the promotion of literature.

Towards this end, Halqa has organized poetry events with the specific purpose of promoting the ethic of respect and tolerance. For example, in October

1999 Halqa organized a *mushaira* in Gilgit in which poets were specifically asked to write on the topic of *Tark-i-Taasobat* (The Ending of Prejudice). A poetry collection based on this *mushaira* was later published by Halqa.[42]

The role of Halqa was especially critical during the textbook conflict in 2005, which I discussed in the previous chapter. Revenge killings had become the norm after the supreme Shia leader in Gilgit, Agha Ziauddin Rizvi, was murdered in January 2005. Twenty days after his murder, some Halqa poets got together and decided that they must intervene. They were not sure what they could do as the atmosphere was filled with fear and people tended to remain in their houses, and within their sect-specific neighborhoods. Working towards peace in such a context was considered cowardice, and worse a betrayal of one's own sect that could result in reputational repercussions from other members of one's community. Even as the poets felt that their 'creativity was deadened by the violence', they thought that they must strive to write and, at a later point, recite. As one of them said to me:

> The *naara-e-ehtiyaat* [the stance of silence] had to go. Even if they died, at least they would have died for the noble cause of building peace.

One of the first poems that became popular at this time was called 'Karbala-e-Jadid' [The New Karbala], and was authored by the Sunni poet Rehman Josh who works as a teacher at a local government school in Gilgit.[43] Below, I provide some verses from his moving elegy:

> *Naya ik Karbala hai shehr mein kyon?*
> *Musalman be-nawa hai shehr mein kyon?*
> *Kisi ka ghar jala hai shehr mein kyon?*
> *Ye matam sa bapa hai shehr mein kyon?*
> *Naya ik Karbala hai shehr mein kyon?*
>
> *Agar Islam hai teray chalan mein*
> *Agar fitna nahin hai teray man mein*
> *Agar anas-o-muhabbat hai vatan mein*
> *Laho itna baha hai shehr mein kyon?*
> *Naya ik Karbala hai shehr mein kyon?*

Musalman ab baraiy deen utho
Badal do uth kay ye aain utho
Utho Iqbal kay shaheen utho
Bana har ik khuda hai shehr mein kyon?
Naya ik Karbala hai shehr mein kyon?

A new Karbala in the city, why?
Voiceless Muslims in the city, why?
A home burns in the city, why?
This air of mourning in the city, why?
A new Karbala in the city, why?

If Islam still lives in your soul
If evil does not rein your heart
If love still remains in the homeland
Then so much blood spilled in the city, why?
A new Karbala in the city, why?

Oh Muslim, now stand up and protect your faith
Stand up and change the constitution, stand up
Stand up, Iqbal's eagles, stand up[44]
Everyone plays God in the city, why?
A new Karbala in the city, why?

—Rehman Josh

Prose along similar themes circulated in the local Urdu newspapers in Gilgit, which were also struggling to play a constructive role in the context of heightened sectarianism. But the most innovative intervention came when Halqa organized a *Gulaman-e-Mustafa* (servants of Prophet Muhammad) recitation conference for the specific purpose of bringing *ulema* or scholars from different sects together in appreciation of a shared Islam. These were followed by other *seerat* (in praise of Muhammad) and *aman* (peace) conferences.

While showing me pictures of these events, Dost Fakir, a founding member of Halqa, narrated:

You can see here, that we have organized a *aman* [peace] conference ...a *seerat* conference [in praise of Prophet Muhammad]...and here's a *mehfil-e-musalama* conference titled '*Hussain sub ka*' [Hussain is for everyone].[45] All to get *maulvis* from the Shia and Sunni sects to sit together. They would of course never come to a regular *mushaira* so we organized events according to their disposition; we talked only about Allah and the Prophet, and compelled them to come. After Agha Ziaduddin's death, there were open killings in Gilgit. *Maulvis* from the two sects even refused to see each other's faces, and there was only talk of revenge and hatred. We tried on our part to break the tension, by organizing a *naatia mushaira* [poetry evening in praise of Prophet Muhammad] in which the religious leaders of both sects came together for the first time since the sectarian situation went bad. At this event, we also invited progressive-minded *alims* [religious scholars] and intellectuals from down-Pakistan who talked about the need for Muslim unity in the face of larger global challenges.

Such efforts to 'break the tension' by creating a space for 'sitting together' and recognizing commonality are of profound value in the sectarianized context of Gilgit. The poetic veneration of common religious figures—even asserting that they are *common*—and a scholarly attention to the larger global context constitute creative strategies for overcoming sectarian conflict and restoring social unity. These strategies are all the more significant for securing the involvement of influential local religious leaders, some of whom have the strongest stake in maintaining sectarian enmity. We might think of such Halqa events as creating what Amin (2002) calls 'micro-publics of banal transgression', where the fixed patterns of interaction between people from different backgrounds may be destabilized and new ways of connecting established.[46]

The cultural activism of Halqa in countering sectarian animosity has elicited a mixed reaction from the religious clergy in Gilgit. As Saqi Jan, a prominent Sunni poet who is also a key official of Halqa, said to me:

There are ulema from both sects who welcome the work of Halqa members, and say 'Recite!' even when we recite verses that poke fun at their sensibilities. But there are others who dismiss poetry altogether, and view culture as a threat to religion. They want us to forget our history and culture, of which religion is a part.

The displeasure of the Sunni clergy has even been vocalized in mosque sermons, in which the Sunni poets of Halqa have been vilified for engaging in the *tauheen* or disrespect of ulema. According to Zaman, verses such as the following have been especially infuriating for the clergy in Gilgit:

Mullah ka yahan pait nikalta hai musalsal
Lekin woh samajhta hai ke imaan bauhat hai

The mullah here has a protruding belly
And he thinks he is filled with faith

More tragically, in 2007, a member of an extremist Sunni religious group was caught before attempting to kill a Halqa-affiliated Sunni poet for 'organizing conferences' and 'uniting sects'. This demonstrates the extent to which extremist Sunni organizations feel threatened by Halqa, and also the considerable risk that Halqa poets have taken to bridge the sectarian divide and recover the ethic of religious harmony in Gilgit.

The efforts of Halqa are also sometimes dismissed by members of the secular–liberal left in Gilgit, as they feel that Halqa events are more about 'entertainment' than 'real change'. As a journalist–activist, Suleman Shah, mentioned to me:

The Progressive Writers Movement took on empire. They invited *mazdoor* [labor] and *kisan* [farmer] leaders as chief guests at their events. Halqa poets invite government officials. They are complacent, and keen on pleasing officials than on boldly challenging them.

Such critiques overlook the fact that entertaining performances also constitute subversive sites of 'real change' and that it is precisely its more mainstream position that enables Halqa to have a wider appeal and reach. More significantly, the majority of poets affiliated with Halqa work for the local government in Gilgit. As government workers, they have severe limitations on political expression, participation, and protest, particularly in a heavily monitored space as Gilgit-Baltistan. Resistance in its directly political form is thus a luxury that they cannot afford, given their political and economic circumstances. In such a context, critical poetry affords a creative means of expressing grievance and protest. The abstractness of poetry means that it is not deemed as threatening as, for example, journalistic accounts, which are regularly repressed in the region. Poetry can be performed in a casual and amused tone, so as not to seriously offend—though at one famed Halqa *mushaira*, the Chief Secretary who also happened to be the chief guest at the occasion felt snubbed, and threatened to leave if 'guests continued to be respected this way'.[47] Halqa poetry thus embodies a critique of, and challenge to authority that can outrage both political and religious power in Gilgit.

The work of Halqa also helps to complicate our understanding of the state, as it contests the assumption that bureaucrats are unthinking state agents who simply represent and reproduce state discourses and practices of rule. The poetry of Halqa may be seen as embodying bureaucratic agency, critique, and subversion in the face of coercive state logics. Yet the poets are not proposing a radical break from state politics. Their poetry, in fact, evokes the same moral values that historically legitimized the ideal of the Pakistani state—as one that embodied humanity, equality, and Muslim unity, instead of the selfishness and violence of power. Hence, the poets are simultaneously local and national; they experience the state as local inhabitants but also embody its ideals and help to execute its policies. From this overlapping position, they seek to create spaces of poetic reflection and critique that can reach the government as well as society. They comment on the callousness of the Pakistan government, as much as they speak of sectarian prejudice amongst the people of Gilgit-Baltistan. The parameters of poetic critique, however, are defined by the poets' ideological positions and by the realities of repression in the region. For example, the military-intelligence regime that dominates state power in Gilgit-Baltistan is never directly criticized; indeed, sacrifices of regional soldiers for the Pakistani army are often glorified. The poets also tend to discuss the region's problems as if they themselves exist outside of and above them, not as those who are embroiled in negotiating these complex realities. However, these are realities that they are moved by, and which they strive to understand and transform through poetry.

It is also important to note that Halqa-e-Arbab-e-Zauq is one amongst several literary organizations in Gilgit-Baltistan that seek to bring about progressive change through poetry. Prominent among these is the *Bazm-e-Ilm-o-Fann* (Bazm) or Society for Knowledge and Art. While Halqa is dominant in Gilgit, Bazm is more active in Skardu. The motto of Bazm reveals the organization's vision: *adab vaseela-e-ittehad, muhabbat vaseela-e-aman*— 'literature is the means for unity, love is the means for peace'. As the head of the organization, Jalal Daanish, described to me:

> Gatherings that are on party or religious basis tend to create groups, and divide people. But our cultural events are open to everyone. There is no *sarhad* [border] in poetry, and this is the first step towards unity.

When I probed him about what 'learning and reflection' Bazm aspires for, he explained:

> Look at the values that have destroyed our region. Like *aksariat aur aqliat ki soch* [the idea of majority and minority]. Why should we ever think in these terms? Everyone has the right to live as they desire, once you accept that, why should numbers matter? In our region, we have so much *taasub* [prejudice] and *hasad* [jealousy/competitiveness] that destroys peace and unity. We want others to fail, so that we can succeed. Schools also promote such thinking. That's one reason I think the literate have done more to promote sectarianism than the illiterate. Instead, we should want ourselves to do well, and same for everyone else. In literature, there is neither space for *taasub* nor for *hasad*. We preach *insaniyat* which is the central message of Islam. We also teach history. At our cultural events, we especially try to target the youth aged 15–26 and talk about events such as the *jang-e-azadi* [Gilgit war of independence] that are absent from their history textbooks. We try to give the region's youth of a sense of local history and culture because they do not get it from schools.

FIGURE 4.2 Poetry festival held at the Karakoram International University, Gilgit, 2006
Source: Author.

There is thus a 'crisis of *insaaniyat*' that Bazm and other organizations seek to address through a literary vision for change.[48] Cultural activists in Gilgit-Baltistan link this crisis particularly to school-based education, which is deemed to promote both majoritarian thinking as I highlighted in the previous chapter, as well as a *taasub*-filled sectarian imaginary which I elaborated in this chapter.[49] However, while literary interventions provide an important antidote, they alone cannot counter the vicious pervasiveness of sectarianism; institutionalized sectarianism itself needs to be rooted out for the sustenance of religious harmony in Gilgit-Baltistan.

CONCLUSION

In this chapter, I have attempted to explore Shia–Sunni sectarianism in Gilgit in its routine enactment and negotiation, in relation to the sectarian imaginaries that structure thought and action, and in terms of emotional experiences of *taasub* instead of those of militant violence. At the same time, I have demonstrated that everyday inter-sect relations in Gilgit continue to entail the realities of a shared cultural ethos, progressive politics, and conscious initiatives for promoting religious pluralism. That people are critically aware of a more harmonious past, recognize the divisive role of the state in creating a tense present and mobilize to work towards a peaceful and egalitarian future offers a source of hope amidst grim realities.

The role of Gilgit-Baltistani poets is particularly significant in this context, and demonstrates a continuity with long-standing poetic traditions of South Asia in which poetry has served as a means of knowledge, ethical reflection, and change. Pakistan is an unfinished project for these poetic social reformers, and they are trying to build more humane communities out of the resources that they have mined.

At the KIU *mushaira* that I discussed earlier, the main banner (Figure 4.2) carried a line from the renowned progressive Pakistani poet Faiz Ahmed Faiz:

> *Hum parwarish-e-lauh-o-qalam karte rahein ge*
> We will continue to nurture the tablet and the pen

Through their verses of interrogation, mockery, and pedagogy, the Halqa poets in Gilgit are thus nurturing their tablets and their pens, and in this process, the very soul of society. In the next chapter, I examine how villagers in Gilgit-Baltistan are likewise engaged in a moral–intellectual struggle of a different order—a struggle for an ecological vision for change that contests institutionalized logics of development and environmentalism.

NOTES

1   Taylor (2007: 29); italics in original.
2   Zaman (1998), Nasr (2000), and Jaffrelot (2002).

3   Gottschalk (2000) for an illuminating discussion of the work of 'multiple identities' in defining everyday inter-community interaction in South Asia.
4   In my discussion of the sectarian imaginary, I am reusing material from a previous article which was published in Current Sociology; See Ali (2010b). My discussion of poetic publics draws upon 'Poetry, Power, Protest: Reimagining Muslim Nationhood in Northern Pakistan' which was originally published in Comparative Studies of South Asia, Africa, and the Middle East, Vol. 32: 1, pp. 13–24. Copyright, 2012, Comparative Studies of South Asia, Africa and the Middle East. All rights reserved. Used by permission of the publisher, Duke University Press.
5   For example, Taylor and Dyke (2004).
6   For an insightful analysis of performative publics, see Wedeen (2008). See also Chuengsatiansup (2001).
7   Pardesi is an Urdu word for 'foreigner' and Javed was termed as one since he is originally from Baltistan, not Gilgit. Mazhabi is an Urdu word for 'religious'; mazhabi type is a hybrid Urdu–English word that denotes a person with a strong religious disposition.
8   Delving further into this incident, I discovered that Javed did not know Kamran from before, and there was no prior case of bitterness between them. They both knew about each other's sectarian affiliation from their respective place of origin, as places in Gilgit-Baltistan tend to be religiously homogenous; hence, it is normal to conclude that a Balti student is Shia and a Chilasi one is Sunni.
9   Das (2007).
10 Cohn (1987).
11 Verdery (1994: 46).
12 Drawing from prominent political, religious, and civil society members from both the Shia and Sunni sects, the Grand Aman Jirga was a large coalition established to resolve the heightened atmosphere of sectarian hostility which emerged in the wake of the textbook controversy in Gilgit.
13 Taylor (2004: 23).
14 This homogenizing narrative of secular modernity has been critiqued, amongst others, by Ashis Nandy (1988) and Talal Asad (2003).
15 Sayer (1994: 374).
16 Freitag (1989).
17 For a detailed examination of the development of indigenous polo traditions in Chitral and Gilgit-Baltistan, see Parkes (1996).
18 A caste group of musicians in Gilgit, placed and imagined as low in the social hierarchy.
19 Ghulamuddin (2001).
20 For critical reflections on the work of the AKDN in Gilgit-Baltistan, see especially Nyborg and Ali (2005) and Hussain (2012).
21 Ferguson (1990) and Gaynor (2010).
22 These were the parties active in 2007 when I was engaged in field research.
23 Ramanujan (1991).

24 Caton (1990).
25 Miller (2007).
26 Wedeen (2008) and Campbell (2009).
27 Anderson (1991).
28 Dabashi (2012).
29 Naim (1989).
30 Marsden (2005).
31 Meeker (1976).
32 Patel (2002) and Dadi (2010).
33 I have replaced the poets' actual names with pseudonyms to protect their identity.
34 'Dogras' refers to the Hindu dynasty that ruled the princely state of Jammu and Kashmir before the 1947 partition of the Indian sub-continent.
35 Rai (2004) and Peer (2010).
36 For a compelling and pioneering analysis of moral sentiments in expressive traditions in South Asia, see Raheja and Gold (1994).
37 I am grateful to Ali Husain Mir for this insight.
38 When I interviewed him, the poet clarified to me that 'enemies of the nation' here primarily refers to the bigoted mullahs (clerics) which may be found in both the Sunni and Shia sects.
39 *Muharram* is a holy month in the Islamic calendar, in which the Prophet's grandson, Hussain, was martyred. *Dargah* refers to the shrine of a revered Muslim saint. For prominent anthropological studies of Muslim piety and reform, see Hirschkind (2001) and Mahmood (2004).
40 See Marsden (2005) for an illuminating exploration of how Islamization is contested in the Chitral area of north-western Pakistan.
41 Kershaw (1992) and Bauman and Babcock (1978: 45).
42 Halqa-e-Arbab-e-Zauq (2000).
43 *Karbala* refers to the battle which took place in 680 AD in the city of Karbala in Iraq, in which the Prophet's grandson and the third Shia Imam, Hussain, was brutally murdered along with his followers.
44 The *shaheen* or eagle is a metaphor for the self-confident, engaged, and socially conscious Muslim in Mohammad Iqbal's poetry. It is a popular reference in Gilgiti poetry as well.
45 'For everyone' here emphasizes that Hussain is not just a revered religious figure for Shias, but for all Muslims. Hussain has a special significance for Shia Muslims as he is their third Imam, and the yearly commemoration of his martyrdom is a key aspect of Shia identity and devotion.
46 Amin (2002).
47 The position of the chief secretary is the highest post in the bureaucratic set-up of Gilgit-Baltistan.
48 Saikia (2010).
49 Such problems of schooling are also recognized and countered elsewhere in Gilgit-Baltistan. For example, in upper Hunza, the Gojal Educational and Cultural

Association (GECA) has long been active in preserving Wakhi cultural identity which is absent from the disconnected, urban-biased school curricula that is taught in both public and private schools. In collaboration with Lok Virsa, GECA also plans to establish folklore societies in three Gojali schools in order to foster a sense of self-awareness and pride amongst Wakhi youth (*Pamir Times Report*, 2009).

PART III

Saving Nature, Saving People

5

THE NATURE OF DEVELOPMENT

༄༅

Neoliberal Environments and Pastoral Visions

As indicated in the introduction, the ecological terrain of struggle is often overlooked in studies of Pakistan as well as of Kashmir, focused as they often are on issues of religion, militarism, and politics. My own work in this book has so far tended to revolve around these topics, albeit highlighting—I hope—some very different representational and ethnographic dynamics emphasizing the political economy and cultural production of feelings, and a particular emphasis on faith-based and poetic struggles. By shifting my attention now to political ecology and international development, I wish to further my analysis of the impact of transnational politics in Gilgit-Baltistan and continue highlighting less-understood struggles that shape life in 'conflict zones'. This is significant not only in and of itself—to understand more deeply the conditions of subjection and change—but also to unsettle hegemonic expectations which prescribe that the 'other' be seen through flattened and familiar narratives. Hence, by broadening our view on society and politics in Pakistan and Kashmir, I hope to unsettle the perniciously rigid understandings of the 'social' that often dominate the study of these contexts.

In this vein, this chapter examines nature, land, and livelihood as terrains of state-making and struggle in Gilgit-Baltistan. As demonstrated in Chapter 1, landscape representations of regional spaces such as Gilgit-Baltistan are integral to realizing the nation-state as they have come to signify the eco-body of the nation—its physio-ecological essence and epitome. I now examine how transnational conservation projects service this process of ecological state-making by actualizing the eco-body on the ground, and producing the region of Gilgit-Baltistan as a manufactured space of nature. Gilgit-Baltistan has thus become a site both for nationalist valorizations of its 'natural beauty', as well as international desires for rendering it a pristine natural area.

Over the last 30 years, almost 40 per cent of the territory of Gilgit-Baltistan has been converted into government-owned protected areas, in the form of national parks, wildlife sanctuaries, game reserves, and hunting areas. Indeed, it is not unusual to hear that state authorities wish to transform the biodiversity-rich Gilgit-Baltistan into a 'living museum' for wildlife. This vision has been critically supported and shaped by international conservation NGOs, particularly the International Union for Conservation of Nature (IUCN) and the World Wide Fund for Nature (WWF), both of which have a major presence in the region. Such a vision, however, has generated complex conflicts and contestations in lived practice. To illuminate, I examine here the very first experiment embracing this vision—the Khunjerab National Park (KNP) founded in 1975—as well as more recent community-based conservation projects of international trophy hunting that have become popular in Gilgit-Baltistan. My focus is on three key concerns: the ideals and ideologies that underpin the projects of biodiversity conservation; the ways in which these projects reconfigure the place of nature as well as the state in the region; and, most importantly, how and why these projects are resisted by the subjects of conservation—the pastoralist villagers of Shimshal whose land provides the very ground on which conservation projects are imagined and executed. The purpose of my inquiry is not to dismiss the necessity of ecological preservation. Rather, I wish to examine the compassionate emotion of *saving nature*, and inquire whether this compassion is the 'apex of affective agency'[1] or has it been used to authorize and mask particular Western notions of conservation that have become dominant in global development practice and in Gilgit-Baltistan.

I argue that national parks and community-based conservation projects such as trophy hunting are deeply problematic, as they are contingent on relinquishing the very land and livelihood on which pastoral communities are founded. Such projects often assume that practices of local societies are the key threats to nature, instead of appreciating that nature is embedded in social relations and cannot be protected without recognizing indigenous values, rights, and ownership. Further, conservation projects such as trophy hunting have introduced a market calculus in the management of nature, by commodifying it for elite, mostly Western tourists. These projects are framed as initiatives for 'sustainable development', but in effect have served to entrench the power of the state and capital over local ecologies and communities. Faced with displacement and distress as a result of conservation projects, villagers of Shimshal in Gilgit-Baltistan have responded with courage and creativity, and hitherto managed to protect their homes and pastures from being taken away in the name of global conservation. They have done this by creating a Shimshal Nature Trust (SNT), which has established indigenous ownership and management of Shimshali ancestral land to counter its appropriation by the Khunjerab National Park. A biodiversity hotspot, owned and managed entirely by a local community, has long been considered unthinkable in global conservation practice, which mandates that the territory be owned by state authorities and managed primarily by national and international conservation agencies. The villagers of Shimshal have hence challenged the fundamental logic of international conservation.

While the Shimshalis have struggled against the KNP in order to protect their land and livelihood, I argue that their struggle is especially significant for it contests the epistemic exclusion of pastoral visions from the very definition of development. It challenges the dominant meanings of nature and conservation in global environmental practice, questions whose knowledge counts as expertise, and contests the very process through which 'global' development ideals and projects are framed. By creating a Shimshal Nature Trust that proposes indigenous *ownership* of local land and ecology—as opposed to a national park or revenue-sharing conservation schemes—Shimshalis are fighting for 'ecological sovereignty' instead of 'community participation'. They are engaging in what Jean Franco has called a 'struggle for interpretive power' (1989), which involves new, modified, or adopted repertoires of representation through which marginalized communities carve a space of manoeuvre within dominant paradigms.[2] This is simultaneously an intimate, cultural struggle. Pastoral visions are subjected to such structural indignity and inequality in the rhetoric of conservation today that just asserting the right to be, is an experience of deep anguish and negative astonishment, as reflected in the ethnographic narrative in this chapter. Shimshalis have had to strategically represent and position themselves in relation to conservation, in order to claim voice and value, and simply, to survive. It is precisely through a language of ecological intimacy, history, and expertise, that they are able to assert their political sovereignty over their ancestral land. Simultaneously, they have managed to puncture the epistemic privilege through which states and international institutions construct particular visions of the world as natural, and particular interests as the right, universal, and inevitable path of 'development'.

FROM NATURAL AREAS TO NEOLIBERAL RESOURCES

To understand the dilemmas that national parks pose for Shimshali villagers in Gilgit-Baltistan, it is important to understand the origins of parks, protected areas, and wilderness spaces. The idea of a 'natural protected area' such as a national park for conservation emerged from an ahistorical Western construction of nature, in which nature was viewed as a pristine, peopleless wilderness instead of a lived social landscape.[3] Inspired by Enlightenment and Romantic values, this imagined wilderness had to be created, scientifically managed, preserved, and toured—primarily by urbanites for their own use and luxury. Such valuations of nature emerged in the context of an ongoing unfolding of liberal capitalist modernity, which produced the 'natural' and the 'social' as separate and distinct realms of existence. The mutual constitution of society and nature had to be discursively and materially disengaged, so that both labour and landscape could be freed up for what Marx called 'primitive accumulation'.[4] Capitalism is thus itself an environmental project that fundamentally operates through the restructuring of society's relation with nature.[5] The social alienation and environmental degradation resulting from early capitalist development was partly the reason behind the conservationist impulse to find and preserve 'untouched' and 'endangered' nature—untouched by, and endangered from capital.

Recent conditions of neoliberal capitalism have further transformed the nature–society relation. 'Neoliberal' here refers to political, economic, and cultural practices that promote the rule of the market, implementing policies such as government deregulation and trade liberalization that maximize corporate profit under the language of efficiency and consumer choice.[6] In the realm of human–environment relations, neoliberalism refers to the transformation of nature from a factor of production external to capital, into a commodity that itself must be bought and sold according to the dictates of capital.[7] In practice, this commodification of nature has been achieved through the institutionalization of tradeable pollution permits, transferable fishing quotas, intellectual property rights over crop varieties, the privatization of public utilities, and other market-based mechanisms for managing nature. Far from the claims of 'efficient' and 'sustainable' use, these practices in effect deepen the exploitation of natural resources and heighten the inequities characterizing their access. Countries in the global south and particularly their indigenous communities who depend directly on natural resources, tend to lose out the most as their rights and use values are delegitimized to make way for the interests and exchange values of global elites.

In the specific arena of biodiversity conservation, neoliberal values have steadily become dominant over the last 40 years. In the 1970s, the protected area model and its conception of nature as divorced from society began to come under severe criticism for being exclusionary and ineffective, both from within the conservation community as well as from rural communities, whose rights were being superseded by the imperatives of biodiversity preservation. By the early 90s, a series of conferences such as the 1982 and 1992 World Congress on National Parks and Protected Areas (WCNPPA) as well as the 1992 Earth Summit in Rio de Janeiro, had decisively transformed the discourse on biodiversity conservation against the 'island mentality' that had hitherto guided the management of protected areas.[8] The aim now was not strict preservation, but rather conservation combined with 'sustainable development'. International conservation organizations such as the Conservation International, WWF, and IUCN subsequently set about investigating how the goals of conservation could be achieved while simultaneously ensuring 'community participation' and 'benefit-sharing'.

Part of the answer that they came up with was decidedly neoliberal: the use of protected areas for the promotion of commercialized ventures, such as ecotourism, trophy hunting, and bioprospecting, which would commodify nature to serve mostly Western consumers, but also give local communities a share in the resulting revenue. This commodification of nature is presented as 'conservation', employing the circular logic of selling nature in order to save it, and saving nature in order to sell it.[9] It is also presented as a form of 'community-based conservation' for 'sustainable development', while simultaneously perpetuating a protected area model of conservation that is fundamentally anti-community: protected areas mostly convert commonly owned pastoral and agricultural land into state-owned territory, in which subsistence-based uses of nature such as grazing and farming are severely curtailed. Frequently, indigenous communities are altogether evicted from their lands in order to create the imagined 'natural' landscape, leading to an alarming number of 'conservation refugees' around the world.[10] Through such logics of protected areas as well as their neoliberal uses, global biodiversity conservation has opened up a new frontier for the appropriation of local space by capital and state, thus embodying a form of 'accumulation by dispossession'.[11] However, it entails the nationalization of community land instead of its privatization as Harvey posits.

The accomplishment of this neoliberal conservation depends critically on the rhetoric of sustainable development and community-based conservation in which it is cloaked. This rhetoric helps to neutralize critique because it seemingly addresses concerns of both ecological damage and social inequality, while simultaneously rendering nature and communities more available to capital. Such incorporations of environmental agendas into neoliberal regimes have arguably done more to sustain neoliberal capitalism than their outright dismissal.[12] The discourse of community-based conservation has also helped to re-legitimize the protected area model, leading to a vigorous expansion of protected areas particularly in the developing world. Between 1986 and 1996, there was a 60 per cent increase in the number of natural protected areas in Asia, Africa, the Middle East, and Latin America.[13] The justification for this increase comes not only from conservation practitioners, who emphasize the role of conservation in the development of the community, but also from experts in the fields of biology, ecology, and environmental studies who draw upon the legitimizing power of science and economics to authorize protected areas as the most effective tools for saving biodiversity. The actual formation of protected areas as well as their neoliberal projects is propagated and implemented by international conservation organizations, as well as by funding mechanisms such as the Global Environment Facility (GEF), which is in turn implemented by other multilateral institutions like the World Bank and the United Nations Environment Programme (UNEP).

While critiques of neoliberalism often target the policies promoted by organizations such as the World Bank and IMF, those of conservation organizations have only recently come to be recognized as linked to the realization of a neoliberal agenda.[14] This is partly due to the ways in which the aim of conserving biodiversity has become naturalized as a common sense feeling and ideal—an abstract, global desire, to be aspired towards by everyone for the sake of the earth as well as for future generations. Certainly, attention to the sustainability of the natural world and equitable access to it is of ultimate significance, and is made possible precisely by a language of environmental conservation that counters the ecologically and socially destructive consumerism of capitalist modernity. However, what this common sense environmental sentiment – ethic has come to embody in actual conservation practice deserves critical study, as the latter constitutes one of the modes through which rural livelihoods around the globe are being superseded by agendas of neoliberalism.[15]

THE CONTEXT OF THE KHUNJERAB NATIONAL PARK

During the colonial era, naturally endowed places such as the regions that today form Gilgit-Baltistan, were of special significance as the control and conservation of nature was directly tied to the political, economic, and cultural imperatives of the empire.[16] Colonial bureaucracies of forest conservation in South Asia helped to secure timber resources for commercial exploitation, and enabled the management of indigenous populations.[17] Numerous parks as well as game reserves were created in Asian and African colonies for the hunting privilege of ruling elites, as well as to service strategic needs.[18] Indeed, the first forest regulations in present-day Gilgit-Baltistan were instituted to meet the fuelwood requirements of the Kashmiri troops stationed at Gilgit.[19] However, as a consequence of the geographical inaccessibility and perceived political sensitivity of the areas that today form Gilgit-Baltistan, the British administration could not establish an extensive regime of forest and wildlife management in the way it had set up in other parts of the Indian subcontinent.

After the 1947 partition of the subcontinent, the Pakistan state gradually began a process of territorialiszation that sought to incorporate the northern frontier region firmly into its circumference of authority. It was during 1972–1974 that—aided by community struggles against the local Rajas—the state was able to abolish the princely states of Hunza and Nagar as well as the regimes of other 'little kings', and create a single, directly ruled administrative division called the 'Northern Areas'. Barely a year later, in 1975, the Northern Areas Wildlife Preservation Act was passed under which the Northern Areas administration could declare any area in its domain as a national park, wildlife reserve, or wildlife sanctuary, and alter the boundaries of such areas as deemed necessary. Through a government notification in the same year, the Khunjerab National Park was subsequently established by the then Prime Minister, Zulfiqar Ali Bhutto, as the first national park in Gilgit-Baltistan.

The KNP covers an area of 2,270 square Kilometres, and comprises the grasslands of the Khunjerab, Ghujerab, and Shimshal valleys in the upper Hunza region of Gilgit-Baltistan. During the time of princely and colonial rule, the village communities who inhabited this area enjoyed grazing rights on its pastures and paid livestock and livestock products as tax to the Mir of Hunza.[20] Some pastures like that of Shimshal had been bought from the Mir and were directly owned by the local agro-pastoral communities. After the abolition of the Hunza state in 1974, other local communities also assumed complete ownership of the lands formerly controlled by the Mir.

The official rationale for the KNP was the protection of the endangered Marco Polo sheep, as well as the preservation of other Asian wildlife species such as the snow leopard, blue sheep, and Himalayan ibex. The park was recommended and delineated by the famous American field zoologist George B. Schaller, who was affiliated with the Wildlife Conservation Society and visited Pakistan several times between 1970 and 1975. It was designated as a Category II park; according to the guidelines provided by IUCN, this meant that human activity such as grazing and hunting would be banned and visitors would be allowed only for 'inspirational, educational, cultural, and recreational purposes at a level which will maintain the area in a natural or near natural state'.[21]

The proposal to create the park was inviting for the Pakistani government as it served to bolster a sense of nation-pride linked to the protection and conservation of the country's natural resources. This was particularly significant in the context of the Bhutto government, which had been implementing an agenda of nationalization in the rest of the country. The government also hoped that the KNP would become Pakistan's first national park to be recognized as a World Heritage Site under UNESCO's World Heritage Convention. In this way, the nation could achieve glory not only within its own boundaries, but also within the global community of nations. The fact that initiatives of national conservation were being undertaken in neighbouring India provided an added impetus.

The creation of the KNP can be seen as a form of 'ecological nationalism'—a useful concept by Cederlof and Sivaramakrishnan (2006) that captures how metropolitan-secular practices of nature devotion such as the establishment of national parks serve to legitimize and consolidate the nation. However, I would argue that their theorization of the connections between nature and the nation is limited due to its lack of attention to the state. The appropriation of nature by the nation-state is not just about the struggle to define the nation in terms of landscape, and to channel this landscape in the service of national development. It is also fundamentally about reordering space and its use to accomplish the territorial sovereignty of the modern state.[22] In many parts of Africa, for example, the creation of an 'artefactual wilderness' through protected areas has been central to the process of colonial and postcolonial state-making, as it strengthens the state's proprietary claims on land by facilitating the enclosure of existing commons.[23]

Likewise, the establishment of the Khunjerab National Park in Gilgit-Baltistan was more than just an expression of ecological nationalism. It embodied a process of ecological state-making, as it helped to affirm and expand the Pakistan state's territorial control in Gilgit-Baltistan. Amongst the communities that came under the sphere of the park, it is still commonly believed that the creation of this park right at the Pakistan–China border was at least partly a move to territorialize this disputed border area by declaring it a natural 'protected area'. After all, the former princely state of Hunza had strong ties with China, and the Chinese government had already established a claim to a part of Gilgit-Baltistan called the Trans-Karakoram Tract.[24] It is also significant that the KNP was formed barely a year after the region was actively reconstructed through a process of renaming the territory, redrawing its administrative boundaries, and radically reconfiguring local systems of authority. The reshaping of landscape through the formation of national parks—intentionally or not—feeds into such modes of spatial regulation that are not only effective in but also constitutive of state rule. Further, practices of ecological state-making in Gilgit-Baltistan have intensified in recent years with the aid of new neoliberal projects of biodiversity conservation, as I discuss later in the chapter.

CONTESTING CONSERVATION

Shimshal is located at the north-eastern periphery of Gilgit-Baltistan, along the border of Pakistan and China. It comprises about 2,700 square Kilomatres of high altitude land in the Central Karakoram region, and is exclusively[25] controlled by an agro-pastoral community of approximately 1,700 people— all adherents of the Ismaili sect of Islam. Within this area, Shimshalis maintain several village settlements, enough irrigated land to fulfill their food requirements, and over a dozen communal pastures for seasonal herding of their sizeable livestock population. While all the other villages that were going to be affected by the Khunjerab National Park eventually accepted the park's authority, the villagers of Shimshal still refuse to cede ownership of their land. This has been a major impediment in the implementation of the KNP, as two-thirds of the park is comprised of Shimshali territory.

Shimshalis offer a number of reasons to explain why they have been resisting the conversion of their territory into a national park. To begin with, people in Shimshal argue that the KNP was created without any consultation with the affected communities regarding its boundaries, regulations, or management. They were simply informed that most of their pastures and even some of their village settlements were now part of a state-owned national park. More importantly, the community of Shimshal serves to lose the most from the park due to its exceptionally high dependence on livestock herding as a source of livelihood. In 1995, Shimshalis owned a total of 4,473 goats, 2,547 sheep, 960 yaks, 399 cows, and 32 donkeys, and they continue to have the largest livestock holdings in the Hunza region.[26] An enforcement of park regulations would

FIGURE 5.1 A village settlement in central Shimshal
Source: Author.

entail a complete ban on grazing and hunting in most Shimshali pastures, so that wildlife species and their habitats can be preserved. This would directly threaten Shimshali livelihoods not only because of the loss of pastures, but also due to the prohibition on hunting certain wildlife predators of livestock such as the snow leopard. As Shimshali villagers commented to me:

> We are supposed to protect the snow leopard, even though it eats up our goats and sheep and causes a huge economic loss for us. Who will compensate us for this loss? We have to pay the price for conservation.

And

First our rights should be honoured, then those of wildlife.

These statements embody a complex challenge to the modernist, universalizing agenda of biodiversity conservation that privileges the protection of wildlife for the 'future of the earth' over the protection of pastoral livelihoods and futures. For Shimshalis, conservation—as promoted by international conservation organizations—is not of inherent local value because it entails an appropriation of their territory, and because one of the rare species that needs to be protected is a deadly predator of livestock. Yet they have to respect the tenets of global conservation because of the consequences that challenging this global value—through local hunting, for example—might entail in a context where it is already threatening them with displacement. Precisely to prevent this displacement by the Khunjerab National Park, Shimshalis have themselves had to appropriate the discourse of conservation through practices such as a self-imposed ban on wildlife hunting. As I was told in a collective meeting in 2006:

> We believe in conservation. That's why we imposed a ban on wildlife hunting ourselves 10 years ago. In other places, if a snow leopard eats up livestock, it tends to get hunted down in a retaliatory killing so that the helpless shepherd can recover his loss by selling the leopard's pelt.

Hence, because of the unequal power relations embedded in global conservation regimes, indigenous communities around the world have had to re-present themselves as environmentally responsible subjects to ensure their survival.[27] A claim to traditional property rights and livelihood dependency has thus increasingly become insufficient for preventing the appropriation of indigenous rights. Though Shimshalis fulfill the responsibilities that modern conservation expects of them, they remain deeply critical of its logic and the unhealthy attitudes towards nature from which it stems.

The Shimshali understanding of nature is encapsulated in the notion of *qudrat*—a term that is common across South Asia. The spiritualism inherent in the term, however, is not captured by English words like 'nature' and 'environment'. Explaining the difference between *qudrat* and modern conservation, a Shimshali development worker Rahim Ali said to me:

> *Qudrat* is God's *rehmat* [blessing], therefore people's relationship with nature is one of respect and thankfulness. We celebrate many festivals thanking God and nature. But one also has to work hard in order to benefit from God's blessings. To get from nature, you have to give to it, and be respectful and thankful. So, there is no need for conservation in *qudrat* because it has an inbuilt mechanism of conservation. But [modern] conservation comes once something is in danger of disappearing or finishing. Things finish when you only get and use, but don't give back.

Such feelings of respect and gratitude towards the divinity of nature are essential to indigenous civilizations around the world, where people know well that they belong to the earth and not the other way around. As Rahim gestures as well, these feelings stand in contrast with the emotion of *saving* that dominates the discourse of environmental conservation, pointing to ontologically different *ways of seeing and caring* for the natural world. Indeed, villagers in Shimshal challenge even this construction of the 'natural world', which entails the dominant tendency of viewing 'nature' as a magically self-existing entity that exists apart from human existence and 'culture', instead of one that is historically produced and fundamentally linked to human labour. For example, some villagers in Shimshal said to me in a simultaneously anguished and assertive tone:

> My ancestors planted the trees in Shimshal. How can someone come and tell me that these trees do not belong to me?

And

> The markhor is alive because of us!

In other words, if Shimshal is a global biodiversity habitat and wildlife species have not disappeared here as in many other parts, surely the Shimshali pastoralists' way of seeing and being needs to be acknowledged as leading to an already harmonious context. These statements can also be read as claims to a nativist form of ecological nationalism, in which the right to place is asserted through a discourse of lived landscape, nature intimacy, and stewardship.[28] To support their assertion of local sovereignty based on a historically grounded, indigenous conservation, Shimshali activists further point out the incompetence of the state and international organizations in conserving nature:

> We have inhabited and tended this difficult terrain for centuries. What does the DFO[29] or the consultant know about conservation? A while back, a park official came and told us that we need to sign an MoU and give up the rights to our territory for the KNP so that wildlife habitats can be protected. I told him, 'Come, I will show you the area where we have protected wildlife.' And he responded, 'I don't think I can trek that far.' Then I politely asked him, 'If you cannot walk to the area, how will you ever conserve it?'

> In areas where the KNP has been implemented, hunting by state officials has become more common and convenient. This is why the wildlife populations have decreased in these areas. And now the government is putting more pressure on us to accept the park so that wildlife in our areas can be exploited. International organizations also want to put pressure on us, because they have killed nature in their own areas.[30]

Such statements assert a local aptitude for conservation that is presented as superior to that of state institutions and international organizations, while challenging the common portrayal of Shimshalis as incapable stewards of nature.[31, 32] This is significant, as the discourse of the state and conservation NGOs in Gilgit-Baltistan is centred precisely on problematizing the 'lack of local capacity' in attaining conservation goals which in turn helps to justify an international organization's own role in creating, planning, and managing state-owned landscape zones.

The role of language is integral to the power of the modern conservation regime, and the delegitimization of the local that it has come to normalize. For example, 'biodiversity' has come to be constructed as a *national* and *global* preserve that needs to be protected mostly from local 'threats' such as 'unsustainable grazing practices'.[33] The very definition of biodiversity thus undermines local subsistence on nature, while sanctioning the role of the nation-state and global organizations on local places. The language of 'managing landscapes' that is endemic to conservation discourse is also problematic as it turns nature into a technical problem that needs expert supervision. This language stems from the Western nature/culture dualism, which is the central prism through which the rest of the world is understood and redesigned. For rural and indigenous citizens, this divide is artificial and nature is not seen as a 'landscape' that needs to be managed or a 'resource' to be used. In Gilgit-Baltistan conservation circles, moreover, I often heard that not only landscapes but also the 'people who live inside protected areas' needed to be managed. This manner of speaking takes for granted that people live inside protected areas, instead of recognizing that protected areas are imposed on the way people are living. Shimshali villagers further argued incisively that traditional practices of communal nature organization are co-opted by international conservation organizations, given fancy labels such as 'multiple use landscapes', 'zoning', and 'eco-agriculture', and then turned into 'new' discourses of management that carve a space for continuing intervention by these organizations. As I discovered in Gilgit-Baltistan, academic knowledge may likewise become co-opted in order to manage and dominate the authority of the locals. While discussing whether Shimshal is truly ecologically responsible or not, Shawna Stefan, a visiting consultant at a prominent international conservation organization in Gilgit, told me that the Shimshali community cannot be trusted with conservation because 'local communities are not homogenous' and 'interest groups within a community can monopolize relations with outsiders to assert their authority'. A rich body of academic research in political ecology has made precisely this argument, as a *critique* of the international conservation regime's instrumental uses of local communities.[34] It was thus striking to see that academic insights about social fissures were being used to *justify* the international conservation regime and to undermine local resistance to it.

The tendency to undervalue the role of local communities in sustaining nature is indeed a constitutive feature of global conservation discourse. It is assumed that the Third World inhabitants lack the values and sentiments of concern and care that are supposedly the preserve only of Western elites.[35] The nature–society relation in communities across continents has thus come to be described through 'degradation narratives' that perpetuate the stereotype of an essentialized, irresponsible native—often without the support of any scientific analysis—as they help to justify national and international interventions for protecting the 'global commons' from its local users.[36] These narratives emerged from, and was built upon a long-standing colonial discourse that helped to legitimize the appropriation of nature for varied interests including commercial exploitation, hunting pleasure, and strategic needs.[37] Today, they continue to thrive in conservation discourse, despite the rhetoric of including and valorizing the 'local community'. Indeed, as I will elaborate later, the rhetoric of community participation not only serves to obscure but also helps to achieve the exclusionary narrative of national and international conservation.

REPRESENTATION AND POWER: THE CASE OF THE SHIMSHAL NATURE TRUST

Until the mid-90s, Shimshali villagers obstructed the implementation of the KNP through informal resistances such as the disruption of information-gathering mechanisms, refusal to follow administrative regulations, and the blocking of government and NGO officials from entering the community.[38] However, the pressures on them to submit to park authorities kept increasing, as new programmes and funds for conservation poured into Gilgit-Baltistan in the wake of a renewed global, and subsequently, national concern for biodiversity preservation. In this context, the confrontational stance of Shimshalis that emphasized a complete rejection of the park was proving to be counterproductive, and served only to reinforce the stereotype of Shimshal as a backward and 'wild' community. Realizing this, a group of men belonging mostly to Shimshal's first generation English-educated elite—and often employed in development NGOs based in Gilgit or Islamabad—began to rally community members around a politics of appeasement and engagement.[39] They strongly felt—and feared—that a small, marginal, border community like Shimshal could eventually suffer repressive state action unless it was able to counter its negative image, and negotiate cordially with conservation organizations. As one of them said to me: they had to 'fight with dialogue'.

After much deliberation, they came up with an answer: a community-based organization called the Shimshal Nature Trust (SNT) that would manage and showcase Shimshal's conservation efforts, and represent the community in dealings with external organizations.

The SNT was founded in 1997, and one of its first moves to protect the commonly held Shimshali land from being declared a national park was to legally establish it as *waqf*—property devoted to religious or charitable projects that is held in trust, and considered inalienable under Islamic law.[40] The key purpose of the SNT was to formally articulate, and give material force to the representational claims discussed in the previous section—claims to livelihood dependency, native authenticity and ownership, environmental responsibility, and a place-based conservation capability. As the 'Fifteen Year Vision and Management Plan' of the SNT explains:

> Our largest challenge is not to develop a system of utilizing the natural surroundings sustainably, but rather to express our indigenous stewardship practices in language that will garner the financial, technical and political support of the international community, and that will persuade Pakistani authorities that we are indeed capable of protecting our own natural surroundings.[41]

The SNT 'management plan' is precisely a response to this representational challenge: how to counter the language, and hence, the power of a global conservation discourse that refuses to acknowledge indigenous values and rights. The plan describes the socio-economic context of the Shimshal, the ways in which its inhabitants have historically practiced a conservation ethic, and the community-initiated programmes through which they envision natural resource management in the future.[42] Following the tropes of developmentalist writing, these programmes are divided into implementation phases, with various activities planned for each phase. The SNT management plan has been distributed to all the major government and non-governmental organizations working on conservation and development in Gilgit-Baltistan, and is also accessible through the Internet. Between 1999–2002, SNT members also conducted a series of 'workshops' in Gilgit with different 'stakeholders' to create awareness and legitimacy for their approach towards conservation.

The very language, format, and content of SNT practices reflect how communities have come to understand, and reconfigure the nature of the power exercised by international conservation organizations. The global discourse of 'community-based conservation' and 'sustainable development' is appropriated by positing Shimshalis as the original and most suitable conservationists, who are equipped to ensure the sustainable future that international conservation NGOs are striving towards. Moreover, the 'participatory' approach adopted by NGOs in recent years—in part a response to the failure of and resistance to earlier development projects—is reconstituted to argue that effective participation must entail *ownership*. As the management plan explains:

> While we appreciate recent efforts by external agencies to develop community-based nature conservation projects …. it is not enough that external initiatives be managed locally; rather, a culturally and contextually-sensitive nature stewardship programme should be developed and initiated, as well as managed, from within the community.[43]

The existence and legitimacy of such a community-centered programme is then established by describing how indigenous ways of environmental management have historically been based on ecologically sound practices such as land-use zoning, as well as on culturally specific values such as the 'Islamic religious ethic of nature stewardship' in which nature is respected as 'God's ultimate creation'.[44] The emphasis on such a 'moral ecology'[45] grounded in faith has an important discursive effect—it provides a way to unsettle the scientific authority of international conservation agencies, by highlighting how interpreting nature and its conservation through ethical values is more locally appropriate and significant than one based on scientific principles.[46] Indeed, local meanings of nature are inseparable from religious sensibilities and cultural practices. The terrain of wildlife such as snow leopards is itself imagined as a sacred space where mountain spirits reign supreme, and need to be appeased for protection. Long-standing religious and cultural institutions have also enabled Shimshalis to collectively organize for conservation efforts ranging from hunting control to pasture management. The SNT itself is managed partly by local volunteer corps and boy scouts, who are affiliated with the *jamat khana* (religious centre) in Ismaili-Muslim practice.

Despite the existence of a cooperative social and institutional structure, however, Shimshal neither constitutes a homogenous community nor an autonomous zone of resistance. Defining a stance towards conservation agencies and establishing the SNT were contentious processes that community members have had to negotiate with much difficulty. According to my interviewees, it was the threat they faced from the KNP and the need to unite against it that brought them together. A sense of community was hence both a driver and an outcome of their struggle.

While the key purpose of SNT is a celebration and vindication of an indigenous, ecological sovereignty, it is also important to note that Shimshalis make this claim as contemporary moderns and not as pristine pastoralists. Exposure to foreign tourists, school-based education, and migrant life in Pakistani cities has served to reshape Shimshali aspirations towards a modern lifestyle, but one that does not compromise their homes, their heritage, and their sense of identity. In other words, Shimshali Muslims blend their affection for their rural life-world with a cosmopolitan understanding of self and future.[47] Shimshali youth in particular critically argue that their fight for preserving their land rights should not have to be hinged on an artificial image of Shimshal as a static, ancient culture that is locked in time and place—even as they recognize that such simplistic caricaturing has been imposed on other rural movements, and sadly become a condition for the audibility of their demands. SNT members further emphasize that foreign scholars from universities in Japan, Canada, and the US have played a critical role in shaping local consciousness and enabling community initiatives, and hence the role of external support has been integral to their 'local' success.[48] Finally, the SNT also acknowledges that for activities such as a wildlife census, as well as in monitoring and evaluation, the support of organizations like the WWF and IUCN is especially needed and welcome.

Unfortunately, such collaborations have been difficult to implement. Even if it is now occasionally acknowledged—as the new rhetoric of respecting the 'community' demands—that Shimshalis have responsibly taken care of the environment, it is argued matter-of-factly that their main livelihood practice of livestock grazing poses a fundamental threat to wildlife survival, and hence they cannot be 'trusted' with the task of conservation.

REORIENTING LIVELIHOODS

I will investigate this 'livestock-as-threat' rhetoric in more detail now, as it has been a cornerstone of conservation discourse and practice in Gilgit-Baltistan, particularly in relation to the Khunjerab National Park.[49] Within the state as well as in the NGO discourse, 'illegal' livestock grazing has been constructed as directly destructive of wildlife security and biodiversity, as precious wildlife species have to compete with livestock for grass, and are also susceptible to diseases that are transmitted by livestock. If only we could restrict the grazing of livestock in protected areas, the argument goes, wildlife and their habitats would remain intact. It is precisely because of this logic that grazing activities are banned under a Category II national park such as the KNP.

As highlighted earlier, 'degradation narratives' that blame environmental loss on marginal communities are deeply embedded in global conservation discourse. The specific case of condemning livestock grazing has a long history in the Indian sub-continent, particularly in areas of the western Himalayas where grazing has been held responsible for causing massive soil erosion in the hills and intensified flooding in the plains. As Saberwal (1999) compellingly demonstrates, such an alarmist discourse is neither borne out by empirical evidence nor by ecological theory; rather, it only serves to empower bureaucratic institutions by enabling them to increase the land under their authority.

In the particular context of the KNP in Gilgit-Baltistan, the conviction with which livestock grazing is claimed as a threat to wildlife is likewise unjustified. First, there is no acknowledgment that at least in the territory of Shimshal, most wildlife populations exist above the level of agricultural land as well as of pasture land, and hence the image of wildlife and livestock competing for the same piece of grass is misleading. Even in areas where wildlife and livestock coexist, it needs to be acknowledged that yaks eat different plants than wildlife and hence, not all livestock is 'competing'. Second, neither the park management nor conservation NGOs have conducted long-term scientific studies that systematically investigate the relations between livestock and wildlife populations in and around the park area. Third, state and NGO officials acknowledge that the populations of wildlife such as the Himalayan ibex have enormously increased since the implementation of the KNP. For example, according to a preliminary scientific estimate, the ibex population in the KNP has gone up from 300 in 1975 to almost 6,000 at present. This increase is attributed to the ban on hunting wildlife that was imposed by the KNP and largely obeyed by the local communities. If, as officials often claim, the ban on livestock grazing has not been similarly respected by communities, then it becomes hard to assume that livestock is a potent threat to wildlife since the latter has continued to grow.

Indeed, the enormous growth in some wildlife species has proved to be more of a threat to livestock instead of the other way around. This is due to the decrease in the availability of grass, as well as a higher rate of predation. The massive growth is also not always in the interest of conserving wildlife, according to a number of Shimshali elders. They point out that the Blue sheep in Shimshal has multiplied in thousands since the ban on hunting, but now it is dying of disease as such large numbers cannot be sustained naturally. They claim that a more sustainable balance between livestock and wildlife was traditionally achieved through local hunting, and now this balance is upset. Interestingly, George Schaller—the initiator of the KNP—also acknowledged that the 'scarcity' of certain wildlife species is inherent in the ecology of the region:

> The answer to the scarcity of the ibex lies in the habitat. In this severe environment, this refuge of the ice age, the habitat is simple and fragmented, tiny meadows scattered among barren expanses. The mountains simply cannot support many ibex, nor, therefore, many snow leopard.[50]

This logic is often ignored by conservation professionals and state officials alike, as they tend to use a numeric increase in rare wildlife species as the predominant metric for successful conservation. Instead of at least recognizing that the death of Blue sheep in Shimshal might be linked to the nature of the habitat or flawed interventionist policies, a state official claimed to me that the Blue sheep is dying in Shimshal as a result of catching a disease from livestock, and hence the government must pressure the Shimshalis to accept the KNP and respect its ban on livestock grazing.

In highlighting these contrasting claims about the livestock–wildlife relation, my purpose is not to unquestioningly uphold the local interpretation and demolish that of the state and global conservation agencies. Sure, livestock grazing might in fact threaten the survival of particular kinds of wildlife in particular areas, and what is actually happening in specific contexts can only be ascertained after an in-depth study. What I wish to emphasize, however, is that ecological change is a complex process that is ridden with considerable uncertainty, and that this uncertainty is hardly conceded in the self-assured claims and prescriptions for protected areas.[51] Indeed, this uncertainty has to be eclipsed in order to produce a simplistic, causal logic of livestock-as-threat, which legitimizes the state-NGO claim over nature and undermines that of local communities. It is also ironic—and fundamentally unjust—that pastoral grazing in a Third World rural context should be so denigrated by Western environmentalist discourses, precisely at a time when the replacement of grazing by corn-fed feedlots in the West have come under heavy criticism for being profoundly damaging to nature and humanity alike.[52] The 'livestock-as-threat' discourse is perhaps more applicable to the livestock that are incarcerated in concentrated animal feedlot operations (CAFOs).

What have been the practical consequences of the 'livestock-as-threat' discourse in Gilgit-Baltistan? The ban on grazing in the KNP was marginally enforced till 1989, when the newly formed government organization—the National Council for Conservation of Wildlife (NCCW)—drafted a plan for a stricter enforcement of the Category II criteria. The affected villages nevertheless continued to practice their customary grazing rights, particularly since the government was not forthcoming with the promised compensation. Things came to a head in 1991, when the government used the paramilitary Khunjerab Security Force to evict herdsman from the park's no-grazing zone and even killed some of their livestock. Eventually, in 1992, all the aggrieved communities except Shimshal signed an agreement with the KNP authorities, that allowed them some concessions on their grazing rights as well a share in park-generated revenue in return for accepting the authority of the park.[53]

While the coercively enforced ban on livestock grazing was somewhat relaxed, it soon gave way to a new emphasis on a reduction in livestock holdings. This reduction has in effect become a pre-condition for obtaining the community share in park-generated revenue such as entry fees. In fact, as a state wildlife official informed me, the very point of sharing the park revenue with the community is to enable them to engage in 'conservation activities such as the reduction of their livestock over a period of time'.

In recent years, this new logic of equating community conservation with livestock reduction—which stems from the livestock-as-threat discourse—has meant that park officials have withheld payment of the community share in KNP's entry fees for long periods on account that the concerned communities are not reducing their livestock.[54] Such a claim about livestock holdings has thus become a tool in the hands of KNP officials to deprive communities of their promised share in the park's entry fees.

The push towards a decreased ownership of livestock as well as the claim that this is not happening is either way problematic, given that the number of people involved in animal husbandry in the Hunza region has already declined substantially over the last thirty years.[55] Even in Shimshal—which has always been exceptionally dependent on a pastoral economy—the trend is changing fast. Community members commonly express that livestock holdings have been on the decline. Shimshali women who historically had the sole responsibility of tending livestock in the summer months, have increasingly begun to stay back in the village instead of going to the pastures with their animals.[56] This reduced involvement in pastoral activity is primarily attributed to the demands of education, agriculture, and off-farm employment. Traditionally, older women went to the pastures with their children, and particularly depended on the support of their daughters. Now, girls are busy in their school routines, while their mothers are occupied in taking care of school-going children, in various household and agricultural tasks, and some also in jobs in government or non-governmental organizations.

While people in Shimshal—old and young, men and women—generally consider livestock as a crucial source of income, insurance, and community identity, many simultaneously feel that it is very difficult to continue with animal husbandry in today's world.[57] There are simply very few people *willing* to take care of livestock. Such changing patterns and perceptions of pastoral activity in Shimshal, as elsewhere, are both a condition and an outcome of the process of becoming 'modern' and 'developed'. In the itinerary of 'development', a pastoral way of being is rendered primitive and almost an antithesis of modernity, whereas an urban, middle-class lifestyle that is divorced from ownership of land or labour is authorized as normative. This delegitimization of pastoral or peasant livelihoods is embedded in the very ideals of capitalist modernity and development, and is propagated through channels such as modern schooling.

Again, I do not wish to romanticize a pastoral life, nor do I intend to argue that the exclusionary ideals of modernity and development are unthinkingly internalized by pastoralists. What I wish to highlight is that under conditions of modernity, where there is already a decline in the appeal and practice of livestock grazing, pastoral livelihoods are further devalued through the discourses and practices of conservation. Perhaps this is to be expected, as the ideals of conservation themselves stem from those of modernity, evidenced for example by the way in which the livestock-as-threat discourse represents and reinforces modernity's denigration of the 'primitive pastoralist'.

Moreover, in the neoliberal context, the livestock-as-threat discourse has proved to be a more powerful discourse of accumulation, facilitating the institutional agendas of state authorities as well as of international conservation organizations. It is not surprising, then, that despite overwhelming evidence of decreasing livestock ownership and grazing in Gilgit-Baltistan, KNP officials continue to claim otherwise in order to retain their hold over communities and their resources. As one KNP higher-up told me:

> I know that livestock holdings have increased in the Khunjerab area. These communities are very smart. If you visit the KNP without informing them, you will see how much livestock they keep in the no-grazing zone. But if you inform them before going, they will hide their animals and make you believe that their animals do not pose a threat to wildlife. Communities cannot keep their animals, and also claim a share in the entry fees.

Conservation NGOs, on the other hand, concede that dependence on livestock herding is indeed decreasing in areas affecting the KNP. This, however, does not necessarily bring any credit for the community. A manager at an international conservation NGO remarked:

> Communities are not reducing their livestock because they care about conservation. It is happening itself because people are increasingly seeking off-farm employment. It is only when they will consciously reduce livestock that we will achieve true community participation.

In other words, it is not just particular conservation outcomes that are desired; rather, a disciplining of community attitudes is being struggled for, and represented as the legitimate form of participation. Community participation is thus reconfigured as a measure of how well people in Gilgit-Baltistan have internalized the international conservation discourse, and sacrificed their own livelihoods for its sake.

Because it is believed that communities are not 'participating' well, international conservation organizations have sought to go beyond the process of awareness-raising regarding the negative impact of livestock on wildlife conservation. They wish to actively steer people away from livestock herding by providing alternate sources of income.[58] These 'alternate livelihoods' must ideally be linked to the implementation of the park, so that people can realize that conservation can be a source of their development as opposed to pastoralism. Linking the global project of conservation to 'income-generating opportunities' at the local level has become known as 'community-based conservation' in the discourse of international conservation NGOs operating in Gilgit-Baltistan—and Community-based Natural Resource Management (CBNRM) more generally—and it is to its contested operations that I now turn my attention.

COMMUNITY-BASED CONSERVATION

One way of providing conservation-related alternate livelihoods is to give people jobs in the very management of protected areas. This was recommended in the WWF-drafted management plan for the Khunjerab National Park,[59] as a means to compensate pastoralists for the loss of grazing rights, as well as an incentive for more pastoralists to give up livestock grazing. Consequently, park jobs have been used by the government Directorate that manages the KNP to lure Shimshalis into accepting the authority of the KNP, and respecting its grazing restrictions. The offer was enticing for around 18 people in Shimshal, who responded to the government's call for job vacancies in the KNP. However, village elders as well as members of the SNT saw the offer as a government tactic, designed to create disunity among Shimshalis. Remarkably, they eventually managed to convince all the applicants to take back their applications in the larger interest of Shimshal. As an SNT member explained:

> We asked these people: 'What jobs could the KNP offer anyway? A guard, or an office boy? The Director of the KNP would never be from Shimshal, would he, even if Shimshal forms two-thirds of the park?' You see people are feeling helpless, and they want jobs to earn cash. But we told them that they should not give up their ancestral land and their yaks for a job of Rs 3,000 per month.

More recently, community-based conservation in Gilgit-Baltistan has become synonymous with the international sport of trophy hunting. The sport has particularly come to dominate the conservation scene in Gilgit-Baltistan over the last twelve years, during which 22 'Community Controlled Hunting Areas' (CCHAs) have been created in the region. These have been established primarily by IUCN, through the GEF/UNDP funded Mountain Areas Conservancy Project. The CCHAs have a strong appeal for communities, as 75 per cent of the revenue generated through trophy hunting goes to the community that manages the relevant area, while the remaining amount goes to the government. The cost of a hunting permit varies with different wildlife species: for an ibex it is $3,000, for a blue sheep it is $6,500, and shooting an Astor Markhor can cost up to $40,000. Communities also earn income through the porters and guides that accompany the hunter. Moreover, hunters are also known to be generous, and might give up to $3,000 as a donation for local development after a successful hunt.

International conservation organizations in Gilgit-Baltistan promote trophy hunting as a form of 'sustainable community development' because of the cash it generates, which is either distributed evenly to all the households in a village, or saved with a recognized community-based organization that can utilize the funds for local development projects. Trophy hunting is also represented as a useful tool for conservation: the income that can be generated by occasionally catering to the needs of rich Pakistani and foreign hunters is deemed to be a significant disincentive for local hunting which might be undertaken for subsistence, cultural significance, pleasure, or trade.

Ironically, conservation agencies perceive no contradiction between projects such as the KNP that seek to preserve landscapes in their 'natural state' for the protection of wildlife, and projects such as the CCHA which turns this wildlife into a commodity that can be killed for pleasure. In many cases, a CCHA is in fact located right alongside the boundaries of a national park, in what is called the 'buffer zone'. It is assumed that the sportive hunting of treasured wildlife in these buffer zones does not disrupt their natural habitats, but the practice of livestock grazing and local hunting—which have been happening for centuries—does. In effect, local use values of nature are delegitimized in order to secure its global exchange value.

This commodification of nature in the name of conservation is perfectly aligned with the interests of hunters. As trophy hunting faces increased resistance in North America and Europe, 'hunters, like multinational industries, flee to grounds where they can escape those restrictive conditions'.[60] The continuation of their sport, however, is dependent on the protection of wildlife in these freer areas from local use and abuse. This link between local conservation and global hunting is captured tellingly in a Safari Club International (SCI)[61] sticker that I saw at the head office of a prominent international conservation organization in Gilgit-Baltistan. It read: 'Conserve Now, Hunt Later'. No wonder that conservation agencies perceive no contradiction between saving nature and selling it: they want nature to be saved precisely so that it can be sold and killed later.

Community-based trophy hunting also serves the interests of the state, and particularly of the local forest bureaucracy that oversees the management of protected areas. It is an important source of revenue for them, and there have been allegations from community members across Gilgit-Baltistan that the forest department retains the hunting revenue in its own account in order to gain interest, before disbursing it to the relevant communities.[62] Trophy hunting also reinforces the power of the state to distribute patronage through the granting of hunting quotas to specific villages and outfitters, while marginalizing others. Finally, it serves as a tool for regulating community behaviour. Indeed, the KNP management has used trophy hunting as a lure to put pressure on Shimshalis for giving ownership of their land to the KNP. As a KNP official explained to me:

> In 2006, we gave a permit to an American hunter to hunt in Shimshal. The community got its due share for the trophy as well. We then allowed

the creation of a Community Controlled Hunting Area as an additional incentive. Since then, we have given more permits, but we will not release the money till Shimshalis sign an MoU in which they accept the KNP and its regulations. We have to bring these communities in line. They think they can extract the benefits of the park, without obeying the writ of the government.

Hence, 'community-based conservation' schemes that provide a community share in trophy hunting and in park entry fees, have come to perpetuate a state–community relation in which the very terms of participation are based on exclusion, as they require communities to surrender ownership of their land on the one hand and abandon their livelihoods on the other. These projects have become forms of political and social control that help to entrench the power of the state over rural spaces and communities, thus extending the ecological state-making that the creation of the KNP already initiated. This ecological control has been further underpinned by more sinister tactics to put pressure on Shimshalis. For example, in 2006, the directorate of the Khunjerab National Park lodged a court case against a number of Shimshali youth for assaulting park rangers who had been sent to Shimshal. Members of the Shimshal Nature Trust, however, contend that there was only a verbal argument between the rangers and local youth, and that the case has been filed only to malign Shimshalis and force them into accepting the authority of the KNP. It needs to be underlined that such a coercive use of the legal and policing apparatus of the state remains integral to the making of environmental subjects under neoliberalism,[63] and is often overlooked in analyses of nature and power in terms of eco-governmentality[64] and environmentality.[65]

Analyses of community-based conservation initiatives elsewhere have also demonstrated how environmental agendas framed in participatory terms have served to intensify state power, often diminishing the political and economic security of rural communities instead of enhancing it.[66] These agendas are defined by a dense network of national and transnational actors that cut across the traditional divides of state, non-governmental organization, and corporation.[67] What is truly baffling and dangerous about the global conservation agenda is its insistence on promoting activities such as trophy hunting—which commodify nature primarily for the leisure of rich, Western consumers—as *sustainable alternatives* to local subsistence-based livelihoods. In this neoliberal logic, the 'sustainable development' of a community becomes equated with the ability to raise cash incomes through the market, and the development of nature is presumed to be achieved by turning it into a commodity that is subject to market forces of production and exchange. Such logics of neoliberal development cannot be implemented without the necessary cultivation and appropriation of local subjectivities. Through promises of 'benefit-sharing', already marginal, local communities are first expected to compromise their own livelihood concerns and take on the burden of conserving 'nature', and then to treat nature as a resource from which they can and must profit from.

The appeal and importance of such market-driven approaches for local communities should not be underestimated. In a context where the state is pushing for park development but shows very little interest in social development, communities like Shimshal tremendously value the revenue that they may get from projects like trophy hunting, as it can be used for self-help initiatives ranging from water channels to health care provision. Indeed, villages elsewhere in Gilgit-Baltistan have been lobbying the government to get parts of their land declared as community-controlled hunting areas because foreign hunting is an important source of immediate cash for them. However, these community-based alternative livelihood projects are particularly problematic when, as I have argued for Shimshal, they are tied to the dispossession of community land and livelihood and serve a nexus of powerful interests including state institutions, hunters, and outfitters. Importantly, they also fail to fulfil their primary aim of maintaining biodiversity, as introducing a market mechanism in the management of nature overvalues some species of wildlife that have a 'demand' from hunters while undervaluing others that do not 'sell'. As Shafqat Hussain has argued, trophy hunting projects in Gilgit-Baltistan have heightened the market value of single species such as the ibex and markhor, while creating disincentives for local communities to conserve the snow leopard which preys on the well-selling species (2007). This has disturbed the balance of the ecosystem, as all species are interdependent and need to be holistically valued.

Apart from upsetting complex systems of local ecology, the commodification of nature also serves to undermine the moral–ecological values that have historically helped to preserve nature in Shimshali territory. For example, at a workshop on conservation that I co-facilitated in Shimshal in November

2006, local men and women were asked to share their understandings of conservation. Several participants defined conservation first and foremost as a 'source of income', because absurdly, this is precisely what conservation has become reduced to—the practice of selling wildlife and earning money through it. This is in sharp contrast with traditional modes of seeing nature, in which the realm of wildlife is deemed sacred, and nature more generally perceived as God's blessing that is to be utilized with care and appreciation. Marketized notions of nature, however, did not exhaust local visions of conservation. At the workshop, a Shimshali woman, Shama Bibi, mentioned that conservation to her means peace—with nature, within the village, and with neighbouring villages. She also expressed doubt as to whether the materialistic notion of conservation that has come to dominate the region achieves this sense of harmony.

Ultimately, the agenda of 'sustainable use' and 'alternative livelihoods' is misguided because it assumes that a pastoral community's relationship with nature is merely about economic need, and hence alternative sources of incomes would, and should automatically translate into a reduced dependence on nature—ideally, a total surrender of it so that it becomes a 'protected area' for state and capital. What is erased in such a discourse is the central role of nature and pastoral activity in defining a community's identity and its forms of belonging. In Shimshal, for example, pastures are not only the material means of production but also symbolic resources that are considered key sites for historical events, spiritual renewal, and cultural celebrations.[68] They are also particularly cherished by Shimshali women as places that provide respite from the constraints and anxieties of village life, by offering a meaningful experience of independence, female solidarity, and peace. Hence, the value of land and nature for Shimshalis is simultaneously material and symbolic, encompassing identity, history, and livelihood.[69] It is the very source and meaning of life, which is why both its commodification and compensation is considered unthinkable.

CONCLUSION

Ten years after the establishment of the SNT, a number of its members expressed to me a sense of disillusionment about their initiative. As one of its key leaders, Amin Ali commented to me:

> We created the SNT to engage with outside interests, and make them understand our concerns. Instead, we have become perceived as more of a threat, and portrayed as anti-state. This is completely false. We are eager to work with the state, and with international NGOs. We know that conservation is important. All we are saying is, don't make a park that will prevent us from owning our lands and living our lives.

These were the last impressions with which I left Shimshal in June 2007. By 2008, however, the tide had fortunately changed. Shimshalis had managed to sign an MoU with the Northern Areas Wildlife and Parks Department, which clearly acknowledged and guaranteed the land use rights and settlements of Shimshal, in return for cooperation in transnational and national conservation efforts. Subsequently, the Khunjerab National Park authorities have also withdrawn their legal case against Shimshali youth. The change in circumstances can be explained by the 'confidence-building measures' that SNT members had been engaging in—such as inviting conservation officials to local celebrations and thus creating opportunities for amicable dialogue. It is also attributable to the fact that conservation organizations claiming to work on 'community-based conservation' are completely hindered without the support of the 'local community', particularly one such as Shimshal which controls a vast territory that is central to multiple conservation projects such as the Khunjerab National Park and the Central Karakoram National Park. SNT members now speak with a sense of relief and hope, instead of frustration and fear. It can thus be argued that the epistemic 'struggle for interpretive power'[70] that Shimshalis engaged in was ultimately successful, though the future course of interactions between Shimshalis, state actors, and international institutions remains to be seen.

Critical struggles from below—like those of Shimshal—have both benefited from, and contributed to peasant struggles elsewhere that have sought to reclaim their space and agency in global development projects.[71] They also create openings for alternate visions of being and becoming in an increasingly marketized world, where power considers rural people as relics of the past and disposable in an industrialized and corporatized future.

It is one of the bewildering ironies of global environmental practice that agendas of conservation and sustainable development continue to be defined by those who have become alienated from the process of living with nature. Meanwhile, communities that continue to inhabit and sustain biodiversity-rich regions are classified as the objects of conservation projects. These communities are often vilified for their reckless attitude towards the environment—tree-cutting, hunting, or grazing—by a modern, Western conservation society that is far more enmeshed in environmental destruction. Even when not vilified, the 'indigenous' might be produced as noble conservationists, and held accountable to misguided and unrealistic ideals of local resource use.[72]

The Shimshali struggle serves to change the dominant 'global' discourse on conservation itself, by arguing that the Shimshalis are central makers of the development project, instead of its beneficiaries, and that they are eager to imagine new social futures with 'government participation' and 'international participation'. This would counteract the existing framework whereby epistemic and material powers are concentrated in the hands of a transnational–national nexus of institutions, the agendas of which are scripted from above while allowing 'community participation'. In effect, like indigenous communities elsewhere, Shimshalis are working towards an ecological sovereignty in which their community governs itself as well the resources on which it depends—as it has always done. Such ecological struggles—at once epistemic and material—point to new imaginings of citizenship that go beyond the institutional parameters of political rights.

Despite the Shimshali achievement, however, the normative narrative of biodiversity conservation remains wedded to projects that act in the name of community, but are unwilling to listen to it. Indeed, what I have tried to point out in this chapter is not only the unwillingness, but the structural *inability* of the global conservation nexus to understand and value the interests of local communities. Embedded in the global discourse of biodiversity conservation and sustainable development are *assumptions*—for example, about nature as divorced from society, and livestock as an irredeemable threat to wildlife—and *interests* such as those of conservation organizations, their corporate financiers, and hunters, which make it *unthinkable* to acknowledge that a local community can own and manage a protected area. What gets authorized, instead, are two linked processes: one is that of ecological state-making which enhances the power of the state to territorialize nature and to regulate subjects through the control of nature. The other is the commodification of nature through an agenda of 'green developmentalism' which 'abstracts nature from its spatial and social contexts ... reinforces the claims of global elites to the greatest share of the earth's biomass and all it contains ... and speeds the extension of market relations into diverse and complex eco-social systems, with material and cultural outcomes that do more to diminish than to conserve diversity and sustainability'.[73] In Gilgit-Baltistan, the end result of these processes is that almost 40 per cent of the territory has been declared as some form of conservation enclosure, most of which seek to commodify nature for global use and exchange value at the cost of local sovereignty and livelihood.

I do not wish to suggest that the role of conservation organizations in Gilgit-Baltistan has been entirely negative. Both the WWF and IUCN are staffed with several local managers who are all too aware of the dilemmas that conservation poses for their region and people, and have pushed their supervisors to be more sensitive to local contexts. These organizations have also undertaken important initiatives that address local needs of conservation, such as trainings of communities in restoring pastures, in protecting livestock from predators, and in addressing concerns of deforestation and overhunting. Importantly, they have also attempted to go beyond the drafting of management plans for protected areas, to undertaking valuable research on topics such as local understandings of ecology and wildlife management. Initiatives such as these have the potential to promote a more meaningful attention to the 'local' in conservation practice.

Ultimately, from the perspective of Shimshalis, they have been conserving all along and cannot understand why they must discontinue their practices *for* the sake of conservation. A shepherd from southern France has poignantly echoed this sentiment: 'shepherds...are trapped between the desire to do what they know and want to do and the requirement to act as a manager of space and biodiversity. The most difficult thing is perhaps to explain that, all told, this is one and the same approach'.[74] Such reflections on biodiversity enable and invite a deeper analysis of environmental issues than that permitted by the dominant conservation discourse that pits nature versus society, and local irresponsibility against global concerns. One hopes that for the cause of environmental sustainability as well as of social justice, such local understandings, values, sentiments, and aspirations are not only researched, but actually allowed a central place in framing the agenda of biodiversity conservation.

In the next and final chapter of the book, I discuss how the 'local' is misunderstood and misrepresented in another form of contemporary development politics in Gilgit-Baltistan—that of humanitarian education as it has come to unfold under the war on terror and neoliberal empire.

NOTES

1. Gilbert and Berlant (2014: 9).
2. Pratt (1999) and Cornwall et al. (2007).
3. Cronon (1995).
4. Marx (1887).
5. McCarthy and Prudham (2004).
6. Harvey (2003).
7. O'Connor (1994).
8. McNeely (1993).
9. McAfee (1999) and Breunig (2006).
10. Geisler (2003).
11. Harvey (2003).
12. McCarthy and Prudham (2004).
13. Breunig (2006).
14. See, for example, McCarthy and Prudham (2004), Igoe and Brockington (2007), Heynen et al. (2007), and Büscher et al. (2014).
15. cf. McMichael (2006).
16. West and Brechin (1991) and Arnold and Guha (1995).
17. Guha (1989), Gadgil and Guha (1995), and Sivaramakrishnan (1999).
18. MacKenzie (1988), Rangarajan (1996), and Rangarajan (2006).
19. Schickhoff (2006).
20. Mock (2008).
21. IUCN (1994).
22. Vandergeest and Peluso (1995) and Peluso and Vandergeest (2001).
23. Neumann (2004).
24. This claim was accepted by the Pakistani government in 1963, leading to the transfer of the Trans-Karakoram Tract to China in return for a Chinese-controlled area that the communities living on the Pakistani side had demanded.

25 'Exclusive' in the sense that only villagers of Shimshal own and manage this vast terrain. The administrative role of the local or the national state has historically been limited, largely due to the rugged, inaccessible terrain of Shimshal. Shimshalis used to pay grazing taxes during the Mir's reign, but after the abolition of the Hunza princely state in 1974, no income taxes are paid to the Pakistani government. This is true of Gilgit-Baltistan in general. Due to the region's ambiguous constitutional status, income taxes are not officially collected from the region's inhabitants though they were imposed in 2012.
26 Ali and Butz (2003).
27 Martinez-Alier (2002).
28 Cerderlof and Sivaramakrishnan (2006).
29 Abbreviation for the District Forest Officer, the key government official responsible for implementing state policies of conservation in the Gilgit-Baltistan.
30 The occurrence of illegal hunting by state officials in the KNP has even been acknowledged by the WWF, which is the main international organization that has been pushing for the formalization of the park (WWF, 1996). Moreover, a higher-up official at WWF also acknowledged that 'wildlife in Shimshal is most likely being conserved well' (personal interview).
31 Butz (1998).
32 Research elsewhere has also demonstrated that replacing local forms of control with state control is not always productive for conserving nature, because the state is generally unable to enforce its own conservation policies (Guha, 1989; Saberwal, 1999; Agrawal, 2001b).
33 IUCN (1999: 31).
34 For example, see Neumann (2001) and Agrawal and Gibson (2001).
35 Gareau (2007).
36 Brockington and Homewood (2001) and Neumann (2004).
37 Rangarajan (2006).
38 Butz (2002).
39 Their intervention was openly vilified at first, particularly by some notable village elders who accused them of being bought by the state and conservation NGOs.
40 Abidi-Habib and Lawrence (2007).
41 SNT (1997).
42 These programmes include a community-enforced ban on wildlife hunting which was mentioned earlier. Keeping local needs in mind, the ban does not apply to the small number of ibex that are hunted for meat by yak herders in the winters.
43 SNT (1997).
44 Ibid.
45 Gold and Gujar (2002: 9).
46 At the same time, a scientific approach is also drawn upon by asserting that nature conservation by the Shimshal community would be based, in the first place, on up-to-date statistical information collected by local youth.

47 See Marsden (2008) for an illuminating discussion of cosmopolitan, rural Muslims in Northern Pakistan.
48 The SNT management plan itself was compiled and edited by David Butz, a geographer who has been working in Shimshal since 1988.
49 In the general conservation discourse in Gilgit-Baltistan, 'indiscriminate hunting' is perhaps regarded as the most significant factor for decreasing wildlife populations. However, state-community conflicts generated by the KNP have revolved more around the issue of habitat loss due to livestock grazing, which is why I have decided to focus on it.
50 Schaller (1980: 112).
51 Saberwal (1999).
52 Pollan (2006).
53 Knudsen (1999).
54 These communities do not include Shimshal; they belong to the seven Upper Hunza villages that accepted the authority of the park, and hence, are entitled to a share in park revenue.
55 Kreutzmann (2006).
56 A number of Shimshali men and women said that in earlier times, 60 to 75 per cent of women used to be in the pastures during summer. By 2007, the percentage had dropped to 25 to 30 per cent.
57 Yaks in particular are highly valued, as each yak can fetch up to Rs 45,000 or $750.
58 WWF (1996).
59 Ibid.
60 MacDonald (2005).
61 SCI is the largest big game hunting organization in the world. It serves as a lobby group for hunters, and also engages in wilderness awareness and conservation projects.
62 Hussain (2007).
63 On the neoliberal creation of environmental subjects and recalibrated relations of nature and power, see Goldman (2001) on eco-governmentality and Agrawal (2005) on environmentality.
64 Goldman (2001).
65 Agrawal (2005).
66 Neumann (2001), Agrawal (2001a), Li (2002), and Breunig (2006).
67 Igoe and Brockington (2007).
68 Butz (1996).
69 cf. Moore (1993).
70 Franco (1989).
71 McMichael (2010).
72 Dove (2006).
73 McAfee (1999: 1–3).
74 Grellier (2006: 163).

6

BOOKS vs. BOMBS?

ಏಓಚ

Humanitarian Education, Empire, and the Narrative of Terror

The representation of a zone of conflict is key to the perpetuation of power over it. I thus began the story of Gilgit-Baltistan in the first chapter by problematizing how the region is constructed within the nationalist/statist imagination of Pakistan, through an exclusionary and silencing narrative of beauty. In this final chapter, I broaden my analytical frame to transnational regimes of knowledge, and demonstrate how Gilgit-Baltistan has been constructed within such regimes through a problematic narrative of terror. My purpose is to emphasize how political subjection in 'hot zones'—such as Gilgit-Baltistan, Kashmir, and Pakistan—is overdetermined by both national and transnational logics of truth and knowledge, and that the affect, effect, and violence of such knowledge must be unravelled in order to demystify the region and its predicament. Moreover, the narratives of beauty and terror themselves produce the region as an affect: regions seem to acquire and produce a feeling—an aura as it were, an aura of space and sociality such that invoking 'Northern Pakistan' or 'Gilgit-Baltistan' conjures immediately a set of images and feelings that shape how one sees, senses, and receives the region. This chapter hence unpacks the image-feelings of fear, terror, and humanitarian care that have recently been carved on the body of Gilgit-Baltistan, under conditions of empire and the so-called war on terror.

The point of entry for my analysis is the immensely popular biography of the American humanitarian Greg Mortenson, *Three Cups of Tea: One Man's*

Mission to Promote Peace ... One School at a Time (2006), which is primarily set in Gilgit-Baltistan, and was originally published in hardcover as *Three Cups of Tea: One Man's Mission to Fight Terrorism and Build Nations ... One School at a Time*. Through this text, Gilgit-Baltistan suddenly became the prime terrain to 'fight terror', 'build nations', and promote peace through schools in Muslim lands, in the context of the US-led war on terror. The text deserves attention not only because it visibilizes Gilgit-Baltistan nationally and globally through a misplaced narrative of terror, but also because it provides a larger template for combining a discourse on terrorism with a discourse on poverty, development, and humanitarianism in the production of Muslim others. Despite the scandal that revealed Mortenson's intellectual and philanthropic deceit—an exposé in which my own writing played a role—the discourse embodied by *Three Cups of Tea* continues to be stable and widespread.[1] With Gilgit-Baltistan as its key ground, the text embodies spatial, political, and cultural assumptions that have morphed into a transnational regime of cultural knowledge for understanding Islam, madrasas, education, development, as well as terrorism in Muslim countries.

I am interested in examining both the politics of representation in this new configuration of transnational cultural knowledge, as well as the relationship between this knowledge and the transnational political economy of militarism in South Asia. In attending to such linkages, I am committed to a feminist, world-historical scholarship that deploys transnational perspectives in order to unsettle nation-centred narratives, and that emphasizes relational histories of power instead of prohibitive ones of place in which 'other' regions are treated as discrete and exceptional.[2] Calling attention to the connections between Mortenson's schools, *Three Cups of Tea*, and the US military, I show how the text facilitated the emergence of a *participatory militarism*, whereby humanitarian work in Gilgit-Baltistan and adjoining areas helped to reinvent the US military as a culturally sensitive and caring institution, in order to justify the project of empire. This meeting of compassion and counter-insurgency in and through Gilgit-Baltistan is important to analyze because it extends my analysis of Chapter 2 where I show how militarism works through a political economy of feeling. The humanitarian-oriented, participatory militarism of the US is also important to examine because its practice has only increased in the last five years, beyond its direct operation in Gilgit-Baltistan, Pakistan, and Afghanistan. Indeed, as Mona Bhan (2013) has forcefully shown, US-style counter-insurgency has become a travelling project, inspiring the Indian military to conduct 'heart warfare' in the zones of Kashmir that it controls. Hence, alongside Bhan, what I am suggesting is that it is not only the practice of the Pakistani or Indian military that we need to understand but also that of the US military, for a fuller understanding of how different forms of militarism affect Kashmir at large.

Such an emphasis is especially significant given the geopolitical realities of Pakistan. As I have argued earlier in the book, the country has long been a 'shadowland of empire', and—perhaps more than any other place in South Asia—cannot be made sense of outside of its relation to US policy. The delusions of empire, in fact, are revealed precisely in its shadowlands. Hence, what McClintock (2009) calls the 'catastrophic self-delusion' of empire, is visible both in the transnational narrative of Islam and terror in Gilgit-Baltistan as constructed through *Three Cups of Tea*, as well as in the transnational, participatory militarism that it has served to engender in the region. Moreover, as I demonstrate later in this chapter, the same narrative of terror that imposes the image-feelings of fear and terror onto Gilgit-Baltistan simultaneously produces the innocence and benevolence of empire.

THE CONTEXT OF THREE CUPS OF TEA

As its central thesis, *Three Cups of Tea*—henceforth TCT—argues that the American humanitarian Greg Mortenson has been effectively countering terrorism in Northern Pakistan and Afghanistan through the creation of schools. The book is co-authored by Mortenson and the journalist David Oliver Relin, and is essentially written as a tribute by Relin to Mortenson's educational efforts in Northern Pakistan and Afghanistan.[3] TCT is the only phenomenally popular text that Americans have read and continue to read about Pakistan—a country that has become a key frontier in the US war on terror. The text was number one on the New York Times bestseller list for several weeks, and honored as *Time Magazine*'s Asian Book of The Year award in 2006. It has been a popular text in US schools for discussing development as well as the war on terror. Indeed, as the official site for TCT tells us, Mortenson has himself 'developed a rubric for the National Education Association to teach the book'. The book also came out in two edited versions for children in 2009— *Listen to the Wind: The Story of Dr. Greg and Three Cups of Tea* for ages four–eight, and *Three Cups of Tea: Young Readers Edition* for ages 8–13 Recognizing his services, the Pakistani government awarded the highest civilian award of Sitara-e-Imtiaz or 'Star of Pakistan' to Greg Mortenson in March 2009.

A significant part of TCT is devoted to Mortenson's personal life. Mortenson spent his early years in Tanzania, where his parents were Lutheran missionaries and teachers. His father co-founded the Kilimanjaro Christian Medical Centre, and served in the US military prior to the family's missionary-humanitarian work in Africa. Mortenson also joined the US army after graduating from high school, and served in Germany for two years. He went on to do his undergraduate degree on a GI scholarship, and later trained to become a medical nurse. In 1993, after the death of his sister Christa, Mortenson decided to climb K2, the second highest peak in the world that forms part of the Karakoram range in Northern Pakistan. But his attempt to scale K2 failed, and his life was saved by the people of Korphe, a remote village in the Baltistan area of Gilgit-Baltistan. In return, he promised to build them a school, and spent the next several years of his life building schools not only in Korphe but also in other parts of Northern Pakistan. In 1996, he went on to establish a non-profit named the Central Asia Institute , which has since built more than 70 schools for girls and boys in Pakistan and Afghanistan, and continues to work in the region.

But *Three Cups of Tea* is not merely about Mortenson's biography and humanitarianism. Despite the revelations in 2011 that tarnished Mortenson's image, the book has become the quintessential text through which Americans have come to see the longest war in US and Pakistan's history. TCT also became a strategic guide for the US military soon after its publication. It is striking, for example, to read on the book's official website that

Three Cups of Tea is required reading for US senior military commanders, for officers in the Norwegian War College, Forsvarsnett, for US Special Forces deploying to Afghanistan, Pentagon officers in counter-insurgency training, and Canadian Defense Ministry members. The book has been read by General David Petraeus–CENTCOM Commander, Admiral Mike Mullen–Chairman

Joint Chief of Staff, and ... several other US military commanders who advocate for building relationships as a part of an overall strategic plan for peace. Mortenson has addressed the National Defense Senior Leadership Conference at the Pentagon, visited over two dozen military bases, NORAD, and been to the Air Force, Naval, and West Point Academies.[4]

In the following sections, I investigate how the simplifications and silences present in TCT create a redemptive narrative of terrorism that enables the text's uptake by the US military, as well as its popularity with the American public.

To elaborate my argument and analyse the spatial, political, and cultural politics of terror enabled through TCT, I ask: how does the text represent the regional space and social context of Gilgit-Baltistan in which Mortenson seeks to intervene? What assumptions about culture, development, and terrorism underpin the way in which the problems of rural Pakistan and Gilgit-Baltistan are framed, and solutions proposed? What silences characterize the representation of the US in the text? And, since the publication of the text, how have Mortenson's development-oriented efforts in education become implicated in militaristic discourses of counter-insurgency?[5] The sections below correspond to each of these concerns, followed by a final section in which I articulate my own experience as a scholar researching a zone of war in this moment.

THE REGION—COLLAPSIBLE AND DANGEROUS

The primary geographical focus of TCT is the terrain of Baltistan, which is located in Gilgit-Baltistan, a region that till 2009 was called the 'Northern Areas' in Pakistan. To avoid confusion, I will use the region's old name since TCT was written before the name change. Mortenson started his educational efforts in the Braldu Valley of Baltistan and then moved on to create schools in other parts of the Northern Areas. Hence, when the book speaks about the 'region', the reference appears to be the Northern Areas as a whole. This is suggested even by the map that is provided at the beginning of the book—a map titled, 'The Northern Areas'. Only some thirty odd pages of the book are devoted to other areas—such as the Pakistani territory of Waziristan and places in Afghanistan—where Mortenson also expanded his educational efforts.

In TCT, the Northern Areas is described as the 'wild country' with 'wild mountain valleys'.[6] It is 'the poorest region of one of the world's poorest countries', a place where there are 'warring sects' and people have been living 'as they have for centuries'.[7] To be sure, TCT has contextual descriptions, often presented in humanizing, positive terms, and 'quite accurate' portrayals of the main characters, as an anthropologist who has worked extensively in Baltistan said to me. However, the overall image conjured is of a barren and backward land waiting to be claimed and tamed. Such imagery contrasts sharply with my own experiences as a researcher in Gilgit-Balistan over the last ten years and with people's self-representations in the region. Filled with historical settlements where people—despite many material needs—pride themselves for the respect and industriousness with which they have tended the land, the region cannot simply be termed 'wild', and their sustainable rural lifestyles dismissed as 'poor' and 'menial'. As highlighted in Chapter 1, images of mountain societies as timeless and history-less are likewise misguided, and typical of the lowland perspective from which social analysis is often written.[8] Particularly in the context of the Northern Areas, this perspective runs counter to local histories of caravan trade, travel, religious conversions, and political and military struggles that formed the heart of the British–Russian Great Game in the nineteenth century.

Along with the essentializing tropes of backwardness—characteristic of development interventions more generally—TCT also invokes fear by portraying the region as 'wild', 'warring', and steeped in ignorance, filled with 'extremist madrassas' that gave 'birth to the Taliban'.[9] For example, the back cover of the book states:

> From eerie blue glaciers, where snow leopards stalk their prey, to high-altitude fundamentalist villages, where the faith is as severe as the surroundings, and down the deadly opium trails of Afghanistan at war, Three Cups of Tea traces Mortenson's decade-long odyssey to build schools, especially for girls, throughout the region that gave birth to the Taliban and sanctuary to Al-Qaeda.

Further, the introduction to the book says

> Slamming over the so-called Karakoram 'Highway' in his old Land Cruiser, taking great personal risks to seed the region that gave birth to the Taliban

with schools, Mortenson goes to war with the root causes of terror every time he offers a student a chance to receive a balanced education, rather than attend an extremist madrassa.[10]

Before examining the book's claims about education and the 'root causes of terror', we need to ask: what is this region that gave birth to the Taliban? To describe the region of the Karakoram Highway (KKH) as one that gave 'birth to the Taliban' is incorrect, and embodies a dangerous jump of geographies and logics. The bulk of the KKH lies in the administrative territory of Gilgit-Baltistan in Pakistan, and the bulk of the book TCT is focused on the region of Baltistan which lies in present-day Gilgit-Baltistan. Baltistan is 95 per cent Shia and, by the book's own admission, the first Wahhabi madrasa was created here in 2001—which too, is not synonymous with the Taliban. Indeed, the Northern Areas/Gilgit-Baltistan as a whole is majority-Shia. To claim that this Shia-majority region is the birthplace of the Sunni fundamentalist, anti-Shia Taliban is simply absurd. The Taliban were predominantly based in the Helmand, Kandahar, and Uruzgan regions of Afghanistan.[11] Their origins are more properly traced to agitations in response to the frustrated nature of Afghan sovereignty, and most decisively to the CIA and ISI production of the mujahideen during the Cold War, through particular kinds of madrasas in some parts of Afghanistan and some parts of western Pakistan that trained and armed Muslim students from around the world in a new, rabidly fundamentalist version of Islam to service the strategic interests of the US.[12] Indeed, an explicitly violent curriculum that was to be used in these madrasas was produced by the University of Nebraska, Omaha, and published in both Dari and Pashto through a USAID grant.[13] As such, one might more appropriately declare the US as the 'region that gave birth to the Taliban'.

However, TCT is a text in which such uncomfortable truths are not present, and indeed, details in general do not matter. Factual errors add to the text's disregard for regional and political context. For example, George Schaller recommended the Khunjerab National Park in the Northern Areas, not the 'Karakoram National Park'[14] as we are told, and Mortenson could not have attended Mother Teresa's funeral in the spring of 2000[15] because she died in the fall of 1997. While we learn about the different places and people that Mortenson encounters during his mission, there is little sense of spatial differentiation in the broad claims of the book—and little desire to do so. The enormous space of Northern Areas, NWFP and FATA in Pakistan—incredibly diverse regions even within their own boundaries and stretching from Pakistan's eastern to northern and western borders—are lumped together as one 'region', and further combined with parts of Afghanistan that have a different historical and cultural context altogether.[16] In this collapsible 'region', the spaces and people appear interchangeable. Because an abstract cultural template of poverty and danger is applied to diverse locations, one gets a sense that there are mobile, multiple enemies all around in Muslim places that are self-evidently poor and ignorant, and thus potentially violent and dangerous. The many references to 'poor Muslims', in fact, makes it seem that the story can be transplanted to any Muslim context. Hence, unsurprisingly, public reviews of the book often mention how the book helps a reader understand not just Pakistan, but Central Asia and the Middle East as a whole.

The most troubling irony is that the focal region of Mortenson's work—the Shia region of Baltistan with its Tibetan-Buddhist heritage—has nothing to do with the war on terror, yet primarily viewed through this lens in TCT. While it has madrasas affiliated with different interpretations of Islam, the Northern Areas more generally is not a terrain teeming with fundamentalist madrasas and Taliban on the loose—the definitive image of the region in TCT, especially in its back cover, its introduction, and in its general publicity. Hence, despite the now characteristic token statements like 'not every madrassa was a hotbed of extremism', the subtext of TCT remains rooted in a narrative of fear and danger through which we are taught to visualize Gilgit-Baltistan.[17]

THE RURAL, IGNORANT, AND EXTREMIST

It is not just that an inaccurate, politically consequential description about being the birthplace of the Taliban is imposed on a rich and diverse landscape such as the Northern Areas, which has an entirely different context than that of the NWFP and FATA in Pakistan—areas that too have a rich and diverse landscape beyond the extremist madrasas introduced primarily in the 1980s. What is all the more striking about TCT is that the blanket claims about an already vast, collapsible region—defined by Mortenson's travels rather than geographical specificity—which is apparently extendible to all of 'rural Pakistan'.

Relin tells us that *The Oregonian* was the first major American newspaper to cover Mortenson's efforts in Pakistan. He goes on to quote from this first story about Mortenson: 'A politically volatile area, rural Pakistan is a breeding ground for terrorists who share anti-American sentiment.'[18]

Hence, not just areas north and west of Pakistan are conflated and reduced to the narrative of terrorism, but all of rural Pakistan is declared a volatile, terrorist zone. Such extensions of logic are made possible by the book itself, which often juxtaposes the 'rural poor', 'madrasas', and 'extremism'. Recall, for example, Mortenson's work in 'fundamentalist villages, where the faith is as severe as the surroundings', which I quoted earlier.

The connection between rurality and extremism deserves close examination, as it is essential to the logical framework of TCT and is also commonly asserted in development as well as liberal-elite discourse in Pakistan about Gilgit-Baltistan and other rural areas. This framework encompasses a series of linked claims. First, people residing in Pakistan's rural areas are poor, illiterate, and therefore ignorant. Second, due to a failed state education system, the rural poor are easily attracted to extremist madrasas that provide free lodging and meals, and hence they are prone to extremism. Finally, creating schools is the best way to counter this extremism, and hence, to fight terrorism. The problem of terrorism is thus defined as a problem of poverty and illiteracy prevalent in rural Pakistan, which inevitably leads to religious extremism.

This equation constructs the rural areas of Pakistan as dangerous spaces that are always already constituted as a threat. Of course, one cannot deny that rural Pakistan has many extremist madrasas—spurred in large part by CIA, ISI, and Saudi sponsorship, that these madrasas are a threat to Pakistani society and international security, and that parents do send children to these madrasas out of poverty. However, imposing this unilinear story on rural Pakistanis denies them dignity and agency, and makes it impossible to apprehend the rural on its own terms outside the narrative of poverty, illiteracy, and terrorism. Because this story is not placed in the larger context of schooling, rurality, and Muslim life-worlds, it ends up reducing a complex reality to a convenient, sanitized account of terrorism.

If one must generalize about religious identity in the diverse rural regions of Pakistan, surely the conclusion would be the opposite of what is claimed by TCT. Rural areas of Pakistan have been known for their adherence to a pluralistic sense of faith in which Islam is perceived as an idiom of morality instead of theology, and devotion is deemed more important than dogma.[19] As demonstrated in the previous two chapters, a poetic-progressive sensibility dominates the region of Gilgit-Baltistan in particular, and far from being illiterate village conformists, Muslims here consider debate and intellectual engagement as an integral element of living their faith.[20] Moreover, as discussed in Chapter 3, even the clergy in the Northern Areas has most recently been known for leading a secular-Shia movement against biased, public school textbooks, and not for creating hubs of anti-school, 'extremist madrasas'.

Madrasas—which literally means 'schools' in Arabic—have a rich and diverse history as centres of Islamic learning in Pakistan, as well as in the Muslim world in general. However, they are most often invoked in TCT with attributes such as 'extremist' and 'fundamentalist', which conveys the sense that the Northern Areas not just teem with madrasas—an incorrect picture of the region to begin with—but with fanatical ones at that. The suggestion is that before Mortenson created schools for the poor, extremist Taliban-producing madrasas were their only choice:

> Vast swathes of the country were barely served by Pakistan's struggling, inadequately funded public schools. The madrassa system targeted the impoverished students the public system failed. By offering free room and board and building schools in areas where none existed, madrassas provided millions of Pakistan's parents with their only opportunity to educate their children.[21]

The proliferation of madrasas is presented as a 'simple matter of economics', leading a military official at one of Mortenson's lectures to ask if a school could be created next to every madrasa—'like a Starbucks'—to drive the 'jihadis out of business'.[22]

The logic of creating a school to counter the madrasa is stupefying even on its own terms. If free room and board is a key attraction of a madrasa, how can schools that parents have to pay for compete against them? Further, while many madrasa students do come from less privileged households, it is incorrect to assume that the 'poorest of the poor' are somehow automatically drawn towards them. They are less likely to attend any school—and this is true especially for remote villages like Korphe where Mortenson built his first school.

Most importantly, even if education is considered, madrasas are hardly the only choice. Many government schools offer incentives such as free books, free uniform, and stipends for girl students. Significantly, private education is a dynamic and growing sector in rural and peri-urban areas of Pakistan, and a low-cost private school is the most preferred option for schooling in these areas.[23] In a comprehensive recent study by Cockroft et al., we learn that 58.8 per cent of Pakistani children were enrolled in a government school, 36.1 per cent in a private school, 3.8 per cent at a madrasa or madrasa-based school, and 1.2 per cent in non-formal and NGO schools.[24] Particularly in the Northern Areas, it is impossible to overlook its inhabitants' intense desire for secular education, and the presence and appeal of a wide range of low-cost government, private, and community schools that have been present in the region since the 1940s. TCT tells us that Pakistanis are attending madrasas without ever acknowledging the reality of these other, far more prevalent forms of schooling—a silence that creates an inflated sense of madrasa presence and popularity in Pakistan in general, and rural Pakistan in particular. This absence is conducive to creating the spectre of rural ignorance and extremism that is central to the text.

TCT further enhances this spectre through slippages between madrasas, extremist madrasas, and terrorism such that any Islamic education appears to be suspect and reducible to terrorist training.[25] In its emphasis on pushing people away from madrasas towards secular schools—considered essential for 'winning the war on terror'—TCT not only demonizes madrasas wholesale, but fails to grasp the simple fact that for a vast majority of rural and urban Pakistanis, a religious education alongside a worldly one is considered normal and desirable. People might send their children to religious specialists and centres, particular to their interpretation of Islam even if their children are attending a good, local school. Because people do not perceive a contradiction between the religious and the secular, it is not surprising that within the small percentage of families that send a child full-time to a madrasa, 75 per cent send their other children to a public or a private school.[26] Most fundamentally, in its insistence on assuming poverty to be a driver for madrasas, TCT refuses to acknowledge any positive parental motivations for madrasa preference—such as Islamic learning and moral discipline—that are in fact elemental to the existence and appeal of madrasas for the poor and rich alike.[27] By further jumping to the conclusion that the rural, illiterate, madrasa-going Muslim is the key driver for terrorism, TCT also fails to acknowledge the political grievances behind acts of terror such as 9/11, as well as the predominantly urban, educated backgrounds of those involved in anti-western Islamist violence.[28]

THE US, INNOCENT, AND BENEVOLENT

In the aftermath of 9/11, the cause for terrorism was traced and confined to the problem of Islam.[29] In part through TCT, this religio-cultural narrative has been complicated by combining the problem of Islam with that of poverty and illiteracy. Muslims are still the problem—no longer because of Islam per se, but because they are poor and ignorant, and easily amenable to extremist interpretations of Islam. Hence, it remains an Islam versus the West narrative, but now combined with the white man's burden. By locating the root cause of terrorism in poverty and ignorance—naturalized as the most defining features of Muslim lands—TCT provides a thoroughly delusional and ahistorical narrative of terrorism in which the devastating effects of US interventionism in the region are erased, and thus the contemporary imperial state of the US rendered innocent.

As highlighted earlier, we are told nothing about how the 'extremist madrasa' that TCT presents as an integral part of the Pakistani landscape, was in fact a product of US foreign policy during 1979–1988. Importantly, the use of Islam as a strategic tool in Afghanistan emerged not in response to the Russian invasion, but prior to it so that the Russians could be drawn into battle, and given their 'own Vietnam war'.[30] Far from being a result of poverty, the mujahideen were produced through the mobilization of tremendous wealth. With the aid of US, Saudi, and Gulf money, the CIA helped to fund, train and arm the Pakistani ISI, the most retrograde 'freedom fighters' like Osama bin Laden and Gulbudin Hekmatyar, and thousands of Muslims from Afghanistan and Pakistan whose religious identities and economic needs were exploited to enlist them in a brutal modern war labeled as jihad. Apart from militarizing and Islamicizing Afghanistan and Pakistan, the Afghan jihad came to produce more than 100,000 foreign Muslim radicals.[31] Indeed, the CIA strategy was to deploy the Afghan jihad as a model for militant, Islamist resistance against the Soviets elsewhere, with the result that mujahideen forces spread beyond Afghanistan to places such as Chechnya and Kosovo.[32]

This story is well known today through several academic, journalistic, and policy writings, yet it remains largely absent from popular, contemporary narratives on the war on terror in the US. If mentioned, the blame for the Cold War production of jihadis tends to get placed entirely on the ISI and the Saudis—still the Muslim others—instead of acknowledging the central role of US funds, arms, and training.[33] In one of the most oft-quoted passages from TCT, Mortenson says:

> I've learned that terror doesn't happen because some group of people somewhere like Pakistan or Afghanistan simply decide to hate us. It happens because children aren't being offered a bright enough future that they have a reason to choose life over death.[34]

One might ask: how is a bright enough future offered to children who have grown up under the systematic destruction of the Cold War and now the war on terror? In portraying terror as exclusively linked to poor, susceptible Muslims, TCT not also conceals the role of the US in sponsoring terror through madrasas but also in backing state terror more generally. For example, at the 'School' of the Americas in Fort Benning, Georgia, more than 60,000 Latin and Central American military, police, and civilian personnel have been trained in techniques of torture, extortion, kidnapping, and assassination.[35] Not surprisingly, the graduates of the School of the Americas have been linked with US-backed dictatorial regimes and severe human rights atrocities. Such schools—not unlike the extremist madrasa—have served the official US foreign policy of securing American strategic and corporate interests by destabilizing the developing world, through creating, arming, and supporting proxy agents of repression or engineered democracies. If 'the enemy is ignorance'—as the title of a chapter in TCT proclaims—the cultivated ignorance of schooled US citizens has done far more to sustain processes of terror than the ignorance attributed to the rural, Pakistani Muslim in the text. Given such political realities, and the fact that the US is the world's biggest arms exporter, it is not unfair to suggest that the US has been at the heart of globalizing terror, violence, and extremism in the world.[36]

If this sounds hyperbolic, it is because the cultural logic of development and imperialism constitutes the political economy of 'objective' knowledge and social science analysis. While affects of care and humanitarianism are validated, even celebrated mediums of development thinking and practice, politicized critique, and anger are invalidated as mediums of 'voice' and 'participation' in theory and practice. This unequal deployment and legitimation of particular affect within disciplinary knowledge helps fetishize certain embodied affects as civil while others are rendered uncivil. Ultimately, this affective fetishism of care and common humanity renders unspeakable the uncivil extremism of the US geopolitical agenda—for which Pakistan has paid a very high price. This unspeakability is increasingly enforced in the academy through several modes of policing knowledge, as several authors reveal compellingly in Chatterjee and Maira (2014).

TCT is perhaps most appealing because it encompasses a sense of self-interrogation about the role of the US in the war on terror, especially its excessive and costly use of military force as well as its lack of attention to local development needs. Compared with the singularly militaristic and Islamophobic rhetoric that dominated the post-9/11 discourse in the US, this critique is undoubtedly significant. Yet the text authorizes another dehistoricized narrative, by reducing terrorism to the spectre of dangerous, illiterate Muslims in undifferentiated landscapes teeming with extremist madrasas. When *books* and *bombs* are seen as comparable strategies for winning an imperialist war, the broader history and logics of which remain unexamined and unchallenged, it reflects 'how far we have fallen' and the poverty of the political discourse rather than a humanistic perspective.[37]

Moreover, if America is a 'deeply divided nation' over how to conduct the war on terror, TCT hits this feeling of national anxiety with just the right notes.[38] It is mildly self-critical about the war on terror, without actually problematizing either terrorism or the war itself. The problem of America's lack of popularity in the Pakistani and Afghani region is presented as mere misunderstanding, stemming from 'their' ignorance—instead of their acute awareness of the hypocrisy and violence of the US policy. But these 'root causes' need not be acknowledged, or addressed. The book suggests that like Mortenson, perhaps all that Americans need to do is bring civilization to Muslims by creating schools, and this will win hearts and minds. Mortenson is quite literally produced as a humanitarian idol in remote, terrorizing lands—a 'real life Indiana Jones' as the back cover of TCT tells us—who is saving Muslims from themselves, and securing America. Through Mortenson's dispositions of care, compassion, and sacrifice, TCT does the crucial work of accomplishing a political economy of feeling that sustains military imperialism: it affirms the inherent goodness of the American character, and serves as a balm for the American conscience by providing a palatable, therapeutic narrative of 'their' terror and 'our' humanitarianism. Indeed, it has also come to facilitate a reinvention of empire, as I elaborate in the next section.

DEVELOPMENT AND THE NEW MILITARY CULTURE OF COUNTER-INSURGENCY

I don't do what I'm doing to fight terror. I do it because I care about kids. Fighting terror is maybe seventh or eighth on my list of priorities.[39]

What's the difference between them [Pakistanis/Afghanis] becoming a productive local citizen or a terrorist? I think the key is education.[40]

The British policy was 'divide and conquer'. But I say 'unite and conquer.[41]

While counter-insurgency is surely not the reason why Mortenson initiated his educational efforts, he increasingly described school-building as the key answer to the problem of terrorism—in TCT itself as well as in the many public and Pentagon lectures that he has given since the publication of the book. Indeed, at one point in the book (third quotation above), Mortenson's voice as a humanitarian development worker morphs clearly into that of a US military strategist, comparing the American strategy of 'conquering' with that of the British colonizers before.

Importantly, Mortenson's solution of schools goes alongside the use of US military force, even though in some parts of TCT and in some media reviews of the text, one gets a sense that he is proposing books in place of force. For example, Mortenson says that he supported the war in Afghanistan, but felt that military campaigns should be accompanied with rebuilding which is essential for 'winning the war on terror'.[42] He thus argues for a more comprehensive approach, in which development becomes the very means for attaining American security—an argument that has found a willing audience amongst military officials in the US. According to Major James Spies, the Counterinsurgency Operations course director at West Point:

> Mortenson's involvement in central Asia is critical to a holistic approach to assisting other countries. The military has re-learned the lessons of counterinsurgency that point out the need to build up the whole of a society to assist them in solving the core problems that created an insurgency.

Hence, even as Mortenson refused funding from the US military to protect the neutrality of his work, his approach and effort has facilitated the re-invention of the military as well as of 'development' and 'reconstruction' in the current moment of empire.

Development in the post 9/11 context has become part and parcel of the project of US military hegemony, particularly in Afghanistan, Iraq, and Pakistan. In Afghanistan, for example, 'development assistance' is not only provided through US corporate contractors via USAID but also through military units called Provincial Reconstruction Teams (PRTs) that build schools, dig wells, and provide medical help. The military also runs agricultural laboratories and drip irrigation projects as a 'security measure' and to 'build a rapport with the villagers through education and employment'.[43] These techniques of 'soft power' resonate with the 'pacification' experiments implemented by the US during the Vietnam War and serve a number of aims. First, they achieve local goodwill and military intelligence so that the efficacy of the war in the occupied territory may be enhanced.[44] Second, the talk of protecting and serving civilians helps to silence critics, and cover up the devastation of lives and homes caused by military bombing. Third, they serve to expand the military's already enlarged existence. Finally, they give a positive image to the occupation at home, helping to justify and extend it.

This new militarism—which the counter-insurgency doctrine calls 'armed social work'—has blurred the lines between military warfare and civilian development. Because aid workers are increasingly seen as combatants, local and international NGO work has become extremely dangerous, aggravating civilian miseries caused by the war.[45] Reconstruction is also a billion-dollar business for American and multinational corporations, which not only profit from large-scale infrastructure projects in the short-term but also ensure continued profiteering by gaining control of land and natural resources, and by reshaping a country's economic policies along neoliberal lines. This 'disaster capitalism' has been implemented especially in Iraq, with territories flattened through intense firepower and local industry destroyed through new laws in order to pave the way for US corporate and military hegemony.[46] Even state-of-the-art health institutions were destroyed by design, with illusory promises that they will be grandly rebuilt.[47] Moreover, the White House now has an Office of the Coordinator of Reconstruction and Stabilization, which has elaborate 'rapid response' reconstruction plans for changing 'the very social fabric of a nation' in up to twenty-five countries that are *not yet* in conflict.[48] The changing of 'culture' is thus presented as a cure for conflict situations, but has effectively become the rationale for imperial expansion.

The discourse of poverty and extremism tremendously helps in entrenching this twenty-first century form of colonialism. Linking terrorism to poverty and ignorance provides a fitting logic for 'changing cultures' through 'reconstruction' activities such as education, which might also serve to create local consent for imperial ventures as it feeds into people's desire for literacy and social mobility. It plays an even more important role in creating consent at home, by producing the image of a benevolent America and its military.

This was strikingly demonstrated in an article by the *New York Times*-journalist, Thomas Friedman, in which he cites the inauguration of a girl's school in Afghanistan—created by Greg Mortenson—as a reason for extending the US presence in the country.[49] Interestingly, and yet not surprisingly—given the strategic blending of the soldier and the humanitarian in the new counter-insurgency approach—the school was inaugurated by Admiral Mike Mullen, the US chairman of the Joint Chiefs of Staff in 2009. Friedman writes:

> When you see two little Afghan girls crouched on the front steps of their new school, clutching tightly with both arms the notebooks handed to them by a US admiral—as if they were their first dolls—it's hard to say: 'Let's just walk away'. Not yet.

And again:

> Mortenson's efforts remind us what the essence of the 'war on terrorism' is about. It's about the war of ideas within Islam—a war between religious zealots who glorify martyrdom and want to keep Islam untouched by modernity and isolated from other faiths, with its women disempowered, and those who want to embrace modernity, open Islam to new ideas and empower Muslim women as much as men. America's invasions of Iraq and Afghanistan were, in part, an effort to create the space for the Muslim progressives to fight and win so that the real engine of change, something that takes nine months and 21 years to produce—a new generation—can be educated and raised differently.

The colonial logic of deploying culture to justify 'the long war' and occupation does not get more straightforward than this.[50] Imperial power as the beacon of modernity, development, civilization, and women's empowerment is precisely the discourse used by British and French colonizers in Egypt, India, and Algeria amongst other places for explaining their occupations.[51] The lives of the same Afghan and Pakistani women and children that Mortenson and others wish to save through education have been thoroughly ravaged by imperial adventures that have unleashed a misogynist Islam for foreign policy interests, and that continue to destroy lives, land, and livelihood through bombs, Predator drones, military bases, and imposed, neoliberal ideologies. Friedman's article goes on to state:

> Mortenson said he was originally critical of the US military in Iraq and Afghanistan, but he's changed his views: 'The US military has gone through

a huge learning curve. They really get it. It's all about building relationships from the ground up, listening more and serving the people of Afghanistan'.

This grassroots, participatory militarism goes alongside the reinvented image of the military as a harbinger of humanitarian development, and helps the military recover from its scarred images of an occupying force committing torture. It is also a project that has long been in the making, as part of what Derek Gregory calls the 'cultural turn in late modern war' whereby cultural knowledge is not 'a substitute for killing but rather, in certain circumstances, a prerequisite for its refinement'.[52] This cultural turn is aided by what I would call an 'ethnographic turn' in empire in which—similar to the ethnographic turn in development—practices of knowing and working with the local express empathy and humanitarian compassion, while effectively re-legitimizing the imperial project through an erasure of power relations and structural inequality.[53]

FALSEHOODS, POWER, AND DELUSION

Before TCT was released in 2006, my friends in Pakistan barely knew about the area where I was conducting my dissertation, signifying the invisibility of the region as I discussed in Chapter 1. After the publication of TCT, however, I started hearing: 'Oh there must be so much poverty and danger there! I learnt from *Three Cups of Tea*'. The text had quickly reached global fame, and educated Pakistanis of a particular class were also suddenly using this book as a reference to understand Gilgit-Baltistan in deeply problematic ways. This prompted me to read the book, and it left me flabbergasted. I could not fathom how such falsehood could be published as non-fiction, let alone become definitive. My Gilgiti activist-friends were even more shocked, as they directly inhabited the landscape which was being portrayed as Taliban-central. They immediately apprehended it as part of the new Great Game, in which the war on terror necessitated new fictions to justify imperial interests. But when we tried to talk to our friends about the level of fabrication in the text, we were treated as suspicious. Here was a good humanitarian man, creating schools, and us researchers and activists only knew critique. Many in Gilgit-Baltistan had simply not read the book, but were happy that some schools were being created, and that more tourists were now interested in visiting the area just to see the schools. Mortenson had become a living legend, and one tourist company in Gilgit was designing a 'Three Cups of Tea Tour' to chart the path that Mortenson had traversed.

I had been trained in development sociology and postcolonial studies, and here was a contemporary white knight fantasy—designed to nourish Western stereotypes and interests—being lived out on the very terrain of my field research. I felt compelled to write a journal article to unpack the multiple problems with the text and its connection to US counter-insurgency and militarism.[54] A short book review would not have sufficed given the extent of misrepresentations, so I undertook a thorough, in-depth analysis. To my dismay, the response—from scholars and the lay audience alike—was a refusal to accept. Indeed, it was hard to get the journal article published, because what I was pointing out was *too much*, and I was pointing it out with the anger and anguish such falsehood elicited. One reviewer wondered if I had even visited Pakistan lately. Implicitly, could my word as a brown local woman be trusted as opposed to that of a Western idol-humanitarian, regarding places in which 'we' were at war?

Once the article was published, however, Gilgiti activists and scholars who had actually read the book were deeply appreciative. A prominent development thinker and practitioner of Gilgit-Baltistan communicated to me that he and some of his colleagues were planning to file a lawsuit against Mortenson for his fabricated text but after my article, they felt heard and affirmed. This was in turn affirming for me, as from most friends and acquaintances in Gilgit-Baltistan and Pakistan, I was facing a backlash. The resistance to my critique revealed to me the sheer force of the savior rhetoric of humanitarianism. It can claim unquestionable moral certainty and superiority, and even serve as a shield and license for disingenuous representation and action. Ten months later, Jon Krakauer released 'Three Cups of Deceit: How Greg Mortenson, Humanitarian Hero, Lost His Way' (2011) which created an immense public outcry over Mortentson's misuse of funds and fudged biographical details in TCT. Within three years, however, Mortenson's reputation was rehabilitated, the falseness of TCT forgotten, and the children's version of the book till today continues to be a top-seller in the US. The core of my own critique — which emphasized the Islamophobia, racism, and militarism embodied in Mortenson's project—continues to remain inaudible.

Following Foucault, much work in social analysis has focused on truth and knowledge as mechanisms and effects of power. It is of critical significance, today, to address falsehood, dishonesty and willful deceit as key ingredients of power and its regimes of knowledge.

We must ask: what does it say about our current imperial moment that such delusional fabrications as that of Mortenson about Gilgit-Baltistan can pass off as truth? Whose truth and voice counts, why, and on what terms? Delusion proper is not just incorrect belief, but 'absolutely unshakeable, quite beyond argument'.[55] In political delusion, one might suggest that its *confidence of non-critiquability* comes from what Mignolo (2010) has termed an 'imperial epistemic supremacy' that defines narratives of poor/indigenous/Muslim others in ways that are always already imperialized, racialized, and gendered. Imperial narratives count as true and valid because they speak from and for power, and hence are rendered unaccountable. Even after they are challenged, they continue to have lasting force as a regime of truth because the underlying logic remains the preferable and palatable interpretation of reality.

My purpose in this chapter has not been to discount the need and value of education and grassroot development work. Books are obviously better than bombs, and this demand has become a key rallying point for peace activists in the US and Pakistan alike. But, as I argued in the previous chapter as well, one has to assess the nobility of a development intervention within the larger politics that it represents and perpetuates. Through the figure and work of Greg Mortenson, *Three Cups of Tea* uses the terrain of Gilgit-Baltistan to produce a narrative about the war on terror that is devoid of history, power, and politics. The text deploys and normalizes particular, decontextualized constructions of culture and underdevelopment to displace blame, defining the American self as well as the Muslim other in ways conducive to US policy, and reassuring for the American public. In doing so, it promotes a liberal interventionism that apparently provides a humane and progressive perspective on terrorism, but, in fact, occludes the complex material and political conditions that engender it. Simultaneously, it reproduces the West-affirming terms of development discourse that 'separate the world's components into bounded units, disaggregate their relational histories, turn difference into hierarchy, and naturalize...[such]...representations'.[56] Even as the text provides a more sympathetic account of Pakistani Muslims—particularly through memorable characters such as Haji Ali—its general depiction of Pakistan remains couched in an otherizing narrative of terror that essentializes the country as a zone of ignorance, backwardness, and extremism. Hence, as a rule, most Pakistanis appear to be pitiable and dangerous, though 'not all'. Mortenson's ethnographic approach and knowledge is precisely what gives this narrative an aura of realism. Finally, TCT has enabled the emergence of a participatory militarism in which an ethnographically sensitive military strives to 'listen' and 'build relationships' to 'serve people'—in order to occupy better, and longer.

There is surely a dire need for humanitarian work and for rebuilding in the wake of a devastating imperial occupation. Hence, the argument is not to exit and forget, but to acknowledge historical and contemporary aggression, be accountable for war crimes and pay reparations, work towards undoing the damage, and take steps at home and abroad so that ruthless foreign policies are not repeated. What needs to be practiced is not a hawkish, colonizing humanitarianism but an 'anti-colonial', 'historicizing humanism' which acknowledges suffering but also the relational histories that have produced it.[57] Moreover, it acknowledges the social life-worlds of others in their own terms and voices, instead of apprehending them solely through the assumed prisms of imperial mercy or disdain.

Finally, we also need to question the affective politics of humanitarianism, particularly as it has come to be understood in situations of political conflict. The label of 'humanitarian' has become an exclusive preserve of Western saviours, who are deemed to care and have compassion as they are building hospitals, schools, and relief camps in darker nations. Simultaneously, labels of 'extremism' and 'violence' have become naturalized properties of poorer regions, as if the political economy of colonial exploitation, neoliberal dispossession, and savage militarism—processes that lie at the heart of Western civilization and its ability to be humanitarian—are not extreme and violent. One wonders why the poor and illiterate villagers of Korphe in Gilgit-Baltistan—who saved Mortenson's life and nursed him back to health by sharing meager resources and giving him their 'finest' possessions—are not considered as having 'humanitarian instincts' but those of Mortenson are readily assumed.[58] After all, Mortenson embarked on his journey because he felt that he must repay the Korphe people for their extraordinary generosity. They had no such obligation.

NOTES

1. On 17 April 2011, the CBS investigative programme '60 minutes' revealed shocking details of alleged misconduct by Greg Mortenson, highlighting how in *Three Cups of Tea*, Mortenson fabricated key stories regarding his personal journeys in Pakistan, and that his charity, the Central Asia Institute, had been involved in serious financial malpractices. This programme was a follow-up to Jack Karakuer's text, *Three Cups of Deceit* which had exposed Mortenson's misdeeds, and used my journal article on the subject as reference (Ali, 2010a).
2. For recent interventions, see especially Visweswaran (2013), Fernandes (2013), and Deeb and Winegar (2015).
3. David Relin committed suicide in 2012, a year after the book turned into a scandal.
4. Taken in 2010 from www.threecupsoftea.com, the official site of the book *Three Cups of Tea*. The link is no longer active.
5. While TCT is reminiscent of the otherizing tendencies of Western Orientalism, it is not my aim to analyze the text through Orientalism as the central lens. TCT is not primarily concerned with producing forms of knowledge about the other, and is not written in overtly racist terms. Rather than invoking Orientalism as imposed conceptual framework, I interrogate the text on its own terms and examine the representational, humanitarian, and military politics that it engenders.
6. Mortenson and Relin, *Three Cups of Tea*, p. 77, p. 200.
7. Ibid., p. 95, p. 189, p. 183.
8. Stellrecht (1997).
9. For a critique of development discourse, see, for example, Ferguson (1990). For a critique of development discourse in the Northern Areas, see, for example, Butz (1998).
10. Mortenson and Relin, *Three Cups of Tea*, p. 5.
11. Rashid (2000).
12. As discussed in Chapter 2, the ISI is the largest intelligence agency in Pakistan. *Mujahideen*, here, refers specifically to the Muslim fighters recruited, funded and equipped by US and Pakistani intelligence services during the 1980s Afghan war. For detailed examinations of the Cold War, see Cooley (2000) and Arne Westad (2007). For a nuanced understanding of the Afghan Taliban, see Crews (2012).
13. Craig (2002).
14. Ibid., p. 116.

15 Ibid., p. 233–235.
16 The collapsing of different regions into a homogenous landscape is characteristic of the security lens through which Pakistan and Afghanistan have been viewed in US policy, most recently crystallized in the political category of 'Af-Pak' under the Obama administration.
17 Mortenson and Relin, *Three Cups of Tea*, p. 243.
18 Ibid., p. 228.
19 Kurin (1986).
20 Marsden (2005).
21 Mortenson and Relin, *Three Cups of Tea*, p. 243.
22 Ibid., p. 243, p. 295.
23 Andrabi et al. (2006).
24 Cockcroft et al. (2009).
25 Such proclamations about Islamic education are prevalent in Western media more generally. For a critique of such representations, see McClure (2009).
26 Andrabi et al. (2006).
27 Cockcroft (2009).
28 According to statements released by Al-Qaeda, these political motivations include opposition to the presence of US military bases and troops in Muslim lands, as well as the US foreign policy towards Israel. For an examination of the class and educational backgrounds of those who engage in Islamist violence, see, for example, Bergen and Pandey (2006).
29 Mamdani (2004).
30 Cooley (2000: 10).
31 Rashid (2000).
32 Blackburn (2002).
33 The history of US foreign policy is mentioned—not critiqued—in only a couple of places in *TCT* through passing, almost submerged references to Stinger missiles, such as on p. 213 and p. 217.
34 Mortenson and Relin, *Three Cups of Tea*, p. 292.
35 Amnesty International (2002) and Gill (2004).
36 Stockholm International Peace Research Institute (2008).
37 Gregory (2008: 45).
38 Mortenson and Relin, *Three Cups of Tea*, p. 301.
39 Ibid., p. 138.
40 Ibid., p. 268.
41 Ibid., p. 189.
42 Ibid., p. 294.
43 GRAIN (2009).
44 Ibid.
45 Omidian (2009).
46 Klein (2007).
47 Al-Kubaisy (2009).

48 Klein (2005).
49 Friedman (2009).
50 Hayden (2009).
51 Abu-Lughod (2002).
52 Gregory (2008: 4).
53 Li (2007).
54 Ali (2010a).
55 Sass (1994: 4).
56 Hart (2006: 997).
57 Razack (2004) and Malkki (1997).
58 Gardner (2006).

CONCLUSION

The Great Media Game

In a *New York Times* (*NY Times*) article titled, 'China's Discreet Hold on Pakistan's Northern Borderlands', published on 27 August 2010 and a subsequent rejoinder published on 9 September 2010, the American foreign policy strategist Selig Harrison painted an astoundingly imaginative picture of Gilgit-Baltistan.[1] He claimed that this region was witnessing a creeping Chinese occupation at the hands of 7,000–11,000 soldiers of the People's Liberation Army, as well as a simmering local rebellion against Chinese and Pakistani control. What was actually happening on the ground was the post-floods repair work by Chinese labourers and engineers, who have been involved in the construction and maintenance of the Karakoram Highway for several decades. The *NY Times* article portrayed this construction activity as a military manoeuvre by the Chinese army, even suggesting that tunnels created as part of a proposed gas pipeline in the region can be used for storing missiles. While berating Pakistan for supporting 'de facto Chinese control' in Gilgit-Baltistan, it simultaneously praised India for promoting supposedly democratic elections and a free media in Indian-controlled Kashmir.

As was the case for *Three Cups of Tea*, what is significant about such imperial discourses is not merely their penchant for monumental myth-making but the larger politics which they service and enable. Harrison's article was lauding India's role in Kashmir at a time when massive street protests had rocked the region, leading to state violence that eventually resulted in more than a hundred deaths and brought critical global attention to India's injustices in Kashmir. To hype up Pakistan's mistreatment of the parts of Kashmir under its control then became an Indian foreign policy need—one that India's intelligence agents, lobbyists, and strategists serviced by promoting a particular kind of intellectual and journalistic discourse on Gilgit-Baltistan. The patently false *NY Times* article was followed by one in *The Guardian* titled, 'China and India: The Great Game's New Players' by former Indian finance and defence minister, Jaswant Singh, which repeated the myth about how thousands of Chinese troops were stationed in Gilgit-Baltistan.[2] By early 2011, an 'Institute for Gilgit-Baltistan Studies' had emerged in Washington. Led by comprador intellectuals, the first major seminar that the Institute organized was titled, 'China's growing presence in Gilgit-Baltistan', at which—no less intriguingly—Selig Harrison quietly apologized for the incorrect information that he had provided in his *NY Times* article barely six months before. The apology was never published in *NY Times*, nor any correction issued.

Activists in Gilgit-Baltistan, however, had no trouble recognizing that the *NY Times* report was an outcome of multiple delusions. It reflected a shared US–India competitiveness against China, and an attempt to maintain the myth of India as a great democracy despite its annihilatory violence on Kashmiri bodies. It was also an attempt to whip up a sense of 'Pakistan-and-India-are-equally-bad-in-Kashmir' so that the devastating scale of Indian military violence in Indian-controlled Kashmir could be erased in global public discourse. Activists in Gilgit-Baltistan saw such myth-making as a continuation of the Great Game. During the imperial rivalry between Britain and Russia in the late nineteenth century, small Central Asian states—including those that today form Gilgit-Baltistan—were used as a playing ground of power, and specious claims about people and places were deployed for justifying imperial interests. This 'Great Game'—as it came to be called with no sense of irony or conscience—continues today with Pakistan, India, China, and the US as the key 'players' that define the geopolitical context of Gilgit-Baltistan. It is as much about the intrigues of states as it is a story of competing representations—a Great Media Game, so to speak. It is a game that is routinely discussed in everyday conversation in Gilgit-Baltistan, and is regarded as a political fact by many in the region. The metaphor is indeed the truth. Then and now, it was literally a game, a sport of state and empire-making, wreaking havoc.

Great delusions have always been central to great games, and the continuing crisis of Kashmir is evidence of such delusions by multiple powers over the last two centuries—delusions that reflect the arrogance of states and their hunger for power; the destructive madness of paranoia and policing; the willful denial of actual subjection; and the false beliefs of grandeur, democracy, and superiority built on histories of violence and occupation. For the people of Gilgit-Baltistan, becoming part of Pakistan was once deemed as an escape from this Great Game, a promise of Muslim solidarity and union. Yet their imbrication in the Kashmir dispute has meant a continued betrayal of their trust in this promise, and a continuation of undemocratic rule and oppression.

The latest, worrying development in this regard is the way in which the Pakistani government is steamrolling the China–Pakistan Economic Corridor (CPEC) throughout its territory, including in Gilgit-Baltistan, which directly borders China and is the most crucial link in this series of infrastructure projects and investments valued at over $50 billion. China was once considered a friend and a good neighbour to Gilgit-Baltistanis in need. Today, people in the region are wary of deep political, social, and climactic consequences of Pakistani and Chinese collaborations. In the name of CPEC, an already severe regime of monitoring of activists in Gilgit-Baltistan has been heightened, involving systematic violation of rights and suppression of dissent. The Human Rights Commission of Pakistan has documented how state agencies have been abusing the anti-terror laws to harass and jail journalists, political workers, and ordinary citizens who have been evicted due to CPEC and are protesting in response.[3] Of special mention here is the creation of what is known as the 'Schedule Four' list for Gilgit-Baltistan under the Anti-Terrorism Act 1997. More than a hundred civil society members and activists have been booked, arrested, and harassed by being placed on this infamous list—without any rationale or proof of fault—and continue to be harassed as they cannot travel without prior approval, let alone gather or protest.

But the voices of these citizens are neither heard in masculinist political narratives focused on 'games' and 'key players' nor in popular nationalist ones which claim Gilgit-Baltistan as a zone of natural beauty and freedom.[4] As I have attempted to demonstrate, the people of Gilgit-Baltistan are silenced and suspected, and seen as traitors, rural backwards, or extremists. The inhabitants of one of the most contested border zones in the world find themselves contained by multiple discourses and interests—disingenuous claims that they must perpetually fend off and defend against. These are claims about their land being a 'paradise on earth' in which their own presence is invisibilized, about their untrustworthiness that merits surveillance instead of rights, about their sectarian difference which needs to be homogenized, about their livelihoods being a threat to biodiversity, and about terror being caused by their assumed ignorance and poverty. They are thus affected and shaped by the tourist gaze, the military-intelligence gaze, the Sunni-fundamentalist gaze, the conservationist gaze and the humanitarian-counterinsurgent gaze. These regimes of representation and control are felt intensely and intimately in Gilgit-Baltistan, evoking an anguished emotionality against multiple forms of injustice. It leads many to despair and cynicism, but many articulate ever more strongly their love and loyalty towards Pakistan—this is simultaneously an expression of local ethical–moral subjectivity; an expression of a historical faith in the project of Pakistan; an outcome of families upon families trained to be loyal due to employment in the military; and a condition of survival in a delusional, surveillance state.

In effect, the multiple positionality of Gilgit-Baltistan's people—as border, religious, and development subjects—has rendered them subject to multiple state and transnational projects of rule, including practices that deny political rights to the region, textbooks that silence Shia identity in discussions of Islam, and national parks that appropriate pastoral land in the name of development. In this book, I analyse such practices in terms of the state-formative processes of representation, militarization, sectarianized education, and international development—seemingly unlinked processes that must be examined relationally in order to grasp the intersecting ways in which rule is accomplished over spaces and subjects. Ultimately, the multilayered, ethnographic analysis of state-making in this book reveals the state not only as a coherent structure of legibility and integration but also as an unwieldy assemblage that operates through illegibility, disintegration, and emotional regulation. Rule here is accomplished through the cultivation of erasure and ambiguity, divisiveness and manipulation, and emotions like loyalty and suspicion that simultaneously produce consent, coercion, concealment, and conflict. Rule is also contested, as revealed through everyday negotiations of power as well as organized struggles for political, cultural, and environmental recognition. What unites these various engagements with power is an intimate quest for a substantive citizenship that embodies dignity, equality, and harmony. People neither wish to reject modernity nor the modern state; rather 'they are struggling for self-determination, that is, significant control over the terms and conditions under which they develop their relations with the nation-state, the global economy... and other historical processes'.[5]

Finally, even though it is a Shia-majority, disputed border zone, Gilgit-Baltistan is not simply an exception or an anomaly in the larger context of the Pakistani nation/state. Rather, I conceive of it as an extraordinary zone were the norms of rule are especially manifest. While the region remains deprived of meaningful citizenship under the garb of the Kashmir dispute and is reduced to a sectarian quagmire, state and nationalist discourse in Pakistan proudly claims ownership of its beautiful mountains, while righteously defending Islam and the 'Kashmir cause' as integral to the meaning of Pakistani nationhood. If national self-definition depends on, and is, sustained by what is denied and depoliticized,[6] then Gilgit-Baltistan provides an exemplary crucible on the back of which the Pakistani nation and state operates.

What, then, is the positioning of the academic-scholar in such a militarized conflict zone? Academic researchers are not just perched above, observing the tensions of the state and empire but also often entrapped in them in ways that call into question their own loyalties. My closest such experience was at an academic conference on Pakistan in Washington DC in 2010. There must have been at least a hundred and fifty people in attendance. When the conference concluded, I and some other presenters were disturbed to see that almost all the audience members who came up to speak to us worked for the US Central Command. One such official who approached me said that he worked in the GIS section, and his latest assignment was to make 'sectarian maps' of Gilgit-Baltistan. Would I assist him? I was relieved to eventually encounter some Muslim students from Georgetown University, but they too, it turned out, were employed for some project or the other related to the US military-intelligence complex. One student pointed out that the previous year, there were two hundred jobs available in this complex for fresh undergraduates who were skilled in 'Muslim' languages—reminding me of the Gilgit taxi driver who had told me how he spied earlier in his life to feed his family. Another student pointed out how academic output is seen as 'open-source intelligence' and that his job was to obtain such intelligence from people like me.

From being an object of suspicion in Gilgit to a source of intelligence in the US—this is the terrain that any academic working on conflict zones must confront. The important thing to highlight is that these contexts are not oppositional—both are connected through a larger political economy of militarism within which an intelligencizing of domestic and foreign policy and a delusional regime of surveillance has become normative. Indeed, in recent years, both the field of anthropology and the academy at large has been subjected to the disciplining of knowledge under militarism, placing ever more demands of survival on scholars themselves.[7]

Perhaps one might learn how to address the situation from people in places such as Gilgit-Baltistan, who have long inhabited strategic terrains and battled political subjection. From poets to preachers, pastoralists to political activists, the dwellers of Gilgit-Baltistan have engaged in ethical–political struggle in the public domain to restore equal rights, dignity, and humanity through dissent and rightful representation of their felt oppression. They have fought against institutionalized ignorance and repression in their educational institutions, channeled their anguish and protest through their poetic expressions, and protected their commons amidst sustained subjugation. The only way forward is to add to the chorus.

NOTES

1 Selig S. Harrison, 'China's Discreet Hold on Pakistan's Northern Borderlands', *The New York Times*, 26 August 2010.
2 Jaswant Singh, 'China and India: The great game's new players', *The Guardian*, 25 September 2010.
3 HRCP (2017).
4 For example, the trailer of the Pakistani movie *Motorcycle Girl* (2018) which sets up Gilgit-Baltistan as the site where Pakistani women might find freedom and fulfillment of desires, even if patriarchal ones. In a number of patriotic music videos over the last few years as well, Gilgit-Baltistan's freedom is ignored to privilege the sense of freedom experienced by elite Pakistani men and women. The emergence of Gilgit-Baltistan as the ground for national and even feminist Pakistani aspirations

is akin to the way Kashmir is routinely used as the backdrop for romance in Indian movies.
5 Pratt, 1999: 39 quoted in Butz 2006.
6 Butler and Spivak (2007).
7 Chatterjee and Maira (2014) and Deeb and Winegar (2015).

BIBLIOGRAPHY

Aase, Tor H. 1999. 'The Theological Construction of Conflict: Gilgit, Northern Areas.' In *Muslim Diversity: Local Islam in Global Contexts*, edited by Leif Manger, 58–79. London: Curzon Press.

Abbas, Hassan. 2005. *Pakistan's Drift Into Extremism: Allah, the Army, and America's War on Terror*. London: M.E. Sharpe.

Abbas, Sarmad. 2005. 'Unending War.' *The Herald*, November.

———. 2006. 'Uneasy Calm.' *The Herald Annual*, January.

Abidi-Habib, Mehjabeen and Anna Lawrence. 2007. 'Revolt and Remember: How the Shimshal Nature Trust Develops and Sustains Social-Ecological Resilience in Northern Pakistan.' *Ecology and Society* 12(2): 35.

Abou-Zahab, Mariam. 2002. 'The Regional Dimension of Sectarian Conflicts in Pakistan.' In *Pakistan: Nationalism without a Nation?* edited by Christophe Jaffrelot, 115–128. New Delhi: Manohar.

———. 2004. 'The Sunni-Shia Conflict in Jhang, Pakistan.' In *Lived Islam in South Asia: Adaptations, Accommodation, and Conflict*, edited by Imtiaz Ahmad and Helmut Reifeld, 135–148. Delhi: Social Science Press.

Abraham, Itty. 2003. 'State, Place, Identity: Two Stories in the Making of Region.' In *Regional Modernities: The Cultural Politics of Development in India*, edited by Kalyanakrishnan Sivaramakrishnan and Arun Agrawal, 404–425. Delhi: Oxford University Press.

Abrams, Philip. 1988. 'Notes on the Difficulty of Studying the State.' *Journal of Historical Sociology* 1(1): 58–89.

———. 1982. *Historical Sociology*. Ithaca, NY: Cornell University Press.

Abu-Lughod, Lila. 1986. *Veiled Sentiments: Honor and Poetry in a Bedouin Society*. Berkeley: University of California Press.

———. 2002. 'Do Muslim Women Really Need Saving? Anthropological Reflections on Cultural Relativism and its Others.' *American Anthropologist* 104(3): 783–790.

Adichie, Chimamanda N. 2009. 'The Danger of a Single Story.' Available at: http://www.ted.com/talks/chimamanda_adichie_the_danger_of_a_single_story. Accessed on 20 February 2017.

Agamben, Giorgio. 1998. *Homo Sacer: Sovereign Power and Bare Life*. Stanford: Stanford University Press.

———. 2005. *State of Exception*. Chicago: University of Chicago Press.

Aggarwal, Ravina. 2004. *Beyond Lines of Control: Performance and Politics on the Disputed Borders of Ladakh, India*. Durham: Duke University Press.

Agrawal, Arun. 2001a. 'State Formation in Community Spaces? Decentralization of Control over Forests in the Kumaon Himalaya, India.' *Journal of Asian Studies* 60(1): 9–40.

———. 2001b. 'Common Property Institutions and Sustainable Development.' *World Development* 29(10): 1649–1672.

———. 2005. *Environmentality: Technologies of Government and the Making of Subjects*. Durham: Duke University Press.

Agrawal, Arun and Clark C. Gibson. eds. 2001. *Communities and the Environment: Ethnicity, Gender, and the State in Community-Based Conservation*. New Jersey: Rutgers University Press.

Ahmad, Iftikhar. 2004. 'Islam, Democracy and Citizenship Education: An Examination of the Social Studies Curriculum in Pakistan.' *Current Issues in Comparative Education* 7(1): 39-49.

Ahmad, Imtiaz and Helmut Reifeld. eds. 2004. *Lived Islam in South Asia: Adaptations, Accommodation, and Conflict*. Delhi: Social Science Press.

Ahmed, Akbar S. 1995 (1983). 'Islam and the District Paradigm: Emergent Trends in Contemporary Muslim Society.' In *Muslim Communities of South Asia: Culture, Society, and Power*, edited by Triloki N. Madan, 63–102. New Delhi: Manohar.

Ahmed, Khalid. 2005. 'The Sectarian State in Gilgit.' *The Friday Times* XVII: 21.
———. 2011. *Sectarian War: Pakistan's Sunni-Shia Violence and its links to the Middle East*. Karachi: Oxford University Press.
Ahmed, Sara. 2004. *The Cultural Politics of Emotion*. New York: Routledge.
Al-Kubaisy, Omar. 2009. 'Iraq: Occupation Year 7.' *Countercurrents.org*, 5 April.
Alavi, Hamza. 1988. 'Pakistan and Islam: Ethnicity and Ideology.' In *State and Ideology in the Middle East and Pakistan*, edited by Hamza Alavi and Fred Halliday, 64–111. New York: Monthly Review Press.
———. 1990. 'Authoritarianism and Legitimation of State Power in Pakistan.' In *The Postcolonial State in South Asia*, edited by Subrata Mitra, 19–71. London: Harvester Wheatsheaf.
Ali, Farman. 2001. 'In Search of Identity.' *Dawn*, 8 April.
Ali, Inayat, and David Butz. 2003. 'The Shimshal Governance Model: A Community Conserved Area, a Sense of Cultural Identity, A Way of Life.' *Policy Matters* 12: 111–120.
Ali, Nosheen. 2008. 'Outrageous State, Sectarianized Citizens: Deconstructing the "Textbook Controversy" in the Northern Areas, Pakistan.' *South Asia Multidisciplinary Academic Journal* 2.
———. 2009. 'States of Struggle: Politics, Religion, and Ecology in the Making of the Northern Areas, Pakistan.' PhD dissertation, Cornell University.
———. 2010a. 'Books vs. Bombs: Humanitarian Development and the Narrative of Terror in Northern Pakistan.' *Third World Quarterly* 31(4): 541–559.
———. 2010b. 'Sectarian Imaginaries: The Micropolitics of Sectarianism and State-Making in Northern Pakistan.' *Current Sociology* 58(5): 738–754.
———. 2014. 'Spaces of Nature: Producing Gilgit-Baltistan as the Eco-body of the Nation.' *Ethnoscripts* 16(1): 115–123.
———. 2016. 'From Hallaj to Heer: Poetic Knowledge and the Muslim Tradition.' *Journal of Narrative Politics* 3(1): 2–26.
Ali, Usman. 1990. *Gilgit ki Rog Kahani*. Lahore: Maqbul Academy.
Amin, Ash. 2002. *Ethnicity and the Multicultural City: Living with Diversity* (report for the Department of Transport, Local Government and the Regions and the ESRC Cities Initiative). London: Sage Publications.
Amnesty International. 2002. *Unmatched Power, Unmet Principles: The Human Rights Dimensions of US Training of Foreign Military, Security and Police Forces*. New York: Amnesty International USA Publications.

Anderson, Ben. 2010. 'Modulating the Excess of Affect: Morale in a State of "Total War". In *The Affect Theory Reader*, edited by Melissa Gregg and Gregory J. Seigworth, 161–185. Durham: Duke University Press.

Anderson, Benedict. 1991. *Imagined Communities: Reflections on the Origin and Spread of Nationalism.* London: Verso.

Andrabi, Tahir et al. 2006. 'Religious school enrollment in Pakistan: A look at the data.' *Comparative Education Review* 50(3): 446–477.

Andreas, Joel. 2004. *Addicted to War: Why the US. Can't Kick Militarism.* Oakland: AK Press.

Anjum, Aaliya and Saiba Varma. 2010. 'Curfewed in Kashmir: Voices from the Valley.' *Economic and Political Weekly* 45(35): 10–14.

Anthias, Floya and Nira Yuval-Davis. 1993. *Racialized Boundaries: Race, Nation, Gender, Colour and Class and Anti-Racist Struggle.* London: Routledge.

Apple, Michael and Linda Christian-Smith. eds. 1991. *The Politics of the Textbook.* New York: Routledge.

Applegate, Celia. 1999. 'A Europe of Regions: Reflections on the Historiography of Sub-National Places in Modern Times.' *The American Historical Review* 104(4): 1157–1182.

Arnold, David and Ramachandra Guha. eds. 1995. *Nature, Culture, Imperialism: Essays on the Environmental History of South Asia.* New Delhi: Oxford University Press.

Asad, Talal. 2003. *Formations of the Secular: Christianity, Islam, Modernity.* Palo Alto, CA: Stanford University Press.

Aziz, Khursheed K. 1993. *The Murder of History: A Critique of History Textbooks Used in Pakistan.* Lahore: Sang-e-Meel Publications.

———. 2004. *The Murder of History. A Critique of History Textbooks Used in Pakistan.* Lahore: Vanguard.

Bacevich, Andrews. 2004. *American Empire: The Realities and Consequences of US Diplomacy.* Boston: Harvard University Press.

Banerjee, Mukulika. 2000. *The Pathan Unharmed: Opposition and Memory in the North West Frontier.* New Delhi: Oxford University Press.

Bangash, Yaqoob K. 2010. 'Three Forgotten Accessions: Gilgit, Hunza and Nagar.' *The Journal of Imperial and Commonwealth History* 38(1): 117–143.

Baringer, Sandra. 2004. *The Metanarrative of Suspicion in Late Twentieth-Century America.* New York: Routledge.

Peer, Basharat. 2010. *Curfewed Night*. New York: Scribner.

Bauman, Richard and Barbara Babcock. 1978. *Verbal Art as Performance*. Rowley, MA: Newbury House Publishers.

Baviskar, Amita.. 2007a. 'The Dream Machine: The Model Development Project and the Remaking of the State.' In *Waterscapes: The Cultural Politics of a Natural Resource*, 281–313. Delhi: Permanent Black.

———. 2007b. 'Water Politics.' *Economic and Political Weekly* 42(11).

Bayat, Asef. 2009. *Life as Politics: How Ordinary People Change the Middle East*. Palo Alto: Stanford University Press.

Bayly, Christopher A. 1996. *Empire and Information: Intelligence Gathering and Social Communication in India, 1780–1870*. Cambridge: Cambridge University Press.

Benbassa, Esther and Aron Rodrigue. 2000. *Sephardi Jewry: A History of the Judeo-Spanish Community, 14th–20th Centuries*. Berkeley: University of California Press.

Berezin, Mabel M. 1999. 'Political Belonging: Emotion, Nation and Identity in Fascist Italy.' In *State/Culture: State-formation after the Cultural Turn*, edited by George Steinmetz, 355–377. Ithaca, NY: Cornell University Press.

Bergen, Peter and Swati Pandey. 2006. 'The Madrassa Scapegoat.' *Washington Quarterly* 29(2): 117–125.

Bhan, Mona. 2013. *Counterinsurgency, Democracy, and the Politics of Identity in India: From Warfare to Welfare?* London: Routledge.

Bhan, Mona and Nishita Trisal. 2017. 'Fluid Landscapes, Sovereign Nature: Conservation and Counterinsurgency in Indian-Controlled Kashmir.' *Critique of Anthropology* 37(1): 67–92.

Biddulph, John. 1880. *Tribes of Hindoo Koosh*. Calcutta: Office of the Superintendent of Government Printing.

Blackburn, Robin. 2002. 'The Imperial Presidency, the War on Terrorism, and the Revolutions of Modernity.' *Constellations* 9(1): 3–33.

Blum, William. 2003. *Killing Hope: US Military and CIA Interventions Since World War II*. London: Zed Books.

Bose, Sumantra. 1997. *The Challenge in Kashmir: Democracy, Self-Determination and a Just Peace*. New Delhi: Sage Publications.

Bourdieu, Pierre. 1977. *Outline of a Theory of Practice*. Cambridge: Cambridge University Press.

———. 1991. 'Identity and Representation: Elements for a Critical Reflection on the Idea of Region.' In *Language and Symbolic Power*, edited by John B. Thompson, 220–228. Cambridge: Harvard University Press.

Bourdieu, Pierre and Loïc J.D. Wacquant. eds. 1992. *An Invitation to Reflexive Sociology*. University of Chicago Press.

Braudel, Fernand. 1972. *The Mediterranean and the Mediterranean World in the Age of Philip II, Volume I*. New York: Harper & Row Publishers.

Brenner, Angie. 2008. 'Greg Mortenson's Mission to Promote Peace, One School at a Time.' *Wild River Review*, 26 February. Available at: https://www.wildriverreview.com/archives/wrratlarge-2008-archive/.

Breunig, Lydia A. 2006. *Conservation in Context: Establishing Natural Protected Areas during Mexico's Neoliberal Reformation*. PhD Dissertation, University of Arizona.

Brockington, Dan and Katherine Homewood. 2001. 'Degradation Debates and Data Deficiencies: The Mkomazi Game Reserve, Tanzania.' *Africa* 71(3): 449–480.

Büscher, Bram, Wolfram Dressler and Robert Fletcher. eds. 2014. *Nature Inc. Environmental Conservation in the Neoliberal Age*. Tuscon: University of Arizona Press.

Buse, Dieter K., Gary Kinsman, and Mercedes Steedman. 2000. *Whose National Security?: Canadian State Surveillance and the Creation of Enemies*. Toronto: Between The Lines.

Butler, Judith. 1997. *The Psychic Life of Power: Theories in Subjection*. Stanford: Stanford University Press.

Butler, Judith and Gayatri C. Spivak. 2007. *Who Sings the Nation-State? Language, Politics, Belonging*. New York: Seagull Books.

Butz, David. 1996. 'Sustaining Indigenous Communities: Symbolic and Instrumental Dimensions of Pastoral Resource Use in Shimshal, Northern Pakistan.' *The Canadian Geographer* 40(1): 36–53.

———. 1998. 'Orientalist Representations of Resource Use in Shimshal, Pakistan, and their Extra-discursive Effects.' In *Karakoram-Hindukush-Himalaya: Dynamics of Change (Part 1)*, edited by Irmtraud Stellrecht, 357–386. Köln: Rüdiger Köppe Verlag.

———. 2002. 'Resistance, Representation, and Third Space in Shimshal Village, Northern Pakistan.' *ACME: An International Journal of Critical Geographies* 1(1): 15–34.

Campbell, Bruce. 2009. 'Assembly Poetics in the Global Economy: Nicaragua.' In *Poetry and Cultural Studies: A Reader*, edited by Maria Damon and Ira Livingston, 177–194. Chicago: University of Illinois Press.

Carter, Paul. 1987. *The Road to Botany Bay: An Essay in Spatial History*. London: Faber and Faber.

Caton, Steven C. 1990. *'Peaks of Yemen I Summon': Poetry as Cultural Practice in a North Yemeni Tribe*. Berkeley: University of California Press.

Chatterjee, Partha. 1993. *The Nation and its Fragments: Colonial and Postcolonial Histories*. Princeton, NJ: Princeton University Press.

Chatterjee, Piya and Sunaina Maira. eds. 2014. *The Imperial University: Academic Repression and Scholarly Dissent*. Minneapolis: University of Minnesota Press.

Chuengsatiansup, Komatra. 2001. 'Marginality, Suffering and Community: The Politics of Collective Experience and Empowerment in Thailand.' In *Remaking a World: Violence, Social Suffering, and Recovery*, edited by Veena Das et al., 31–75. Berkeley: University of California Press.

Cederlof, Gunnel and Kalyanakrishnan Sivaramakrishnan. eds. 2006. *Ecological Nationalisms: Nature, Livelihoods, and Identities in South Asia*. Seattle: University of Washington Press.

Cockcroft, Anne et al. 2009. 'Challenging the Myths about Madaris in Pakistan: A National Household Survey of Enrolment and Reasons for Choosing Religious Schools.' *International Journal of Educational Development*, 29(4): 342–349.

Cohn, Bernard S. 1987 (1967). 'Regions Subjective and Objective: Their Relation to the Study of Modern Indian History and Society.' In *An Anthropologist among the Historians and Other Essays*, 100–135. Delhi; New York: Oxford University Press.

———. 1987 (1967). 'The Census, Social Structure and Objectification in South Asia.' In *An Anthropologist among the Historians and Other Essays*, 224–253. Delhi; New York: Oxford University Press.

Cohen, Saul B. and Nurit Kliot. 1992. 'Place-Names in Israel's Ideological Struggles over the Administered Territories.' *Anals of the Association of American Geographers* 82(4): 653–680.

Connor, Walker. 1972. 'Nation-Building or Nation-Destroying.' *World Politics* 24(3): 319–355.

Cooley, John K. 2000. *Unholy Wars: Afghanistan, America, and International Terrorism*. London: Pluto Press.

Cooper, Frederick and Ann Stoler. 1997. 'Between Metropole and Colony: Rethinking a Research Agenda.' In *Tensions of Empire: Colonial Cultures in a Bourgeois World*, edited by Frederick Cooper and Ann Stoler, 1–56 Berkeley: University of California Press.

Copland, Ian. 2000. 'The Political Geography of Religious Conflict: Towards An Explanation Of the Relative Infrequency Of Communal Riots in the Indian Princely States.' *The International Journal Of Punjabi Studies* 7(1): 1–27.

Cornwall, Andrea, Elizabeth Harrison and Ann Whitehead. 2007. *Feminisms in Development: Contradictions, Contestations, and Challenges*. London; New York: Zed Books.

Coronil, Fernando and Julie Skurski. eds. 2006. *States of Violence*. Ann Arbor, MI: University of Michigan Press.

Corrigan, Philip and Derek Sayer. 1985. *The Great Arch: English State Formation as Cultural Revolution*. Oxford: Basil Blackwell.

Craig, Davis. 2002. '"A" Is for Allah, "J" Is for Jihad.' *World Policy Journal* 19(1): 90–94.

Crews, Robert D. 2012. 'The Taliban and Nationalist Militancy in Afghanistan.' In *Contextualizing Jihadi Thought*, edited by Jeevan Deol and Zaheer Kazmi, 343–368. London: Hurst & Company.

Cronon, William. 1995. 'The Trouble with Wilderness; or, Getting Back to the Wrong Nature.' In *Uncommon Ground: Rethinking the Human Place in Nature*, edited by William Cronon, 69–90. New York: W.W. Norton.

Dabashi, Hamid. 2012. *The World of Persian Literary Humanism*. Cambridge: Harvard University Press.

Dadi, Iftikhar. 2010. *Modernism and the Art of Muslim South Asia*. Carolina: University of North Carolina Press.

Daechsel, Markus. 2009. *The Politics of Self-Expression: The Urdu Middleclass Milieu in Mid-Twentieth Century India and Pakistan*. London; New York: Routledge.

Daily Times. 2004. 'Syllabus Protests Paralyse Business and Traffic.' 1 June.

———. 2005. 'Story of Gilgit Death Foretold.' 10 January.

Dani, Ahmad H. 2001. *History of Northern Areas of Pakistan: Up to 2000 A.D.* Lahore: Sang-e-Meel Publications.

Das, Veena and Deborah Poole. 2004. 'State and its Margins: Comparative Ethnographies.' In *Anthropology in the Margins of the State*, 3–33. New Mexico: School of American Research Press.

Das, Veena. 2007. *Life and Words: Violence and the Descent into the Ordinary*. Berkeley: University of California Press.

Dawn. 2004. 'Hunger Strike.' 20 May.

———. 2005. 'Eight Religious Leaders Held.' 16 October.

Deeb, Lara, and Jessica Winegar. eds. 2015. *Anthropology's Politics: Discipline and Region through the Lens of the Middle East*. Stanford: Stanford University Press.

de Mel, Neloufer. 2007. *Militarizing Sri Lanka: Popular Culture, Memory, and Narrative in the Armed Conflict*. New Delhi: Sage.

Deleuze, Gilles and Félix Guattari. 2009. 'What is a Minor Literature?' In *Poetry and Cultural Studies: A Reader*, edited by Maria Damon and Ira Livingston, 56–60. Chicago: University of Illinois Press.

Derrida, Jacques. 1986. 'Declarations of Independence.' *New Political Science* 7(1): 7–15.

Devji, Faisal. 2013. *Muslim Zion: Pakistan as a Political Idea*. Cambridge: Harvard University Press.

Dharwadker, Vinay. 2010. 'Nations, Modernisms, Anti-Nations: Five theses on South Asian Arts and Cultures.' Keynote Address at the Conference on *Nationhood and Nation-building in South Asia*, Stanford University, 28–30 April.

Dodds, Klaus. 2008. 'Hollywood and the Popular Geopolitics of the War on Terror.' *Third World Quarterly* 29(8): 1621–1637.

Donnan, Hastings and Thomas M. Wilson. 1999. *Borders: Frontiers of Identity, Nation, and State*. Oxford: Berg.

Dove, Michael. 2006. 'Indigenous People and Environmental Politics.' *Annual Review of Anthropology* 35: 191–208.

Duara, Prasenjit. 1996. *Rescuing History from the Nation: Questioning Narratives of Modern China*. Chicago: University of Chicago Press.

———. 2003. *Sovereignty and Authenticity: Manchukuo and the East Asian Modern*. Lanham: Rowman & Littlefield.

Durkheim, Emile. 1976. *The Elementary Forms of the Religious life*. London: George Allen and Unwin Ltd.

Edney, Matthew H. 1997. *Mapping an Empire: The Geographical Construction of British India, 1765–1843*. Chicago: University of Chicago Press.

Falkoff, Marc. 2007. 'Poems from Guantanamo.' *CagePrisoners*, 11 May.

Feldman, Allen. 2008. 'Animality and the Inhumanization of Sovereignty: A Visual Culture of Bared Life.' University Lecture for Workshop on *Militarizing Everyday Life*, Cornell University, 3 October.

Ferguson, James. 1990. *The Anti-Politics Machine: 'Development', Depoliticization, and Bureaucratic Power in Lesotho*. Cambridge: Cambridge University Press.

Fernandes, Leela. 2013. *Transnational Feminism in the United States: Knowledge, Ethics and Power*. New York: New York University Press.

Foucault, Michel. 1977. *Discipline and Punish: The Birth of the Prison*. New York: Pantheon Books.

———. 1980. *Power/Knowledge. Selected Interviews and Other Writings, 1972–1977*, edited by Colin Gordon. New York: Pantheon.

———. 1983. 'Afterword: The Subject and Power.' In *Michel Foucault: Beyond Structuralism and Hermeneutics* (second edition), edited by Hubert L. Dreyfus and Paul Rabinow, 208–226. Chicago: University of Chicago Press.

Franco, Jean. 1989. *Plotting Women: Gender and Representation in Mexico*. New York: Columbia University Press.

Fraser, Nancy. 1992. 'Rethinking the Public Sphere: A Contribution to the Critique of Actually Existing Democracy.' In *Habermas and the Public Sphere*, edited by Craig Calhoun, 109–142. Cambridge: MIT Press.

Friedman, Thomas L. 2009. 'Teacher, Can We Leave Now? No.' *The New York Times*, 18 July.

Freitag, Sandra. 1989. *Collective Action and Community: Public Arenas and the Emergence of Communalism in North India*. Berkeley: University of California Press.

Gadgil, Madhav and Ramachandra Guha. 1995. *Ecology and Equity: The Use and Abuse of Nature in Contemporary India*. New York: Routledge.

Gana, Nouri. 2010. 'War, Poetry, Mourning: Darwish, Adonis, Iraq.' *Public Culture* 22(1): 33–65.

Ganguly, Sumit. 1997. *The Crisis in Kashmir: Portents of War, Hopes of Peace*. Cambridge: Cambridge University Press.

Gardner, Marilyn. 2006. 'A Gift For an Entire Village.' *The Christian Science Monitor*, 12 September. Available at: http://www.csmonitor.com/2006/0912/p17s01-bogn.html.

Gareau, Brian J. 2007. 'Ecological Values amid Local Interests: Natural Resource Conservation, Social Differentiation, and Human Survival in Honduras.' *Rural Sociology* 72(2): 244–268.

Gaur, Ishwar D. 2008. *Martyr as Bridegrooms: A Folk Representation of Bhagat Singh*. Delhi: Anthem Press.

Gaynor, Niamh. 2010. 'In-active Citizenship and the Depoliticization of Community Development in Ireland.' *Community Development Journal* 46(1): 27–41.

Geertz, Clifford. 1973. 'The Integrative Revolution: Primordial Sentiments and Civil Politics in the New States.' In *The Interpretation of Cultures*, 255–310. New York: Basic Books Inc.

Geisler, Charles. 2003. 'A New Kind of Trouble: Evictions in Eden.' *International Social Science Journal* 55(175): 69–78.

Gilbert, Paul and Lauren Berlant. eds. 2014. *Compassion: The Culture and Politics of an Emotion*. New York: Routledge.

Gill, Lesley. 2004. *The School of the Americas: Military Training and Political Violence in the Americas*. Durham: Duke University Press.

Gill, Stephen. 2003. *Power and Resistance in the New World Order*. Houndmills: Palgrave MacMillan.

Gilmartin, David. 1998. 'Partition, Pakistan, and South Asian History: In Search of a Narrative.' *The Journal of Asian Studies* 57(4): 1068–1095.

Gilmartin, David and Bruce Lawrence B. eds. 2000. *Beyond Turk and Hindu: Rethinking Religious Identities in Islamicate South Asia*. Gainesville: University Press of Florida.

Giroux, Henry. 2015. 'Totalitarian Paranoia in the Post–Orwellian Surveillance State.' *Cultural Studies* 29(2): 108–140.

Gold, Ann G. and Bhoju R. Gujar. 2002. *In the Time of Trees and Sorrows: Nature, Power, and Memory in Rajasthan*. Durham: Duke University Press.

Gold, Ann G. 2006. 'Love's Cup, Love's Thorn, Love's End: The Language of Prem in Ghatiyali.' In *Love in South Asia: A Cultural History*, edited by Francesca Orsini, 303–330. Cambridge: Cambridge University Press.

Goldman, Michael. 2001. 'Constructing an Environmental State: Eco-governmentality and Other Transnational Practices of a "Green" World Bank.' *Social Problems* 48(4): 499–523.

Good, Mary-Jo and Byron J. Good. 1988. 'Ritual, the State, and the Transformation of Emotional Discourse in Iranian Society.' *Culture, Medicine and Psychiatry* 12(1): 43–63.

Gottschalk, Peter. 2000. *Beyond Hindu and Muslim: Multiple Identity in Narratives from Village India*. New York: Oxford University Press.

Government of Pakistan. 1971. *Report of the Committee of the Northern Areas*. Islamabad: Government of Pakistan.

Government of Pakistan and IUCN. 2003. *Northern Areas State of Environment and Development*. Karachi: IUCN Pakistan.

GRAIN. 2009. 'The Soils of War.' *GRAIN*, 9 March. Available at: http://www.grain.org/article/entries/128-the-soils-of-war. Accessed on 20 February 2017.

Gramsci, Antonio. 1971. *Selections from the Prison Notebooks of Antonio Gramsci*. London: Lawrence & Wishart.

———. 1977. *Selections from Political Writings 1910–1920*. London: Lawrence & Wishart.

Grellier, Bernard. 2006. 'A Transhumant Shepherd on Mount Aigoual: Sheep Transhumance and the Shepherd's Knowledge.' *International Social Science Journal* 58 (187): 161–164.

Gregg, Melissa and Gregory J. Seigworth. eds. 2010. *The Affect Theory Reader*. Durham: Duke University Press.

Gregory, Derek. 2008. '"The Rush to the Intimate": Counterinsurgency and the Cultural Turn in Late Modern War.' *Radical Philosophy* 150: 8–23.

Guha, Ramachandra. 1989. *The Unquiet Woods: Ecological Change and Peasant Resistance in the Indian Himalaya*. Delhi: Oxford University Press.

Gupta, Akhil. 2012. *Red Tape: Bureaucracy, Structural Violence, and Poverty in India*. Durham: Duke University Press.

Habermas, Jürgen. 1989. *The Structural Transformation of the Public Sphere: An Inquiry into a Category of Bourgeois Society*. Cambridge: MIT Press.

Haines, Chad. 2000. *Re-routing/Rooting the Nation-State: The Karakoram Highway and the Making of the Northern Areas of Pakistan*. PhD Dissertation, University of Wisconsin-Madison.

———. 2012. *Nation, Territory, and Globalization in Pakistan: Traversing the Margins*. London; New york: Routledge.

Hall, Stuart. 1992. 'The Questions of Cultural Identity.' In *Modernity and its Futures*, edited by Tony McGrew, Stuart Hall and David Held, 274–325. Cambridge: Polity Press.

Halqa-e-Arbab-e-Zauq. 2000. *Tark-i-Taasoobat*. Gilgit: Baha'i Publishing Trust.

Handler, Richard. 1988. *Nationalism and the Politics of Culture in Quebec*. Madison: The University of Wisconsin Press.

Hansen, Thomas B. and Finn Stepputat. eds. 2001. *States of Imagination: Ethnographic Explorations of the Postcolonial State*. Durham: Duke University Press.

Haqqani, Husain. 2005. *Pakistan: Between Mosque and Military*. Lahore: Vanguard.

Harley, John B. 1989. 'Deconstructing the Map.' *Cartographica* 26(2): 1–20.

———. 2001. *The New Nature of Maps: Essays in the History of Cartography*. Baltimore: Johns Hopkins University Press.

Haroon, Sana. 2007. *Frontier of Faith: Islam in the Indo-Afghan Borderland*. New York: Columbia University Press.

Harper, David. 2008. 'The Politics of Paranoia: Paranoid Positioning and Conspiratorial Narratives in the Surveillance Society.' *Surveillance & Society* 5(1): 1–32.

Hart, Gillian. 2006. 'Denaturalizing Dispossession: Critical Ethnography in the Age of Resurgent Imperialism.' *Antipode* 38(5): 997–1004.

Harvey, David. 2003. *The New Imperialism*. Oxford; New York: Oxford University Press.

Hasan, Mushirul. 2004. *From Pluralism to Separatism: Qasbas in Colonial Awadh*. New Delhi: Oxford University Press.

Hasan, Mushirul and Asim Roy. eds. 2005. *Living Together Separately: Cultural India in History and Politics*. New Delhi: Oxford University Press.

Hayden, Tom. 2009. 'Understanding the Long War.' *The Nation*, 7 May.

Hechter, Michael. 1998 (1975). 'Introduction.' In *Internal Colonialism: The Celtic Fringe in British National Development, 1536–1966*, 3–14. Berkeley: University of California Press.

———. 1998 (1975). 'Towards a Theory of Ethnic Change.' In *Internal Colonialism: The Celtic Fringe in British National Development, 1536–1966*, 15–46. Berkeley: University of California Press.

Heynen, Nik et al. eds. 2007. *Neoliberal Environments: False Promises and Unnatural Consequences*. New York: Routledge.

Hirschkind, Charles. 2001. 'The Ethics of Listening: Cassette Sermon Audition in Contemporary Egypt.' *American Ethnologist* 28(3): 623–649.

Ho, Elaine LE. 2009. 'Constituting Citizenship through the Emotions: Singaporean Transmigrants in London.' *Annals of the Association of American Geographers* 99(4): 788–804.

Hobsbawm, Eric and Terence Ranger. eds. 1983. *The Invention of Tradition*. Cambridge: Cambridge University Press.

Hochschild, Arlie R. 1983. *The Managed Heart: Commercialization of Human Feeling*. Berkeley: University of California Press.

Hoffman, Bruce and Haley Duschinski. 2014. 'Contestations over Law, Power and Representation in Kashmir Valley.' *Interventions: International Journal of Postcolonial Studies* 16(4): 501–530.

Human Rights Commission of Pakistan (HRCP). 2010. *Gilgit-Baltistan Elections 2009: Report of HRCP Observers' Mission*. February.

———. 2017. *Gilgit-Baltistan: Aspirations for Identity, Integration & Autonomy: Report of an HRCP Fact-Finding Mission to Gilgit-Baltistan*.

Human Rights Watch. 2000. *Reform of Repression?: Post-Coup Abuses in Pakistan* 12(6 C).

———. 2006. *'With Friends Like These...' Human Rights Violations in Azad Kashmir* 18(12 C).

Husain, Irfan. ed. 1997. *Pakistan*. Karachi: Oxford University Press.

Hussain, Rifaat. 2004. 'Pakistan's Relations with Azad Kashmir.' *Regional Studies* 21(4): 82–97.

Hussain, Shafqat. 2007. 'Do Economic Incentives Work (in conservation)?' *India Seminar* 577: 39–44.

———. 2012. 'Multiple Sovereignty and Transnationalism in a Nation-State: Aga Khan Development Network in Hunza, Pakistan.' In *Democracy at Large. The Sciences Po Series in International Relations and Political Economy*, edited by Boris Petric, 191–204. New York: Palgrave Macmillan.

——. 2015. *Remoteness and Modernity: Transformation and Continuity in Northern Pakistan*. New Haven: Yale University Press.

Ibrahim, Farhana. 2004. 'Cartographic Control and a Matter of Representation: A "Restricted Zone" in Western India.' Conference Paper, 33rd Annual South Asia Conference, University of Wisconsin-Madison.

Igoe, Jim and Dan Brockington. 2007. 'Neoliberal Conservation: A Brief Introduction.' *Conservation and Society* 5(4): 432–449.

Islah-e-Nisab Committee Shumali Ilaqajaat. 2003. 'Humara Mutalba! Sab Kay liye Qabil-e-Qabool Nisab-e-Taleem (Our Demand! A Curriculum that is Acceptable to All).' Gilgit: Markazi Imamia Jam-e-Masjid.

Ispahani, Mahnaz Z. 1989. *Roads and Rivals: The Political Uses of Access in the Borderlands of Asia*. Ithaca, NY: Cornell University Press.

IUCN. 1994. *Guidelines for Protected Area Management Categories*. Gland: IUCN.

——. 1999. *Central Karakoram National Park: Draft Management Plan*. Gland: IUCN.

——. 2003. *Customary Laws: Governing Natural Resource Management in the Northern Areas*. Karachi: IUCN.

——. 2004. *Environmental Law in Pakistan* Vol 1 Part 6: Northern Areas. Karachi: IUCN

Jaffrelot, Christophe. ed. 2002. *Pakistan: Nationalism Without a Nation?* New Delhi: Manohar.

Jagger, Alison M. 1996 (1989). 'Love and Knowledge: Emotion in Feminist Epistemology.' In *Women, Knowledge and Reality: Explorations in Feminist Philosophy*, edited by Ann Garry and Marilyn Pearsall, 166–190. New York: Routledge.

Jalal, Ayesha. 1990. *The State of Martial Rule: The Origins of Pakistan's Political Economy of Defence*. Lahore: Sang-e-Meel.

Jamal, Arif. 2009. *Shadow War: The Untold Story of Jihad in Kashmir*. Brooklyn: Melville Publishing House.

James, Alexa. 2009. 'Author, Peace Activist Greg Mortenson to speak at West Point.' *Times Herald-Record*, 9 March.

Jenkins, J. Craig and Charles Perrow. 1977. 'Insurgency of the Powerless: Farm Worker Movements 1946–1972.' *American Sociological Review* 42(2): 249–268.

Johnson, Mark. 2008. *The Meaning of the Body: Aesthetics of Human Understanding*. Chicago; London: University of Chicago Press.

Jones, Justin and Ali U. Qasmi. eds. 2015. *The Shi'a in Modern South Asia: Religion, History and Politics*. Cambridge: Cambridge University Press.

Joseph, Gilbert M. and Daniel Nugent. eds. 1994. *Everyday Forms of State Formation: Revolution and the Negotiation of Rule in Modern Mexico*. Durham: Duke University Press.

Kabir, Ananya J. 2009. *Territories of Desire: Representing the Valley of Kashmir*. Minneapolis: University of Minnesota Press.

Kak, Sanjay. ed. 2011. *Until My Freedom Has Come: The New Intifada in Kashmir*. Delhi: Penguin.

Kamal, K. L. 1982. *Pakistan: The Garrison State*. New Delhi: Intellectual Publishing House.

Kaul, Suvir. 2017. *Of Gardens and Graves: Kashmir, Poetry, Politics*. Durham: Duke University Press.

Kedourie, Elie. 1960. *Nationalism*. London: Hutchinson.

Kershaw, Baz. 1992. *The Politics of Performance: Radical Theatre as Cultural Intervention*. New York: Routledge.

Khan, Fazle K. 1991. *A Geography of Pakistan: Environment, People and Economy*. Karachi: Oxford University Press.

Khan, Mahmood H. and Shoaib S. Khan. 1992. *Rural Change in the Third World: Pakistan and the Aga Khan Rural Support Program*. New York: Greenwood Press.

Khan, M. Ilyas. 2002. 'The Pariahs of Pakistan.' *The Herald*, October 2002: 74–75.

Khan, Naveeda. 2003. *Grounding Sectarianism: Islamic Ideology and Muslim Everyday Life in Lahore, Pakistan*. PhD Dissertation, Columbia University.

———. 2006. 'Of Children and Jinn: An Inquiry into an Unexpected Friendship during Uncertain Times.' *Cultural Anthropology* 21(2): 234–264.

———. 2012. *Muslim Becoming: Aspiration and Skepticism in Pakistan*. Durham: Duke University Press.

Khan, Zaigham. 2014. *The Unholy War: Religious Militancy and Sectarian Violence in Pakistan*. Islamabad: Centre for Democratic Governance.

Kennedy, Charles H. 1989. 'Towards the Definition of a Muslim in an Islamic State: The Case of the Ahmadiyya in Pakistan.' In *Religious and Ethnic Minority Politics in South Asia*, edited by Dhirendra Vajpeyi and Yogendra Malik, 71–108. New Delhi: Manohar.

Kidder, Tracy. 2003. *Mountains beyond Mountains: The Quest of Dr. Paul Farmer, a Man Who Would Cure the World*. New York: Random House.

Kingsnorth, Paul. 2012. 'Confessions of a Recovering Environmentalist.' *Orion Magazine*. Available at: http://www.orionmagazine.org/index.php/articles/article/6599. Accessed on 20 February 2017.

Klein, Naomi. 2005. 'The Rise of Disaster Capitalism.' *The Nation*, 14 April. Available at: http://www.thenation.com/article/rise-disaster-capitalism. Accessed on 20 February 2017.

———. 2007. *The Shock Doctrine: The Rise of Disaster Capitalism*, New York: Metropolitan Books.

Knudsen, Are J. 1999. 'Conservation and Controversy in the Karakoram: Khunjerab National Park, Pakistan.' *Journal of Political Ecology* 6(1): 1–29.

Kolhatkar, Sonali and Mariam Rawi. 2009. 'Why Is a Leading Feminist Organization Lending Its name to Support Escalation in Afghanistan?' *AlterNet*, 7 July. Available at: http://www.alternet.org/story/141165/why_is_a_leading_feminist_organization_lending_its_name_to_support_escalation_in_afghanistan. Accessed on 20 February 2017.

Krakauer, Jon. 2011. *Three Cups of Deceit: How Greg Mortenson, Humanitarian Hero, Lost his Way*. Byliner.

Kreutzmann, Hermann. 1991. 'The Karakoram Highway: The Impact of Road Construction on Mountain Societies.' *Modern Asian Studies* 25(4): 711–736.

———. 2006. 'High Mountain Agriculture and its Transformation in a Changing Socio-economic Environment.' In *Karakoram in Transition: Culture, Development, and Ecology in the Hunza Valley*, edited by Hermann Kreutzmann, 329–358. Karachi: Oxford University Press.

———. 2008. 'Kashmir and the Northern Areas of Pakistan: Boundary-making along Contested Frontiers.' *Erdkunde* 62(3): 201–219.

Kurin, Richard. 1986. 'Islamization: A view from the Countryside.' In *Islamic Reassertion in Pakistan: The Application of Islamic Laws in a Modern State*, edited by Anita Weiss, 115–128. Syracuse: Syracuse University Press.

Lamb, Alastair. 1991. *Kashmir: A Disputed Legacy, 1846–1990*. Hertingfordbury: Roxford Books.

Laszczkowski, Mateusz and Madeleine Reeves. 2015. 'Affective States: Entanglements, Suspensions, Suspicions.' *Social Analysis* 59(4): 1–14.

Lentz, Sabine. 1997. 'British Officers, Kashmiri Officials, Adultery and "Customary law"'. In *Perspectives on History and Change in the Karakorum, Hindukush, and Himalaya*, edited by Irmtraud Stellrecht and Matthias Winiger, 401–416. Köln: Rüdiger Köppe Verlag.

Li, Tania M. 2002. 'Engaging Simplifications: Community-Based Resource Management, Market Processes, and State Agendas in Upland Southeast Asia.' *World Development* 30(2): 265–283.

———. 2007. *The Will to Improve: Governmentality, Development, and the Practice of Politics*. Durham: Duke University Press.

Lieberman, Robbie. 1995. *My Song is My Weapon: People's Songs, American Communism, and the Politics of Culture 1930–1950*. Champaign, IL: University of Illinois Press.

Lipman, Pauline. 2004. 'Education Accountability and Repression of Democracy Post-9/11.' *Journal for Critical Education Policy Studies* 2(1).

Los, M. 2004. 'The Technologies of Total Domination.' *Surveillance & Society* 2(1): 15–38.

Lutz, Catherine. 1999. 'Ethnography at the War Century's End.' *Journal of Contemporary Ethnography* 28(6): 610–619.

———. 2004. 'Militarization.' In *A Companion to the Anthropology of Politics*, edited by David Nugent and Joan Vincent, 318–331. London: Blackwell.

Lutz, Catherine and Lila Abu-Lughod. eds. 1990. *Language and the Politics of Emotion*. Cambridge: Cambridge University Press.

Lyon, David. 2003. 'Surveillance after September 11, 2001.' In *The Intensification of Surveillance: Crime, Terrorism and Warfare in the Information Age*, edited by Kirstie Ball and Frank Webster, 16–25. London: Pluto Press.

Maass, Citha. 1994. 'Confidence-Building Measures and Finding Solutions.' In *Perspectives on Kashmir*, edited by K.F. Yusuf. Islamabad: Pakistan Forum.

MacDonald, Kenneth I. 2005. 'Global Hunting Grounds: Power, Scale, and Ecology in the Negotiation of Conservation.' *Cultural Geographies* 12(3): 259–291.

MacKenzie, John M. 1988. *The Empire of Nature: Hunting, Conservation, and British Imperialism*. Manchester: Manchester University Press.

Mahmood, Saba. 2004. *Politics of Piety: The Islamic Revival and the Feminist Subject*. Princeton: Princeton University Press.

Malik, Jamal. 1996. *Colonization of Islam: Dissolution of Traditional Institutions in Pakistan*. New Delhi: Manohar.

Malkki, Liisa H. 1997. 'Speechless Emissaries: Refugees, Humanitarianism and Dehistoricization.' *Cultural Anthropology* 11(3): 377–404.

Mamdani, Mahmood. 2004. *Good Muslim, Bad Muslim: America, the Cold War, and the Roots of Terror*. New York: Pantheon Books.

Markazi Shia Tulba Action Committee. 2004. 'Kab Tak?' Gilgit.

Marsden, Magnus. 2005. *Living Islam: Muslim Religious Experience in Pakistan's North-West Frontier*. Cambridge: Cambridge University Press.

———. 2008. 'Muslim Cosmopolitans? Transnational Life in Northern Pakistan.' *Journal of Asian Studies* 67(1): 213–247.

Martinez-Alier, Joan. 2002. *The Environmentalism of the Poor: A Study of Ecological Conflicts and Valuation*. Cheltenham: Edward Elgar Publishing.

Marx, Gary T. 1988. *Undercover: Police Surveillance in America*. London: University of California Press.

Marx, Karl. 1906 (1887). *Capital: A Critique of Political Economy*. Translated from the 3rd German Edition by Samuel Moore and Edward Aveling, edited by Frederick Engels. New York: Random House Inc.

Mayaram, Shail. 1997. *Resisting Regimes: Myth, Memory and the Shaping of a Muslim Identity*. Delhi: Oxford University Press.

———. 2003. *Against History, Against State: Counter-perspectives from the Margins*. New York: Columbia University Press.

McAfee, Kathleen. 1999. 'Selling Nature to Save it? Biodiversity and the Rise of Green Developmentalism.' *Environment and Planning D: Society and Space* 17(2): 133–154.

McCarthy, James and Scott Prudham. 2004. 'Neoliberal Nature and the Nature of Neoliberalism.' *Geoforum* 35(3): 275–283.

McClintock, Anne. 2009. 'Paranoid Empire: Specters from Guantánamo and Abu Ghraib.' *Small Axe* 13(1): 50–74.

McClure, Kevin R. 2009. 'Madrasas and Pakistan's Education Agenda: Western Media Misrepresentation and Policy Recommendations.' *International Journal of Educational Development*, 29(4): 334–341.

McLeod, Gordon and Martin Jones. 2001. 'Renewing the Geography of Regions.' *Environment and Planning D: Society and Space* 19(6): 669–695.

McMichael, Philip. 1990. 'Incorporating Comparison within a World-Historical Perspective: An Alternative Comparative Method.' *American Sociological Review* 55(3): 385–397.

———. 1995. 'Introduction.' In *Food and Agrarian Orders in the World-Economy*, edited by Philip McMichael, ix–xvi. Westport, CT: Greenwood Press.

———. 2006. 'Peasant Prospects in a Neo-liberal Age.' *New Political Economy* 11(3): 407–418.

———. 2010. *Contesting Development: Critical Struggles for Social Change*. New York: Routledge.

McNeely, Jeffrey A. 1993. *Parks for life: Report of the IVth World Congress on National Parks and Protected Areas*. Gland: IUCN.

Meeker, Michael E. 1976. 'Meaning and Society in the Near East: Examples from the Black Sea Turks and the Levantine Arabs.' *International Journal of Middle East Studies* 7(2): 243–270.

Mehkri, Ishtiaq A. 2001. 'A Simmering Issue.' *Dawn*, 15 April 2001.

Metcalf, Barbara. 2005. 'The Study of Muslims in South Asia.' Talk delivered at the University of California at Santa Barbara, 2 December. Available at: www.columbia.edu/itc/mealac/pritchett/00islamlinks/ikram/parto_metcalfintro.html. Accessed on 20 February 2017.

Meyer, David S. 1990. *A Winter of Discontent: the Nuclear Freeze and American Politics*. New York: Praeger.

Mian, Ajmal. 1999. *Al-Jehad Trust versus Federation of Pakistan 1999 SCMR 1379*. Islamabad: Supreme Court of Pakistan.

Mignolo, Walter. 2010. 'Introduction.' In *Indigenous and Popular Thinking in America*, edited by Rodolfo Kusch, xiii–liv. Durham: Duke University Press.

Miller, Flagg. 2007. *The Moral Resonance of Arab Media: Audiocassette Poetry and Culture in Yemen*. Boston: Harvard Center for Middle Eastern Monographs.

Mills, C. Wright. 1956. *The Power Elite*. New York: Harper.

Misri, Deepti. 2014. *Beyond Partition: Gender, Violence and Representation in Postcolonial India*. Illinois: University of Illinois Press.

Mitchell, Timothy. 1988. *Colonising Egypt*. Cambridge: Cambridge University Press.

———. 1991. 'The Limits of the State: Beyond Statist Approaches and Their Critics.' *American Political Science Review* 85(1): 77–94.

———. 1999. 'Society, Economy, and the State Effect.' In *State/Culture: State-Formation after the Cultural Turn*, edited by George Steinmetz, 76–97. Ithaca, NY and London: Cornell University Press.

Mock, John. 2008. 'Mountain Protected Areas in Northern Pakistan: The Case of the National Parks.' In *Proceedings of the Third International Hindukush Cultural Conference*, edited by Israr-ud-Din, 30–39. Karachi: Oxford University Press.

Moore, Donald S. 1993. 'Contesting Terrain in Zimbabwe's Eastern Highlands: Political Ecology, Ethnography, and Peasant Resource Struggles.' *Economic Geography* 69(4): 380–401.

Morarji, Karuna. 2005. *The Moral of the Story: Schooling, Development, and State Formation in India*. Master's Thesis, Cornell University.

Mortenson, Greg and David O. Relin. 2006. *Three Cups of Tea*. New York: Viking.

Mufti, Aamir. 2010. 'Towards a Lyric History of India.' In *Beyond Crisis: Re-Evaluating Pakistan*, edited by Naveeda Khan, 177–209. New Delhi: Routledge.

Munasinghe, Viranjini. 2002. 'Nationalism in Hybrid Spaces: The Production of Impurity out of Purity.' *American Ethnologist* 29(3): 663–692.

Murakami Wood, D. ed. 2006. *A Report on the Surveillance Society*. Wilmslow UK: Office of the Information Commissioner/Surveillance Studies Network.

Naim, Choudhri M. 1989. 'Poet-audience Interaction at Urdu Musha'irahs.' In *Urdu and Muslim South Asia: Studies in Honour of Ralph Russell*, edited by Christopher Shackle, 167–173. London: School of Oriental and African Studies, University of London.

Nandy, Ashis. 1988. 'The Politics of Secularism and the Recovery of Religious Tolerance.' *Alternatives: Global, Local, Political* 13(2): 177–194.

Nasr, Seyyed V.R. 2000. 'International Politics, Domestic Imperatives, and Identity Mobilization: Sectarianism in Pakistan, 1979–1998.' *Comparative Politics* 32(2): 171–190.

———. 2002. 'Islam, the State and the Rise of Sectarian Militancy in Pakistan.' *Pakistan: Nationalism without a Nation?*, edited by Christophe Jaffrelot, 85–114. New Delhi: Manohar.

Navaro-Yashin, Yael. 2002. *Faces of the State: Secularism and Public Life in Turkey*. Princeton: Princeton University Press.

Nawaz, Shuja. 2007. *Crossed Swords: Pakistan, its Army, and the Wars Within*. Karachi: Oxford University Press.

Nayyar, Abdul H. and Ahmad Salim. 2003. *The Subtle Subversion. The State of Curricula and Textbooks in Pakistan, Urdu, English, Social Studies and Civics*. Islamabad: Sustainable Development Policy Institute.

Nelson, Matthew. 2009. 'Dealing with Difference: Religious Education and the Challenge of Democracy in Pakistan.' *Modern Asian Studies*, 43(3): 591-618.

Neumann, Roderick P. 1995. 'Local Challenges to Global Agendas: Conservation, Economic Liberalization and the Pastoralists' Rights movement in Tanzania.' *Antipode* 27(4): 363–382.

———. 2001. 'Disciplining Peasants in Tanzania: From State Violence to Self-Surveillance in Wildlife Conservation.' In *Violent Environments*, edited by Nancy L. Peluso and Michael Watts, 305–327. Ithaca, NY: Cornell University Press.

———. 2004. 'Nature-State-Territory: Toward a Critical Theorization of Conservation Enclosure.' In *Liberation Ecologies: Environmernt, Development, Social Movements*, edited by Richard Peet and Michael Watts, 195–217. New York: Routledge.

Nyborg Ingrid and Jawad Ali. 2005. 'Exploring Nature, Wealth and Power Issues in Agriculture and Resource Management: A Case Study on the Aga Khan Rural Support Program, Northern Pakistan.' Noragric Working Paper, 39. Noragric/Norwegian University of Life Sciences.

Nyers, Peter. 2007. 'Why Citizenship Studies?' *Citizenship Studies* 11(1): 1–4.

O'Connor, Martin. ed. 1994. *Is Capitalism Sustainable? Political Economy and the Politics of Ecology*. New York: Guilford Press.

Omidian, Patricia. 2009. 'Living and Working in a War Zone: An Applied Anthropologist in Afghanistan.' *Practicing Anthropology* 31(2): 4–11.

Paasi, Anssi. 1986. 'The Institutionalization of Regions: A Theoretical Framework for Understanding the Emergence of Regions and the Constitution of Regional Identity.' *Fennia* 164(1): 105–146.

Pakistan Times. 2005. 'Schools Re-Open Today in Northern Pakistan After OneYear.' 27 April.

Pamir Times Report. 2009. 'GECA and National Book Foundation Join Hands.' *Pamir Times*, 14 July.

Pandey, Gyanendra. 1992. 'In Defense of the Fragment: Writing about Hindu-Muslim Riots in India Today.' *Representations* 37: 27–55

———. 2001. *Remembering Partition: Violence, Nationalism and History in India*. Cambridge: Cambridge University Press.

Parkes, Peter. 1996. 'Indigenous Polo and the Politics of Regional Identity in Northern Pakistan.' In *Sport, Identity and Ethnicity*, edited by Jeremy MacClancy, 43–67. Oxford: Berg.

Patel, Geeta. 2002. *Lyrical Movements, Historical Hauntings: On Gender, Colonialism and Desire in Miraji's Urdu Poetry*. Palo Alto: Stanford University Press.

Peluso, Nancy L. and Peter Vandergeest. 2001. 'Genealogies of the Political Forest and Customary Rights in Indonesia, Malaysia, and Thailand.' *Journal of Asian Studies* 61(3): 761–812.

Pigg, Stacey L. 1992. 'Constructing Social Categories through Place: Social Representations and Development in Nepal.' *Comparative Studies in Society and History* 34(3): 491–513.

Pollan, Michael. 2006. *The Omnivore's Dilemma: A Natural History of Four Meals*.New York: Penguin Press.

Population Census Organization. 2001. *1998 Census Report of Pakistan*. Islamabad: Population Census Organization, Statistics Division, Government of Pakistan.

Poulantzas, Nicos. 1973. *Political Power and Social Classes*. London: Verso.

Pratt, Mary L. 1999. 'Apocalypse in the Andes: Contact Zones and the Struggles for Interpretive Power.' *Americas* 51(4): 38–47.

Qazi, Shams-ul-Haq. 2003. *The Constitution of the Islamic Republic of Pakistan*. Lahore: Irfan Law Book House.

Qureshi Ishtiaq H. 1975. *Education in Pakistan: An Inquiry Into Objectives and Achievements*. Karachi: Ma'aref.

Qureshi, Salim. 1989. 'The Politics of the Shia Minority in Pakistan: Context and Developments.' In *Religious and Ethnic Minority Politics in South Asia*, edited by Dhirendra K. Vajpeyi and Yogendra K. Malik, 109–138. New Delhi: Manohar.

Rabbani, Muhammad I. 2003. *Introduction to Pakistan Studies*. Lahore: The Caravan Press.

Radcliffe, Sarah A. 2001. 'Imagining the State as a Space: Territoriality and the Foundation of the State in Ecuador.' In *States of Imagination: Ethnographic Explorations of the Postcolonial State*, edited by Thomas B. Hansen and Finn Stepputat, 123–145. Durham: Duke University Press.

Rafiq, Arif. 2014. *Pakistan's Resurgent Sectarian War*. Peace Brief 180. United States Institute of Peace.

Raheja, Gloria G. and Ann G. Gold. 1994. *Listen to the Heron's Words: Reimagining Culture and Kinship in North India*. Berkeley: University of California Press.

Rahman, Fazlur. 1953. *New Education in the Making in Pakistan: Its Ideology and Basic Problems*. London: Cassell.

Rahman, Khalid and Ershad Mahmood. 2000. *Shumali Ilaqajaat: Haqaiq, Masail, Aur Hal Kay Liyey Sifarishaat (Northern Areas: Realities, Issues, and Suggestions for a Solution)*. Islamabad: Institute of Policy Studies.

Rajaram, Prem K. and Carl Grundy-Warr. eds. 2007. *Borderscapes: Hidden Geographies and Politics at Territory's Edge*. Minneapolis: University of Minnesota Press.

Rai, Mridu. 2004. *Hindu Rulers, Muslim Subjects: Islam, Rights and the History of Kashmir*. Delhi: Permanent Black.

Ramanujan, Attipate K. 1991. 'Toward a Counter-System: Women's Tales.' In *Gender, Genre, and Power in South Asian Expressive Traditions*, edited by Arjun Appadurai, Frank J. Korom and Margaret A. Mills, 33–55. Philadelphia: University of Pennsylvania Press.

Rangarajan, Mahesh. 1996. *Fencing the Forest: The Colonial State and the Forests of the Central Provinces 1800–1947*. Delhi: Oxford University Press.

———. 2006. 'Battles for Nature: Contesting Wildlife Conservation in 20th Century India.' In *Shades of Green: Environmental Activism Around the Globe*, edited by Christof Mauch, Nathan Stoltzfus and Douglas R. Weiner,161–182 . New York: Rowman & Littlefield.

Rashid, Ahmed. 2000. *Taliban: Militant Islam, Oil and Fundamentalism in Central Asia*. New Haven: Yale University Press.

Ray, Sangeeta. 2000. *En-Gendering India: Woman and Nation in Colonial and Postcolonial Narratives*. Durham: Duke University Press.

Razack, Sherene. 2004. *Dark Threats and White Knights: The Somalia Affair, Peacekeeping, and New Imperialism*. Toronto: University of Toronto Press.

Razvi, Mujtaba. 1971. *The Frontiers of Pakistan: A Study of Frontier Problems in Pakistan's Frontier Policy*. Karachi: National Publishing House Ltd.

Rieck, Andreas. 1995. 'Sectarianism as a Political Problem in Pakistan: The Case of Northern Areas.' *Orient* 36(3): 429–448.

———. 1997. 'From Mountain Refuge to Model Area: Transformation of Shi'i Communities in Northern Pakistan.' In *Perspectives on History and Change in the Karakorum, Hindukush, and Himalaya*, edited by Irmtraud Stellrecht and Matthias Winiger, 215–231. Köln: Rüdiger Köppe Verlag.

———. 2000. 'The Struggle for Equal Rights as a Minority: Shia Communal Organizations in Pakistan, 1948–1968.' In *The Twelver Shia in Modern Times: Religious Culture and Political History*, edited by Werner Ende and Rainer Brunner, 271–287. Leiden: Brill.

———. 2014. *The Shias of Pakistan: An Assertive and Beleaguered Minority*. London: Hurst & Company.

Ring, Laura A. 2006. *Zenana: Everyday Peace in a Karachi Apartment Building*. Blooomington: Indiana University Press.

Rizvi, Hasan A. 2000. *The military and politics in Pakistan : 1947–1997*. Lahore: Sang-e-Meel Publications.

Rizvi, Hasan A., et al. 2003. *Pakistan Studies: Class X*. Lahore: Punjab Textbook Board.

Robinson, Cabeiri d. 2013. *Body of Victim, Body of Warrior: Refugee Families and the Making of Kashmiri Jihadists*. Berkeley: University of California Press.

Rose, Jacqueline. 1996. *States of Fantasy*. Oxford: Clarendon Press.

Roseberry, William. 1994. 'Hegemony and the Language of Contention.' In *Everyday Forms of State Formation: Revolution and the Negotiation of Rule in Modern Mexico*, edited by Gilbert M. Joseph and Daniel Nugent, 355–366. Durham: Duke University Press.

Rostami-Povey, Elaheh. 2007. *Afghan Women: Identity and Invasion*. New York: Zed Books.

Roy, Anindyo. 2005. *Civility and Empire: Literature and Culture in British India, 1822-1922*. New York: Routledge.

Saberwal, Vasant K. 1999. *Pastoral Politics: Shepherds, Bureaucrats, and Conservation in the Western Himalayas*. Delhi: Oxford University Press.

Saeed, Khalid. 1998. 'The Heart of the Pakistan Crisis.' *Dawn*, 14 August.

Saeed, Sadia. 2007. 'Pakistani Nationalism and the State Marginalisation of the Ahmadiyya Community in Pakistan.' *Studies in Ethnicity and Nationalism* 7(3): 132–152.

Sahlins, Peter. 1998. 'State formation and National Identity in the Catalan Borderlands during the Eighteenth and Nineteenth Centuries.' In *Border Identities: Nation and State at International Frontiers*, edited by Thomas M. Wilson and Hastings Donnan, 31–61. Cambridge: Cambridge University Press.

Said, Edward W. 1978. *Orientalism*. New York: Vintage Books.

———. 1993. *Culture and Imperialism*, New York: Knopf.

Saigol, Rubina. 1994. 'Boundaries of Consciousness: Interface Between the Curriculum, Gender and Nationalism.' In *Locating the Self: Reflections on Women and Multiple Identities*, edited by Nigat S. Khan, Rubina Saigol and Afia S. Zia, 41–76. Lahore: ASR.

———. 2000. *Symbolic Violence: Curriculum, Pedagogy and Society*. Lahore: Society for the Advancement of Education.

———. 2003. *Becoming a Modern Nation: Educational Discourse in the Early Years of Ayub Khan (1958-1964)*. Islamabad: Council of Social Sciences, Pakistan.

Saikia, Yasmin. 2010. 'Listening to the Enemy: The Pakistani Army, Violence and Memories of 1971.' In *Beyond Crisis: Re-evaluating Pakistan*, edited by Naveeda Khan, 177–209. Delhi: Routledge.

———. 2011. *Women, War, and the Making of Bangladesh: Remembering 1971*. Durham, NC: Duke University Press.

Sass, Louis A. 1994. *The Paradoxes of Delusion: Wittgenstein, Schreber, and the Schizophrenic Mind*. Ithaca, NY: Cornell University Press.

Sayer, Derek. 1994. 'Everyday Forms of State Formation: Dissident Remarks on Hegemony.' In *Everyday Forms of State Formation: Revolution and the Negotiation of Rule in Modern Mexico*, edited by Gilbert M. Joseph and Daniel Nugent, 367–378. Durham: Duke University Press.

Schaller, George B. 1980. *Stones of Silence: Journeys in the Himalaya*. New York: Viking Press.

Schickhoff, Udo. 2006. 'The Forests of Hunza Valley: Scarce Resources under Threat.' In *Karakoram in Transition: Culture, Development, and Ecology in the Hunza Valley*, edited by Hermann Kreutzmann, 123–144. Karachi: Oxford University Press.

Schofield, Victoria. 2010. *Kashmir in Conflict: India, Pakistan, and the Unending War*. London: I.B. Tauris.

Schomer, Karine et al. eds. 1994. *The Idea of Rajasthan: Explorations in Regional Identity*. New Delhi: Manohar.

Scott, David. 1995. 'Colonial Governmentality.' *Social Text* 43: 191–220.

Scott, James C. 1986. *Weapons of the Weak: Everyday Forms of Peasant Resistance*. New Haven: Yale University Press.

———. 1990. *Domination and the Arts of Resistance: Hidden Transcripts*. New Haven: Yale University Press.

———.1998. *Seeing Like a State: How Certain Schemes to Improve the Human Condition Have Failed*. New Haven: Yale University Press.

———. 2009. *The Art of Not Being Governed: An Anarchist History of Upland South East Asia*. New Haven: Yale University Press.

Secor, Anna J. 2007. 'Between Longing and Despair: State, Space, and Subjectivity in Turkey.' *Environment and Planning D: Society and Space* 25(1): 33–52.

Shah, Aqil. 2014. *The Army and Democracy: Military Politics in Pakistan*. Cambridge: Harvard University Press.

Shaikh, Farzana. 1989. *Community and Consensus in Islam: Muslim Representations in Colonial India 1860–1947*. Cambridge: Cambridge University Press.

Sharma, Aradhana and Akhil Gupta. eds. 2006. *The Anthropology of the State: A Reader*. Oxford: Blackwell.

Shehzad, Muhammad. 2003. 'Textbook Controversy in Gilgit.' *The Friday Times* XV: 19.

Shekhawat, Seema. 2014. *Gender, Conflict and Peace in Kashmir: Invisible Stakeholders*. Delhi: Cambridge University Press.

Shimshal Nature Trust (SNT). 1997. *Shimshal Nature Trust: Fifteen Year Vision and Management Plan*.

Shorrock, Tim. 2008. *Spies for Hire: The Secret World of Intelligence Outsourcing*. New York: Simon & Schuster.

Siddiqa-Agha, Ayesha. 2001. *Pakistan's Arms Procurement and Military Buildup, 1979–99: In Search of a Policy*. London: Palgrave Press.

———. 2007. *Military Inc.: Inside Pakistan's Military Economy.* Karachi: Oxford University Press.

Sivaramakrishnan, Kalyanakrishnan. 1999. *Modern Forests: Statemaking and Environmental Change in Colonial Eastern India.* Stanford: Stanford University Press.

Sivaramakrishnan, Kalyanakrishnan and Arun Agrawal. 2003. 'Regional Modernities in Stories and Practices of Development.' In *Regional Modernities: The Cultural Politics of Development in India,* 1–61. Delhi: Oxford University Press.

Snedden, Christopher. 2011. *The Untold Story of the People of Azad Kashmir.* New York: Oxford University Press.

Sökefeld, Martin. 2003. 'Selves and Others: Representing Multiplicities of Difference in Gilgit, Northern Areas of Pakistan.' In *Ethnic Revival and Religious Turmoil: Identities and Representations in the Himalayas,* edited by Marie Lecomte-Tilouine and Pascale Dollfus, 309–336. New York: Oxford University Press.

———. 2005. 'From Colonialism to Postcolonial Colonialism: Changing Modes of Domination in the Northern Areas of Pakistan.' *Journal of Asian Studies* 64(4): 939–973.

———. 2014. 'Disaster and (im)mobility: Restoring mobility in Gojal after the Attabad landslide.' *Ethnoscripts* 16(1): 187–209.

———. 2017. '"Not Part of Kashmir, but of the Kashmir Dispute": The Political Predicaments of Gilgit-Baltistan.' In *Kashmir: History, Politics, Representation,* edited by Chitralekha Zutshi, 127–144. Cambridge: Cambridge University Press.

Starr, Amory and Jason Adams. 2003. 'Anti-Globalization: The Fight for Local Autonomy.' *New Political Science* 25(1): 19–42.

Starrett, Gregory. 1998. *Putting Islam to Work: Education, Politics, and Religious Transformation in Egypt.* Berkeley: University of California Press.

Steinmetz, George. ed. 1999. *State/Culture: State-Formation after the Cultural Turn.* Ithaca, NY: Cornell University Press.

Stellrecht, Irmtraud. 1997. 'Dynamics of Highland-Lowland Interaction in Northern Pakistan since the 19th Century.' In *Perspectives on History and Change in the Karakorum, Hindukush, and Himalaya,* edited by Irmtraud Stellrecht and Matthias Winiger, 3–22. Köln: Rüdiger Köppe Verlag.

Stöber, Georg 2000. 'Structural Change and Domestic Agriculture in Yasin.' In *Mountain Societies in Transition: Contributions to the Cultural Geography of the Karakoram*, edited by Andreas Dittmann, 235–256. Köln: Rüdigerd. ZGU" Köppe Verlag.

———. 2007. 'Religious Identities Provoked: The Gilgit "Textbook Controversy" and its Conflictual Context.' *International Schulbuchforschung* 29: 389–411.

Stockholm International Peace Research Institute (SIPRI). 2008. *SIPRI Yearbook 2008: Armaments, Disarmament, and International Security*. Oxford: Oxford University Press.

Stoler, Ann L. 2004. 'Affective State's.' In *A Companion to the Anthropology of Politics*, edited by David Nugent and Joan Vincent, 4–29. Oxford: Blackwell.

Subramanian, Ajantha. 2009. *Shorelines: Space and Rights in South India*. Palo Alto: Stanford University Press.

Sundar, Nandini. 1997. *Subalterns and Sovereigns: An Anthropological History of Bastar, 1854–1996*. New York: Oxford University Press.

Suvin, Darko. 1997. 'On Cognitive Emotions and Topological Imagination.' Background Paper for *After Postmodernism Conference*, 14–16 November, University of Chicago.

Talbot, Sally E. 2000. *Partial Reason: Critical and Constructive Transformations of Ethics and Epistemology*. Westport, CT: Greenwood Publishing Group.

Taylor, Charles. 2004. *Modern Social Imaginaries*. Durham: Duke University Press.

———. 2007. 'On Social Imaginaries.' In *Traversing the Imaginary: Richard Kearney and the Postmodern Challenge*, edited by Peter Gratton and John P, Manoussakis, 29–47. Evanston, IL: Northwestern University Press.

Taylor, Verta and Nella V. Dyke. 2004. '"Get up, Stand up": Tactical Repertoires of Social Movements.' In *The Blackwell Companion to Social Movements*, edited by David A. Snow, Sarah A. Soule and Hanspeter Kriesi, 262–293. Oxford: Blackwell.

Thiranagama, Sharika and Tobias Kelly. eds. 2010. *Traitors: Suspicion, Intimacy and the Ethics of State-Building*. Philadelphia: University of Pennsylvania Press.

Tilly, Charles. 1978. *From Mobilization to Revolution*. Reading, MA: Addison-Wesley.

Toor, Saadia. 2012. *The State of Islam: Culture and Cold War Politics in Pakistan*. London: Pluto Press.

Trouillot, Michel-Rolph. 1995. *Silencing the Past: Power and the Production of History*. Boston: Beacon Press.

———. 2001. 'The Anthropology of the State in the Age of Globalization.' *Current Anthropology* 42(1): 125–138.

Tsing, Anna. 1993. *In the Realm of the Diamond Queen: Marginality in an Out-of-the-way Place*. Princeton: Princeton University Press.

Turner, Victor. ed. 1967. 'Betwixt and Between: The Liminal Period in Rites de Passage.' In *The Forest of Symbols: Aspects of Ndembu Ritual*. Ithaca, NY: Cornell University Press.

Turner, Simon. 2007. 'Suspended Spaces: Contesting Sovereignties in a Refugee Camp.' In *Sovereign Bodies: Citizens, Migrants, and States in the Postcolonial World*, edited by Thomas B. Hansen and Finn Stepputat, 93–111. Ithaca, NY: Cornell University Press.

Vandergeest, Peter and Nancy L. Peluso. 1995. 'Territorialization and State Power in Thailand.' *Theory and Society* 24(3): 385–426.

Verdery, Katherine. 1994. 'Ethnicity, Nationalism, and State-Making.' In *The Anthropology of Ethnicity: Beyond Ethnic Groups and Boundaries*, edited by Hans Vermeulen and Cora Govers, 35–58. Amsterdam: Het Spinhuis.

Verkaaik, Oskar. 2001. 'The Captive State: Corruption, Intelligence Agencies, and Ethnicity in Pakistan.' In *States of Imagination: Ethnographic Explorations of the Postcolonial State*, edited by Thomas B. Hansen and Finn Stepputat, 345–364. Durham: Duke University Press.

Visweswaran, Kamala. ed. 2013. *Everyday Occupations: Experiencing Militarism in South Asia and the Middle East*. Philadelphia: University of Pennsylvania Press.

Wacquant, Loic. 2008. *Urban Outcasts: A Comparative Sociology of Advanced Marginality*. Cambridge: Polity Press.

Wax, Emily. 2010. 'In Kashmir, Stone Throwers Face Off with Indian Security Forces.' *The Washington Post*, 17 July.

Weber, Max. 1964. *The Theory of Social and Economic Organization*. New York: Free Press.

Wedeen, Lisa. 2008. *Peripheral Visions: Publics, Power, and Performance in Yemen*. Chicago: University of Chicago Press.

Weiss, Anita M. ed. 1986. *Islamic Reassertion in Pakistan: Application of Islamic Laws in a Modern State*. Syracuse, NY: Syracuse University Press.

———. 1994. 'The Society and its Environment'. In *Pakistan: A Country Study*, edited by Peter R. Blood, 75–146. Washington, DC: Federal Research Division, Library of Congress.

West, Harry G. and Todd Sanders. 2003. 'Power Revealed and Concealed in the New World Order'. In *Transparency and Conspiracy: Ethnographies of Suspicion in the New World Order*, edited by Harry G. West and Todd Sanders, 1–37. Durham: Duke University Press.

West, Patrick C. and Steven R. Brechin. eds. 1991. *Resident Peoples and National Parks: Social Dilemmas and Strategies in International Conservation*. Tucson: University of Arizona Press.

Westad, Odd A. 2007. *The Global Cold War: Third World Interventions and the Making of our Times*. New York: Cambridge University Press.

Whittlesey, Derwent. 1954. 'The Regional Concept and the Regional Method'. In *American Geography: Inventory and Prospect*, edited by Preston E. James and Clarence F. Jones, 19–68. Syracuse, NY: Syracuse University Press.

Winichakul, Thongchai. 1994. *Siam Mapped: A History of the Geo-Body of a Nation*. Honolulu: University of Hawaii Press.

Williams, Brackette. 1989. 'A Class Act: Anthropology and the Race to Nation across Ethnic Terrain'. *Annual Review of Anthropology* 18: 401–444.

Williams, Raymond. 1977. *Marxism and Literature*. Oxford: Oxford University Press.

Wilson, Thomas M. and Hastings Donnan. eds. 1998. 'Nation, State and Identity at International Borders'. In *Border Identities: Nation and State at International Frontiers*, 1–30. Cambridge: Cambridge University Press.

Wirsing, Robert G. 1985. *Pakistan's Security under Zia, 1977–1988: The Policy Imperatives of a Peripheral Asian State*. New York: St. Martin's Press.

WWF. 1996. *Management Plan: Khunjerab National Park*. Gilgit: WWF.

Yuldoshev S. A. 1999. 'Abu Nasr Fārābī and Muhammad Iqbal on Ideal Society'. *Iqbal Review* 40(1).

Yuval-Davis, Nira. 2006. 'Belonging and the Politics of Belonging'. *Patterns of Prejudice* 40(3): 197–214.

Zaman, Muhammad. 1998. 'Sectarianism in Pakistan: The Radicalization of Shia and Sunni Identities'. *Modern Asian Studies* 32(3): 687–716.

Zia, Ather. 2016. 'The Spectacle of a Good-Half Widow: Women in Search of their Disappeared Men in the Kashmir Valley'. *Political and Legal Anthropology Review* 39(2): 164–175.

Zutshi, Chitralekha. 2003. *Languages of Belonging: Islam, Regional Identity, and the Making of Kashmir*. Delhi: Permanent Black.

———. 2014. *Kashmir's Contested Pasts: Narratives, Sacred Geographies, and the Historical Imagination*. New York: Oxford University Press.

INDEX

accumulation by dispossession, 200
Afghanistan, 56, 58, 80
   development assistance by US, 246
   Islamist groups expansion in, 121
   mujahideen forces spreading in, 243
   Pakistan-sponsored movements in, 95
   US invasion of, 100
Aga Khan Development Network (AKDN), 19, 167, 190n20
Aksai Chin frontier, 49
All Jammu and Kashmir Muslim Conference, 15
All Pakistan Education Conference (1947), 133
ameer-e-waqt (or 'Ruler of the Time'), 177
Anderson, Benedict, 62
Anti-Terrorism Act 1997, 259
armed social work, 247
Azad Kashmir (AK), 16, 35, 44, 47, 56, 61, 64, 74n60, 75n74, 75n78
Azad Kashmir High Court, 47

Baad-e-Shumaal weekly newspaper, 166
Balawaristan National Front (BNF), 47–48, 169, 171

Balochistan province, 41, 44, 108n17, 109n31
Balti, 13, 41, 190n8
Bang-e-Sahar, 166
Bazm-e-Ilm-o-Fann (Society for Knowledge and Art), 187–188
Bedaar weekly newspaper, 166
Beyond Lines of Control (Ravina Aggarwal), 11
Bhasha Dam, 171
Bhutto, Zulfiqar, 101–102, 142, 202
Biddulph, John, 117
biodiversity conservation, 12, 196, 199–200, 204, 206, 226, 228
Boloristan, 33
Boloristan Labor Party, 169
Boloristan monthly magazine, 166
Bolor Research Forum, 167
Bolor Thinkers Forum, 167
Braldu Valley of Baltistan, 235
Buddhism, 13
Burushaski, 13

calculated ambiguity, 53
capitalism, 133, 198, 200, 247
capitalist modernity, 198, 201, 217

cartographic censorship, 57
census classifications, classified nature of, 57–61
census-taking, 61–62
Central Karakoram National Park, 225
Chataan weekly newspaper, 166
China (Peoples Republic), 36, 49, 58–59, 257–259
China-Pakistan Economic Corridor (CPEC), 259
CIA, 109n41, 237, 239, 242
  strategy to deploy Afghan jihad, 243
Cold War, 8, 24, 80, 103, 121, 243
communism, 134
community-based
  conservation, 196, 212, 219–224
  Community-based Natural Resource Management (CBNRM), 219
  community-based trophy hunting, 221, 223
Community Controlled Hunting Areas (CCHAs), 220–221
community participation, 197, 199, 210, 218–219, 226
concentrated animal feedlot operations (CAFOs), 216
crisis of *insaaniyat*, 188
cultural
  intervention, 181
  reproduction, 141–143
  rhythms, 163–168
  struggle, 197

Dardistan, 73n19
degradation narratives, 210, 214
District Monitoring Teams (DMTs), 82
Dogra rulers of Jammu, 14, 27n18, 63, 65, 74n70 178, 191n34

Earth Summit (1992), Rio de Janeiro, 199
East Pakistan, 137–138
eco-body of the nation, 25–26, 36, 43, 62, 195–196
  configuration of, 10–11

Northern areas constructed as, 31, 37, 60, 71
ecological
  nationalism, 203
  sovereignty, 197, 213
education and Pakistan state, 132–139
emotion/emotional, 2, 9, 11, 24, 48, 77, 98, 144, 161, 163, 189
  aspirations, 5
  attachment, 1, 3, 10, 90
  bond, 87
  deception, 47
  disposition, 94
  histories, 3
  ill-will, 9, 162
  imaginary, 16
  logics, 8
  of political love, 48
  reactionary, 24
  regulation, 10, 78, 107, 260
  of saving, 207
  selves, 123
  shared, 170
  sensibilities of listeners, 176
  subjectivities, 78
  tenor, 159
empire, 7, 11, 24, 26, 43, 63, 80, 99–100, 185, 201, 228, 231–233, 245–246, 249, 258, 261
environmental conservation, global NGO discourse on, 43
environmental degradation, 198

Faiz, Faiz Ahmed, 189
FATA, 56, 58, 67–68, 72n8, 238
Federally Administered Northern Areas (FANA), 33–34, 38–39, 44, 56, 58, 67–68, 72n8
Field Monitoring Coordination Cell (FMCC), 82–83
firqavariat, 162
Force Command Northern Areas (FCNA), 81–82, 103, 106
Foucault, Michel, 62, 98, 251

Frontier Corps, 82, 121
Frontier Crimes Regulation (FCR), 65, 101–102
Frontier Works Organization (FWO), 82, 84–85
Gandhi, 5
garrison state, Pakistan as, 81–85, 95
GEF/UNDP funded Mountain Areas Conservancy Project, 220
gender/gendered, 21, 24, 94, 115, 146, 167–168, 251
  humiliation, 101
  mainstreaming, 168
  relations, 17
General Mushrraf, 82, 89, 167
General Zia, Islamization agenda/programme of, 103, 114, 120, 138, 147
Gilgit Agency, 33, 38, 50, 53–54, 57–58, 63, 75n72, 85, 117
Gilgit-Baltistan, 64–65
Gilgit-Baltistan Council, 35
Gilgit Baltistan Democratic Alliance (GBDA), 169, 171–172
Gilgit-Baltistan Legislative Assembly (GBLC), 35, 85, 97–98
Gilgit-Baltistan National Alliance (GBNA), 169
Gilgit-Baltistan region, 6, 17, 196
  agro-pastoral population, 12–13
  army role in regional administration of, 85–88, 82–83
  geographical location of, 12
  humanitarian development in, 12
  indigenous ethno-linguistic groups, 13
  and intelligence agencies
    production of sectarian suspicion and tension, 100–105
    role of, 95–100
  and Kargil conflict, 89–90
  land distribution in, 13
  living museum for wildlife, 196
  lowland nationalist discourse on, 43
  pluralistic religious sensibility, 119
  political repression in, 10

sectarian/sectarianism, 116–119, 147, 155–157
  divide and conquer, 140
  formation of difference between students, 157–159
  maps, 261
Gilgit-Baltistan Students Association, Karachi University, 166
Gilgit Scouts, 85–86
Gilgit Wazarat, 50, 63, 74n72
Global Environment Facility (GEF), 201
Gojal Educational and Cultural Association (GECA), 191–192n49
Grand Aman Jirga, 190n12
green developmentalism, 227
Guantanamo prison, 7, 100

Halqa-e-Arbab-e-Zauq (Halqa), 155, 175–176, 187
Harrison, Selig, 257–258
Hasan, Mushirul, 118–119
heart warfare, 233
Hindu-Muslim communalism, 144
humanitarian/humanitarianism, 11–12, 24, 26, 228, 231, 232, 234, 244–249, 250, 252, 253n5, 260
  work in Gilgit-Baltistan region, 232
Human Rights Commission of Pakistan, 259
Hunzakuts, longevity and tranquility of, 41

ilaqiat, 118
imagined communities, 146
imambargas (Shia mosques), 120
imperial, 8, 24, 242, 247–249, 252, 257–258
  conservation, 26
  epistemic supremacy, 251
  humanitarianism, 26
  master, 80
  politics, 11–12
Indo-Persian cultural landscape, 174
insaaniyat (humanism), 5, 181, 187–188

International Union for Conservation of Nature (IUCN), 196, 199, 202, 220, 227
Inter-Services Intelligence (ISI), Pakistan, 95, 121, 237, 239, 242
intra-Islam differences, 144
Introduction to Pakistan Studies (Muhammad Ikram Rabbani), 38
Islah-e-Nisab (correction of curriculum) Committee, 126–127, 150n33
Islam, 5, 13, 32
   inter-sect relations within, 177
   and Pakistan state, 132–139
   pluralistic vision of, 179
Islamabad, 32, 44, 60
Islamic
   content of Pakistani textbooks, 114
   curriculum, 139
   democracy, 134
   ideology, 134, 136, 138–139
   religious ethic of nature stewardship, 212
   social democracy, 136
   socialism, 136
Islamist militancy, 121
Islamization, 103, 113–114, 120, 147, 191n40
island mentality, 199
Ismaili/Ismailis/Ismaili Muslims, 13, 117, 123, 150n11

jagirdari (feudal) system, 65
Jamaat-e-Islami (JI), 137–138, 169
jamat khana (religious centre), 212
Jamhoor quarterly magazine, 166
jihad, 120
Jinnah, Muhammad Ali, 132
JUI party, 138

K2 daily newspaper, 166, 234
K2 mountain, 36, 48, 52, 56, 59
Karachi, 20–21, 34
Karachi Agreement of 1949, 15, 171
Karakoram Highway (KKH), 13, 36, 60, 84–85, 167, 236–237

Karakoram mountain, 37, 39
Karakoram National Movement (KNM), 169
Karakorum International University (KIU), 122, 188–189
karbala, 191n43
Karbala-e-Jadid (The New Karbala), 182–183
Karbala paradigm, 119
Kargil, 11
   conflict of 1999, 86, 88–92, 167
Kargil monthly magazine, 167
Kashmir
   as disputed territory, 50–52
   ecological terrain of struggle in, 11
   Harrison's article on India's role in, 257–258
   heart of hostility between India and Pakistan, 27n1
   historical conditions and understandings of, 27n18, 178
   hypocrisy of Pakistan official line, 45
   Islamist groups expansion in, 121
   and Indian state, 2
   Northern Areas link with, 64
   and Pakistan, 261
      claim on Muslim identity basis, 1–2
      state building, 15
Kashmiri Muslims, 178
Khan, Ayub, 142
Khan, Baccha, 5
Khan, Liaqat Ali, 137
khelna, 4
Khowar group, 13
Khunjerab National Park (KNP), 196–197, 201–204, 206, 208, 213, 220–221, 225, 230n49, 237
   community-based conservation schemes, 219–224
   livestock grazing in, 214–216, 218
   occurrence of illegal hunting by state officials, 229n30
Khunjerab Security Force, 216

khutba (sermon), 106
Kyber-Pukhtoonkhwa province, 34, 68, 83

labour rights, 136
Laden, Osama bin, 243
Lahore, 34
legendary lovers, struggles of, 3
Line of Control (LoC), 50, 88
literary nations, 173
Living Islam (Magnus Marsden), 11
Lok Virsa, 192n49
Lord Mountbatten, 13
love (*muhabbat*), 2, 5
    characteristics of, 3–4
    cultural-poetic constellation of, 4
    manipulation of love in Gilgit-Baltistan by Pakistan, 4
    -martyrs, 3
    -offerings, 5
Love in South Asia: A Cultural History (Ann G. Gold), 4

madrasa/madrasas, 232
    curricula and education in Pakistan, 114, 153–154
    proliferation of, 114, 240
Maharaja Hari Singh, 13–14, 41
majalis (religious gatherings) in *muharram*, 116
majority and minority distinction in region, reasons for, 145–147
managed pluralism, 118
map(s)
    China, depicting Aksai Chin frontier as territory of, 49
    clear representation on maps of India and Pakistan in Kashmir, 49–51
    -making, 61–62
    Northern Areas, 1, 15, 25, 27n18, 31–43, 46–50, 52–61, 63–64, 66–72, 72n6, n8, 74n59, 113, 115–116, 118–119, 121, 123–126, 132, 138–139, 141, 144–145, 167, 171–172, 202, 235–238, 240–241

    role in shaping state-formation and interstate relations, 49
    totemic symbols of nation, 49
Markazi Imamia Jam-e-Masjid (central Shia mosque), 126
Markazi Shia Tulba Action Committee (2004), 150n33
masla-e-Kashmir (Kashmir Problem), 16
McClintock, Anne, 99–100
McMichael, Philip, 7
micro-publics of banal transgression, 184
militarization of Pakistan, 78–81
Ministry of Kashmir Affairs and Northern Areas (KANA), 66, 102, 109n44, 121, 123, 139
Mitchell, Timothy, 61–62
mobile services, introduction in Gilgit, 109n23
moral
    ecology, 212
    regulation, 139
Motorcycle Girl, Pakistani movie, 262n4
muharram, 181, 191n39
mujahideen, 88, 242, 253n12
multiple use landscapes, 209
mushairas (or gatherings), 174–176, 189

naara-e-ehtiyaat (the stance of silence), 182
Naji, Nawaz Khan, 47–48, 169
Naqqara weekly newspaper, 166
national language controversy over Urdu and Bangla (1947-1952), 137–138
national parks, 196, 198–206
Nawab Akbar Khan Bugti, 109n31
Nawaz Sharif-Vajpayee bus diplomacy, 89
neoliberal
    capitalism, 198
    resources, 198–201
New York Times (NY Times), 247, 257–258
non-governmental organization (NGO), 17–18, 20–21
Northern Areas (NA), 1, 25, 27n18, 32–33,

35–37, 40, 61, 74n60, 115–116, 235, 238. *See also* Gilgit-Baltistan region
  absent from depictions of people and culture, 41
  administrative units information about, 74n59
  cartographic representations of, 48–57
  communities of, 42
  definition of, 38–39
  delinking of Northern Areas from Kashmir, 53
  and Pakistan
    Census Report of Pakistan 1998, 57–60
    official map of, 54
  political status of, 40–42
  practice managed pluralism, 118
  representational illegibility of, 67–71
Northern Areas Council Legal Framework Order of 1994, 46
Northern Areas Public Works Department (NWPWD), 83–84
Northern Areas Wildlife Preservation Act 1975, 202
Northern Light Infantry (NLI), 86, 88–90, 109n27
North-West Frontier Province (NWFP), 15, 34, 39–41, 44, 67, 69, 72n4, 75n78, 119, 137, 238
Nurbakhshi, 13
NWFP Textbook Board, 114

open-source intelligence, 262
Orientalism, 253n5

Pakistan/Pakistani, 23, 28n25, 31, 56
  -administered Kashmir, 17, 53, 55–56
    Census Report of Pakistan 1998, 57–60
  Constitution of Pakistan (1973), 44–45
  intimately structured by US foreign policy, 8
  Islamist groups expansion in, 121
  literary humanism in, 179
  machinery of paranoia and surveillance, expansion of, 8
  promotion of militaristic interpretation of Islamic ideology in textbooks, 138–139
  support for Kashmiri haq-e-khud-iradiyat, 15
  and US, connections between, 7
paranoia, 107
  destructive madness of, 259
  and militarism, 8, 100
  sectarian, 162
  and state, 95–100
  and surveillance, 8, 95
participatory militarism, 232, 249, 252
partition of 1947, 64, 150n14
pastoral/pastoralism, 219
  delegitimization of, 217
  economy, 217
  grazing, 216
  visions, 197–198
poetic/poetry in Gilgit region
  festivals in Gilgit, 155
  interventions of Halqa, 155
  life of, 173–174
  role as form of social struggle and resistance, 154
politically organized subjection, 139
politics of nomenclature, in disputed territories, 32
politics of representation, 232
primitive accumulation, 198
Progressive Writers Movement, 175, 185
Progressive Youth Front, 169
Provincial Reconstruction Teams (PRTs), 246
Punjab, 41, 44, 83, 137

qoum identity, 118
qudrat, notion of, 206–207

Radcliffe Line, 49

Rahman, Fazlur, 133–136
Report of the Committee of
    Gilgit-Baltistan, 102
Rizvi, Agha Ziauddin, 124, 126, 182, 184

Sadaa-e-Gilgit weekly newspaper, 166
Saigol, Rubina, 139
sarfi saqafat (consumer culture), 166
saviour nationalism, 15–17
Schaller, George B., 202, 215
sectarian/sectarianism/sectarianized, 188
    identity, 103
    imaginary, 153, 161–163
    micro-politics of, 163
    othering, 158
    peace, 118
    prejudice, 177
    riots, 151n71
    sentiments, 163
    violence, 158
secular-nationalist party activism,
    168–172
Seeing Like a State (James Scott), 31, 62
Seminar on National Question of
    Gilgit-Baltistan, 171
Shia Muslims in Gilgit region, 9, 13, 19, 96,
    102–103, 141
    agitation against changed curriculum
        of government schools, 113–114
    secularism, 130–131
Shia Mutalibat Committee (Shia Demands
    Committee), 142
Shia-Sunni discord on curriculum
    changes, 113
Shia-Sunni sectarian conflict, 144
Shia Tulba Action Committee (Shia
    Students Action Committee), 172
Shimshalis/Shimshal village, 196, 204
    agro-pastoral community of, 26, 196,
        202, 204, 207
    fighting for ecological sovereignty, 197
    geographical location of, 204
    and qudrat, notion of, 206–207

resistance for territory conservation
    into national park, 204–205, 210
Shimshal Nature Trust (SNT), 197,
    219–220, 222
    establishment of, 211
    management plan, 211–212, 230n48
Shina, 13, 41
Siachin, 53, 74n49
Silk Route Festival, 164–165
Sindh, 41, 44
Sino-Indian war of 1962, 49
Sino-Pakistan Agreement of 1963, 49
Sipah-e-Sahaba Pakistan (SSP), 114, 120, 169
siyasat bezari (depoliticization), 166
Skardu, 12, 23, 36, 39–40, 48–49, 68–69,
    89, 166, 171, 187
soft power, 246
South Asia, 4, 12, 174, 179, 189, 190n3,
    191n36, 206, 233
    colonial bureaucracies of forest
        conservation in, 201
    literary nations, 173
    love significance in, 3
    maps role in shaping state-formation
        and interstate relations, 49
    social emotionality in, 5
    transnational political economy of
        militarism in, 232
Special Communications Organization
    (SCO), 82, 109n23
structural adjustment programmes, 166
struggle for interpretive power, 197
Sunni Muslims in Gilgit region, 9, 13,
    19, 102–103. *See also* Textbook
    controversy, in Gilgit region
suspended spaces, 32
suspicion, 2, 8–10, 12, 18–19, 26, 78,
    95–100, 104–105, 107, 153, 159,
    161–162, 169, 260–262
sustainable development, 212

taasub, 162, 179–180, 188–189
Taliban, 137, 236–237

Tark-i-Taasobat (The Ending of
    Prejudice), 182
Taylor, Charles, 153, 161
Tehrik-e-Jafaria Pakistan (TJP), 114, 142,
    151n69, 169
textbook controversy, in Gilgit region,
    113–114, 144, 148
  agitation by Shia students against
    curriculum changes, 123–126
  atthasi ka waqia or atthasi ka tension of
    1998, 119–123
  citizenship versus sectarianism, 143–145
  objections raised by proponents on
    curriculum, 126–132
textbooks/textbook representation
  constitutes micro-practice of
    regulation, 115
  Gilgit movement against changes in
    curriculum, 115
  Islam, 115
  negative impact of discriminatory
    representation on Shia dwarfs, 141
  reinforce existing social inequalities, 115
  Shia and Sunni Islam on, 115
  Sunni orientation of, 140

Three Cups of Tea (TCT): *One Man's
    Mission to Fight Terrorism and
    Build Nations …One School at a
    Time*, 26, 231–235, 237–238, 251,
    253n5, 257
  appealing due to sense of
    self-interrogation, 244
  blanket claims of region, 238–239
  enabled emergence of participatory
    militarism, 252
  invokes fear, 236
  political economy of feeling, 245
Trans-Karakoram Tract, 203, 228n24
transnational cultural knowledge, 232

transnational US-Pakistan-Saudi political
    alliance, 121
trophy hunting, 196

United Nations Commission for India
    and Pakistan (UNCIP), 15
United Nations Environment Programme
    (UNEP), 201
US, 23–24, 99, 245, 250
  9/11, 242
  -backed dictatorial regimes, 243
  corporate and military hegemony,
    246–247
  foreign policy during 1979-1988, 242
  geopolitical agenda, 244
  invasions of Afghanistan and Iraq, 100
  militarization in, 79–81
  -style counter-insurgency, 233

Vietnam war, 242, 246

Waadi weekly newspaper, 166
Wakhi, 13, 41, 192n49
war between India and Pakistan
  in 1965, 88
  in 1999, 88–92
war on terror, 6–7, 12, 24, 26, 68, 147, 228,
    231–234, 238, 241, 243–244, 246,
    249, 251
Waziristan, 67
West Pakistan, 138
Wildlife Conservation Society, 202
World Bank, 201
World Congress on National Parks and
    Protected Areas (WCNPPA) in
    1982 and 1992, 199
World Wide Fund for Nature (WWF),
    196, 199, 219, 227, 229n30

yaum-e-azadi, 14